READ, LEARN, LAUGH;
REPEAT !

Sandy

# RETAIL
# SCHMETAIL™

ONE Hundred Years
TWO Immigrants
THREE Generations
FOUR Hundred Projects

## Sanford Stein

ISBN 13: 978-1-59298-956-0

Library of Congress Catalog Number: 2013922417

Printed in the United States of America

First Printing: 2013

17 16 15 14 13      5 4 3 2 1

Cover and interior design by Sanford Stein and Laura Drew.
Cover photo of Sandy Stein (age 15) working at Jewelry and Toy Center, 1965.
For a full list of interior photograph copywrite information see pages: iv, and v.

Beaver's Pond Press
7108 Ohms Lane
Edina, MN 55439–2129
952-829-8818

To order, visit www.BeaversPondBooks.com
or call 1-800-901-3480. Reseller discounts available.

## DEDICATION

This book is dedicated to my wife Cheryl
and our two daughters Ariel and Brianna.

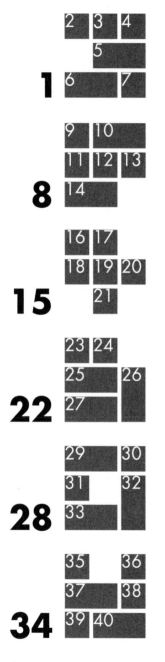

## CHAPTER ONE
**1 Peter Bootzin's General Store Advertisement, April 22, 1931| © *"Curtiss Advance"* (Curtiss, Hoard Twp., Clark Co., Wis.)** 2 Stein Twins with Toddlers Sandy and Suzy, 1949| Source Unknown 3 Jewelry and Toy Center, 1963| Source Unknown 4 Al Stein in Uniform, 1942| Source Unknown 5 Ben Semon (Far Left) and Peter Bootzin (Far Right), Circa 1920| Source Unknown 6 International Civil Rights Museum, Greensboro, NC (Site of 1960 Sit-in at F. W. Woolworth Co.| © Leon Reed 7 Bootzin's Bean Pot; holiday giveaway | 1920s and '30s | © Sanford Stein

## CHAPTER TWO
**8 Jewelry and Toy Center Going Out of Business, 1964 | Source Unknown** 9 Twins on Honeymoon, 1946 | Source Unknown 10 Milwaukee War Memorial, Remember Them All | © CJ Schmidt Photography 11 Pill & Puff Delivery Truck, 1972 | Source Unknown 12 Pill & Puff, West Wisconsin Ave, Milwaukee, WI, 1972 | © Sanford Stein 13 Southdale Mall, Edina, MN, 1956| Source Unknown 14 1957 Ford Skyliner Retractable | © Archivea Inc. DBA Ford Images

## CHAPTER THREE
**15 Ray Eames, | © Eames Office, LLC (eamesoffice.com)** 16 Lounge Chair Metal | Photograph by Grant Tayler, Courtesy of JF Chen © Eames Office, LLC (eamesoffice.com) 17 Peter Seitz, 1984 | Courtesy of Peter Seitz | source unknown 18 "Norby" Wisconsin State Sculpture Competition, 1971, St Norbert College, Green Bay, WI | © Sanford Stein" 19 InterDesign Inc. Logo, 1970 | Courtesy of Peter Seitz 20 North Trek Kiosk—Minnesota Zoo, 1977 by InterDesign Inc. 21 Josefs—Pavilion Place, Roseville, MN, 1986 by SteinDesign | Photograph by Phillip MacMillan James

## CHAPTER FOUR
**22 Brunswick Pavilion, Wilmette, IL, 2003 by Stein LLC | Photograph by Doug Snower** 23 Bucky 71, Spoof on the Impending '72 Elections | by R. Buckminster Fuller 24 Goodman Jewelers, Ridgedale Mall, 1986 | by SteinDesign | George Heinrich Photography 25 Dymaxion Car, by R. Buckminster Fuller 26 Wild Pair—Columbus Ave., NY, 1990 by SteinDesign, Photograph by Phillip MacMillan James 27 Apollo™ Brunswick™ Contender® Series by Stein LLC

## CHAPTER FIVE
**28 Crate and Barrel—Chicago, IL, 1962; © Crate and Barrel** 29 Target—Roseville, MN, 1962 | © Target Brands, Inc 30 01-01-00™ The Novel of the Millenium © Rogelio J. Pineiro 31 Motorola DynaTAC 8000X, 1983 | © Motorola Solutions Heritage Archives 32 The Metreon, San Francisco, CA | © Sony Corporation 33 Walmart, Rogers, AR, 1962 | © Wal-Mart Stores, Inc.

## CHAPTER SIX
**34 SteinDesign Office—Minneapolis, MN, 1985 by SteinDesign, Photograph by Phillip MacMillan James** 35 BEST Indeterminate Façade, Houston, TX, 1974 | Project & Photo: SITE 36 Dimitrius—St. Anthony Main, Minneapolis, MN, 1985 by SteinDesign | Photograph by Phillip MacMillan James 37 Junkyard—Mall of America, Bloomington, MN, 1993 by SteinDesign, Photograph by George Heinrich Photography 38 Dimitrius—Axonometric Drawing 39 Terry Anne Meeuwsen, 1973 Miss America with Al Stein 40 Record Shop, 1992 by SteinDesign | Photograph by Phillip MacMillan James

# Photo Credits

## CHAPTER SEVEN
**41 The Filling Station, '50s era| Source Unknown** 42 Joe Friday, Dragnet, NBC, 1951-1959 | © Milwaukee Historical Society 43 The Milky Way Drive In, Milwaukee, WI | Photograph by Bernice Kiedrow 44 Select Comfort—Prototype Various Locations, 1994-1998 by SteinDesign 45 Runkel Bros. American Garage—Mall of America, Bloomington, MN,1994 by Stein LLC | Photograph by George Heinrich Photography 46 Runkel Bros. American Garage—Mall of America, Bloomington, MN 47 Clark Super 100 Station, Circa 1950s | Source Unknown

## CHAPTER EIGHT
**48 Stein Speaking Badges by Sanford Stein** 49 Dësq, Edina, MN, 1997 by SteinDesign; Photograph by George Heinrich Photography 50 Bnai-Emanuel Bowling Team, 1953 51 The Third Place 52 Starbucks Oak Street Flagship Store—Chicago, IL | Retail Environments, March 2013, Photograph by Ari Burling Photography, Brooklyn, NY. 53 First Starbucks Coffee Shop © Jason Waltman Photography

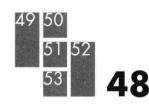

## CHAPTER NINE
**54 Montgomery Ward's 1934 Catalog** 55 GI Generation | © Lori Semprevio 56 Matures or Silent Generation | www.flickr.com © bluvampier 57 MEtail Service Mark Registered by STEIN LLC, March 201158 Baby Boomer | www.flickr.com © Kathryn Barry 59 Generation X, Unknown Couple | www.flickr.com © oven pop 60 Generation Y| www.flickr.com © penpalme 61 Generation Z | www.flickr.com © :: U N I Q U E :: 62 Social Media Logos

## CHAPTER TEN
**63 Brunswick Home & Billiard, Wilmette IL 2003, by Stein LLC | Doug Snower Photography** 64 Life Enhancements, Southdale Shopping Center, Edina, MN, 1993 by SteinDesign | George Heinrich Photography 65 EQ Life—Richfield, MN, 2005 © Best Buy Corp. 66 Brunswick Home & Billiard | Doug Snower Photography 67 Whole Foods Logo | Rupert Ganzer 68 4 Fitness—St. Anthony Main, Minneapolis, MN, 1986 by SteinDesign | Photograph by Phillip MacMillan James

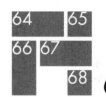

## CHAPTER ELEVEN
**69 Northridge Mall, Milwaukee WI, 2009; © Brian Ulrich, Photographer** 70 Red Wing Store—Mall of America, Bloomington, MN, 1999 by SteinDesign | George Heinrich Photography 71 Red Wing Shoe Craftsmen Finishing A Boot © Red Wing Shoe Company Historical Archives 72 Red Wing Store—Mall of America, Bloomington | George Heinrich Photography 73 Pike Place Market | © Jason Waltman Photography 74 Pontiac Chieftain | Photograph by Mathew Ward, Classic American Cars 75 Penzeys Spices | www.flickr.com © jamimyoung

## AFTERWORD
**76 "Papa Al's Ties," Ariel Stein, Left | Brianna Stein, Right, 2013 | Photo by Sanford Stein**

# RETAIL SCHMETAIL™ CONTENTS

| | |
|---|---|
| **Acknowledgments** | **2** |
| **Foreword by Jack El-Hai** | **4** |
| **Chapter One: Street-Smart Entrepreneurs** | **8** |
| RETAILING'S ORIGIN AND EVOLUTION | 9 |
| RETAIL ROOTS | 11 |
| OFF TO WAR | 15 |
| MERE FORMALITY | 16 |
| FOUR-WHEEL LOVE AFFAIR | 20 |
| DOWNTOWN IS GOING DOWN | 24 |
| RURAL AMERICANA | 25 |
| **Chapter Two: From Downtown to the Mall** | **30** |
| A SOLITARY GUY | 31 |
| THE CREATIVE CURSE | 33 |
| EARLY INSPIRATION | 36 |
| THE END OF JEWELRY AND TOY CENTER | 37 |
| A BONA FIDE BRAND IS BORN | 41 |
| STYLISH REINVENTION | 43 |
| ENTERING AN EVOLVING DESIGN FIELD | 44 |
| AN EYE-OPENING INTERNSHIP | 47 |
| A MODEL RETAIL PLAN | 50 |
| **Chapter Three: Heroes and Mentors** | **58** |
| ORIGIN OF DIS-EASE | 61 |
| GETTIN' INTO PLASTICS | 62 |
| FRESH START AND A NEW MENTOR | 67 |
| MEDITATION | 70 |
| **Chapter Four: The Design Process** | **76** |
| IMMERSION | 76 |

# Table of Contents

## Chapter Four: The Design Process (continued)

CONTEXT ............................................................. 79
OPENNESS ......................................................... 87
STYLE ................................................................. 90
COMMUNICATION ............................................. 95

## Chapter Five: Branding 101      102

A PERSONAL BRAND STAND ............................ 102
IDENTITY ............................................................ 103
NUANCE ............................................................ 105
TRANSCENDENCE ........................................... 108
EMOTION ........................................................... 112
RELEVANCE ...................................................... 115
DESIGN, ENDURANCE, SOUL ......................... 121

## Chapter Six: Retail Matures      130

OUT AND BACK ................................................ 132
THE OLD IS NEW .............................................. 136
GREENER PASTURES ...................................... 138
STEINDESIGN  RHYME, RHYME ...................... 141
BEST FOOT FORWARD ..................................... 144
ADAPTIVE REUSE OPPORTUNITIES CONTINUE ... 147
SITE OF MINNEAPOLIS'S ORIGINS .................. 149
RHYTHMS OF LIFE AND BUSINESS ................. 151
RESIDUAL EFFECT ........................................... 153

## Chapter Seven: Branded Environments and Experiential Retailing      158

WHY DOES IT MATTER? ................................... 161
P & G'S 4E'S .................................................... 161
STAGING EXPERIENCES .................................. 163
THE DICHOTOMY OF THE SERVICE ECONOMY ... 165
BING...DING ...................................................... 166

## Chapter Seven: Branded Environments (continued)

THESE WERE HAPPY DAYS                                      169
RETRO FIT                                                 171
CREATE THE HOOK                                           172
TAKING SERVICE TO A (MUCH) HIGHER LEVEL                   174
ANOTHER CHANGE 'AGENT'                                    177
SPEAKING IN ONE VOICE                                     180

## Chapter Eight: Formats in Flux/Changing Channels        186

IN SEARCH OF THE NEW 'THIRD PLACE'                        186
TREND CONVERGENCE                                         187
BOWLING TEAMS AND OFFICE FOURSOMES BE GONE                189
AMAZON—LIKE THE RIVER                                     190
THE INTERNET PURE PLAY                                    191
QUICK EDUCATION                                           192
GENERATION FLUX                                           194
TOYS R LATE!                                              195
NEW RULES                                                 196
WOW, NOW, AND HOW OF RETAIL RELEVANCE                     198
GETTING VERTICAL                                          199

## Chapter Nine: Market of One                             204

GETTING VERY SOCIAL                                       204
DIGITAL DIVIDE AND CONQUER                                209
FROM MULTICHANNEL TO CROSS-CHANNEL                        210
TO OMNICHANNEL
METAIL^SM—CAUSE OR ANTIDOTE TO SHOWROOMING?               212
EXPERIENTIAL RATHER THAN PRICE DRIVEN                     213
SOLUTION-BASED VS COMPONENT-BASED RETAILING               214
INDIVIDUALIZING THE EXPERIENCE—BEING THE EXPERT           215
LIVING IN A MOBILE WORLD                                  215
WHOLE NEW VOCABULARY                                      216
BRICK AND MOBILE                                          221

Table of Contents

RESHAPING THE FOUR P'S OF RETAILING                 223
ASSISTED DISCOVERY                                  224
LEPSync                                             225

**Chapter Ten: Fads, Trends, and Pretenders         232**

MORE OR LESS                                        233
WHOLE NEW APPROACH                                  234
KARMIC COINCIDENCES                                 237
READING THE SIGNS                                   238
THE LARGER PLAN                                     240
CHANGE OF STATE                                     241
WHAT'S IN A NAME?                                   244
TAPPING A TREND                                     245
THE DICHOTOMY OF CHOICE                             246
RALPH AND MARTHA                                    248
COBALT & SCARLET[SM]                                251
COMING BACK HOME                                    254
A MOST MEMORABLE MEETING                            257
WHERE AMERICA USED TO SHOP                          260

**Chapter Eleven: The Future of Retailing           266**

AMERICA THE OVER RETAILED                           266
BIG TO SMALL                                        268
GENERALIZED TO SPECIALIZED                          271
NATIONAL TO LOCAL                                   276
SYNTHETIC TO AUTHENTIC                              287
STATIC TO KINETIC                                   292
DISCARD TO REPURPOSE                                299
THE TRIPLE BOTTOM LINE                              305

**Afterword: Tying Up Loose Ends                    310**
**Glossary of Terms                                 312**
**Works Cited                                       318**

## ACKNOWLEDGMENTS

It's impossible to recognize all of the people I have collaborated with over the course of five decades; that became the basis for this book. On a personal note I must honor Al and Lou Stein for providing me with a career launch pad as well as the book's inspiration. I must also pay tribute to my mom, Maxine Stein Tishberg, who kept the "wheels on the family bus" so that both my sister Debbie Silberman and I had a loving and stable home life.

I have been particularly blessed to be able to follow my passions due entirely to the love and support of my dear wife Cheryl and our two fabulous daughters Ariel and Brianna; these three women have brought me the greatest joy imaginable.

I must acknowledge the support and friendship of my clients who often made great leaps of faith to follow a "vision" and pathway to places unknown. These include: Greg Adler, Steve de Alcala, Dale Bachman, Les Cherry, Margaret Everist, Mort Gerber, Arthur Goodman, Tracy Handt, Hank Harris, Dan Hunt, Brent Hutton, Amit Kleinberger, Mary Ann Levitt, Ginny Miller, Cari Johnson Pelava, Dave Rittenhouse, Craig Runkel, Ryan Stick, John Stransky, and David Workman, among many others.

I am particularly indebted to mentors, valued colleagues and dear friends whose energies, insights, wisdom, and love have guided me through life and business including: David Alter, Damon Farber, Josh Fogelson, Joel Gedan, Tom Gegax, John Herman, Bob Lapkin, Marshall Lehman, Cotty Lowry, Reuven Rahamim, Peter Seitz, Robert Schultz, Jim Smart, Gunther Stern, Irvine and Charlotte Stein, Kenneth Walker, and Jerry Zweigbaum. And I thank my invaluable TAB group: Mark Komen, Dave Kapell, Kurt Kaiser, Jacque Lee, Jonathan McDonagh, Susan McPherson, and Dan Yaman.

The numerous projects discussed in this book are the work of many talented individuals, whose collaborative efforts have transformed concepts to working realities, including: Jeremiah Albrecht, Jeffrey Agnes, Harris Birkeland, Amanda Davis Taylor, Craig Cherry, Jim Cordaro, Anthony Desnick, Jan Dufault, Angela Ford, Jules Friedman, David Frum, Laila Gatts, Chris Gorney, Henry Grabowski, Ryan Haro, Nick Hemer, Diane Ivens, Karen James, Jessica Kohl Nielsen, Scott Laxton, Rick LaMuro, Chad Omon, Barry Ringland, Bruce Rubin, Anne Serio, Kris Stansberry, Andy Weaverling, Joel Woodward, and Mike Wong.

A decade and a half ago, writer and author Jack El-Hai had the audacity to "envision" a book based on the cacophony of family stories, business, and personal experiences that was and is my life. I thank Jack for inspiring me, and for his beautiful foreword that launches us into the world of Jewelry and Toy Center, circa 1958. I am indebted to the entire Beaver's Pond Press family including Lily Coyle, Laura Drew, Alicia Ester, Tom Kerber, and Wendy Weckwerth. I must also recognize my intrepid editor Anne Hodgson for taking the book (and me) on, along with my team of editors, readers, proofers, and endorsers for their time and interest including: Brent Hutton, Jessica Kohl Nielsen, Cari Johnson Pelava, Joe Pine, Teri Ross, Robert Stephens, Brianna Stein, John Stransky, Kenneth Walker, David Wexler, and Bruce Wright.

FOREWORD

It is 12:15 p.m. on an early autumn afternoon in downtown Milwaukee. A breeze from Lake Michigan snaps the painted fabric of the shop awnings. Bug-like buses roar down Wisconsin Avenue, downtown's main street. Doctors, secretaries, shipping clerks, stenographers, messengers, lawyers, and office workers hurry along the sidewalks in search of a place to eat lunch, something to buy. The wind pulls at their hats, lifts their neckties, billows their scarves. The year is 1958.

At the southwest corner of Second Street and Wisconsin Avenue, between Gimbels and the Boston Store, people stop to look at a crazy set of display windows. In the past, these twelve-foot-high windows displayed an upscale clothier's fashionable suits, dresses, and hats. The stainless steel at the edge of the glass used to shine in the sun, and the marble beneath the windows had a rich polish. Now the chrome is pitted. Every third screw holding it in place is missing. The marble veneer under the curved glass is cracked and chipped, exposing the masonry and old construction adhesive beneath.

Inside the windows, a carnival is in progress. Lights flash behind the glass and hand-lettered signs in a variety of sizes shout messages. Merchandise sits atop build-ups of plywood and colored foil and trim paper—a chaotic mass of goods too jumbled to comprehend in a glance. There are rings, watches, scatter pins, ceramic trinkets, toys, and tools. The build-ups rise in steps nearly seven feet, and the merchandise faces the sidewalk like a pulsating wall.

My Uncle Lou stands in a corner of one of the windows holding the Big Gun, a chrome stapler that mounts trim to the build-ups and attaches banners and signs to the display. These signs race with red letters traced in black. They say: SALE, MARKDOWN, 25% OFF, and LOOK. (The double-O has eyes painted in it.) Uncle Lou wields the big gun like a Wild West sheriff: bang, bang, fold, pull, bang, bang.

Some of the pedestrians pull on the clear glass and stainless steel handles of the door to enter this bizarre retail emporium, the Jewelry and Toy Center, which my father, Al Stein, owns with his brother Lou.

Jewelry and Toy Center is a refuge from the world outside—a place where jewelry always glitters and everything's always a bargain. Dad and Lou worked hard to create it. In 1953 they had opened their first store a couple of blocks away, at 4th and Wisconsin. Schlitz Brewing owned that building and rented the shop space to the brothers on a short-term basis. My dad and Lou started selling earrings for forty-nine cents, which angered the owners of the higher-end jewelry stores on the block. The other retailers got a court injunction against Al and Lou, aimed at ousting them as transient merchants, but it was too late. The brothers had already secured a year's lease from Schlitz. They stayed for three years, but eventually moved down the block to take advantage of the heavier foot traffic.

—Jack El-Hai

# CHAPTER
ONE

# STREET-SMART
ENTREPRENEURS

Al and Lou Stein were like many other small, independent retailers in the latter half of the twentieth century. My father and uncle were first-generation Americans whose immigrant parents came to the U.S. from Eastern Europe to escape religious persecution and they became a part of the American dream. Their path to that dream, like that of both of my grandfathers before them, was through entrepreneurial means. There is a lot of scientific evidence to suggest that entrepreneurs think and behave differently; they have strong powers of deductive reasoning and, in general, a greater risk tolerance. The Stein twins were consummate entrepreneurs; they would never seek to become a part of an established company, punch a time clock or "work their way up" in a business, even another retail business; it wasn't who they were. They were street-smart guys who had retailing in their guts, like the Gershwin brothers had music in their souls. The Steins also came along at a time in American retailing when they could use the marketplace as their school of trial and error.

The twins' initial retail business endeavor, Jewelry and Toy Center, was a decade-long experiment in ad hoc, from-the-gut retailing. It was not pretty, not planned, just out there for the curiosity and indulgence of Milwaukeeans; it mixed consumption, entertainment, and oddity. The business venture that followed was a bona fide branded concept: Pill & Puff became a defining brand and a new niche concept that was as simple and elegant in its conception and execution as Jewelry and Toy was ugly and primitive. I was born and raised in the retail Petri dish that brought both entities to life. I lived it—we lived it—in the stores and at the kitchen table, the highs and the lows, successes and failures. It was formative, sometimes brutal, but always interesting. It also gave me a unique perspective on retailing and brand building that has served me well over my four-decade career.

## RETAILING'S ORIGIN AND EVOLUTION

While the retail marketplace is centuries-old, retailing as we know it today largely grew from the seeds of commerce planted at the later half of the nineteenth century. As America moved from an agrarian to an industrialized society, our first modern retail pioneers were getting a footing in population centers around the country. In 1852 a gentleman named Potter Palmer opened a dry goods store in Chicago that eventually became Marshall Field's. Joseph L. Hudson opened his first store in Detroit in 1881 and Richard Sears and Alvah Roebuck joined forces in 1886. David May opened his first department store in 1887, and F. W. Woolworth opened his first in 1897.

During the first decade of the twentieth century many other names emerged that have become synonymous with American retailing. W. J. Nordstrom in Seattle was founded in 1901, while out west in Wyoming J. C. Penney got its start in 1902, and Carson Pirie Scott had its beginnings in Chicago in 1903. In Dallas in 1907, Herbert Marcus Sr. along with his sister Carrie Marcus Neiman and her husband A. L. Neiman opened the first Neiman Marcus store. In Boston in 1908, Edward Filene began selling excess merchandise out of the basement of his father's store. In New York City between 1914 and 1915, B. Altman's, Lord & Taylor, Saks Fifth Avenue, Stern's, and R. H. Macy's all operated stores in Manhattan between 34th and 52nd Streets. The stories of these families and how they shaped American's tastes and shopping habits are legendary.

The growth of these new urban shopping districts was fueled by the influx of European immigrants and rural Americans as well. But they were further enhanced by other key technological developments, including electric streetlights and new public transportation,

**Pill & Puff became a defining brand and a new niche concept that was as simple and elegant in its conception and execution as Jewelry and Toy was ugly and primitive.**

such as streetcars, that replaced horse-drawn buggies. In some cities, elevated railroads were followed closely by the first subways. So significant was the change to major population centers around the country that a new word was being used to identify the retail phenomenon: *downtown*.

These new department stores with their enormous scale and grandeur were attractions to many, but they were not loved by all. Their emergence and rapid growth was often at the expense of the small independent retailers who made up the very fabric of commerce and trade in the cities. They were the dry goods retailers, grocers, haberdashers, tailors, confectioners, and bookstore and shoe-store owners. Most were family owned, family run, and specialists in their chosen product, service, or craft. These small merchants could not buy in the volume or at the low prices that the great mass merchants could. And they could not afford to sell at the slim margins that were often being offered by the new retail havens next door or just down the street. Often it was the boldly stated intention of the new retail kings to drive a neighborhood pawn out of business; some things never change. Ironically, some of the same merchants who were responsible for building the great new urban department stores were themselves the product of small independent origins. But with the help of key backers or financiers, they were able to build these first great temples of consumerism, squarely aimed at the newly emerging American middle class.

Many of America's first merchants came from modest means and some were "right off the boat," as my dad used to say in reference to the large number of immigrants at the turn of the last century. Often, they may have gotten a meager start, such as selling pieces of fruit on a street corner out of boxes. With a little success, the box would turn into a cart and the cart into a small storefront shop. And the storefront shop occupied by the often-struggling merchant was invariably in front of or beneath the very home where the family lived. In many cases it was an extended family, two and three generations of folks speaking a "foreign" language. A language that was both foreign to settled Americans and equally unfamiliar to other immigrants in another neighborhood only a dozen blocks away or so. This was the patchwork that was being played out in American cities up and down the East Coast and very soon in the American heartland as well.

> These new department stores with their enormous scale and grandeur were attractions to many, but they were not loved by all.

## RETAIL ROOTS

My dad and his brother came from just such a family. Jacob and Elizabeth Nomakstonsky fled from persecution in Minsk, Russia, to Stockholm, Sweden, at the turn of the twentieth century. Like many Eastern European Jews, they dreamed of starting a new life in America, but needed a sponsor who could vouch for them. They had friends from Russia who had already emigrated to the U.S. and set up residency in Milwaukee, Wisconsin. In 1906, Jacob was able to come to the States and begin a career as a tailor.

Jacob started working in a tailor shop in Russia at the age of twelve. For the first year he did nothing but sweep floors, but by the age of thirteen he began his apprenticeship under the guidance of a master tailor. He learned his craft well and once in the U.S., he was hired by a major suit-maker in Milwaukee. Immediately, Jacob acquired the nickname "Stonsky" from his shop buddies, who didn't remember let alone attempt to pronounce his full name; and in the spirit of American change, he decided to go a step further and shorten it to Stein.

By 1908 Jacob wired for my grandmother and their two small children, Herman and Nettie, to make the voyage to the States. They boarded the Lusitania, which was dubbed "Greyhound of the Seas" because it was one of the fastest ocean liners afloat. The

Lusitania had made its maiden voyage just a year earlier and with its 68,000-horsepower engines it was capable of up to 25 knots. The ship was secretly built to Admiralty specifications, as it was destined for British government service in the impending war. The crossing was very hard for Elizabeth and she was quite ill during the entire voyage. A kind stranger took care of her two young children for the entire crossing.

The spirit of entrepreneurship is deeply ingrained in my family for many generations and on both sides. Soon after my grandmother was able to join my grandfather in America, they began a business of their own. By this time, Jacob's skills and artistry had been finely honed and he opened his first tailor shop in downtown Milwaukee on Cass Street north of Wisconsin Avenue, Milwaukee's main business artery. He worked hard to acquire the pressing work for two of Milwaukee's leading hotels of the day, the Knickerbocker and the Astor. Often Jacob would get a call at 4:00 a.m. to come to one of the hotels to retrieve suits that needed to be pressed and returned by 9:00 that same morning. On numerous occasions there were special jobs for the likes of Herbert Hoover and other notables who warranted additional attention. However, from what I've been told, Jacob only knew one way to do things and that was with painstaking attention to detail—sometimes at his own expense.

As the business grew, so did Jacob and Elizabeth Stein's family. They soon welcomed their second daughter, Betty, in 1911, and four years later twin brothers Al and Lou were born. Al made his way out of the birth canal first and for the rest of their lives, his was the dominant personality. The twins stayed together virtually their entire lives, separated only briefly during World War II. They were in business together, got married together, and had their kids together.

As Milwaukee grew in the 1920s, the city's outskirts expanded as well. Townships outside of the city limits became known as suburbs and on Milwaukee's north shore, beside the banks of Lake Michigan, the well-to-do were building stately homes in Shorewood. Jacob was very sensitive to trends and business opportunities, so he decided that he would become the first tailor to take advantage of the trade moving north. In 1925 he opened a shop on Maryland Avenue and Capitol Drive. He subsequently sold the business and opened another shop at 4495 North Oakland Avenue, which is where he, Elizabeth, and their six children lived and worked.

My grandmother's one dream through all those years was to have her own house, but it was not to be. Even though Jacob was doing rather well in his trade, a home was not his priority; cars, however, were. And just as entrepreneurship is a multigenerational phenomenon in my family, so too is the dominant car gene! Jacob always had a new and fancy runabout. As an expression of his personal style (and brand), he made alterations to his vehicles decades before the notion of customizing had its roots in the American automobile culture. He would fabricate special, upholstered kickplates to cover the face of the running boards, lovingly stitching them on his machine as if preparing them for a client or family member to wear with pride.

Jacob became a well-respected tailor among his clientele, which included captains of industry, judges, and other men of means. Among his peers he was a leader, serving as the president of the state's Master Tailors Association. But Jacob could also be the master of his own undoing if his vision did not match that of his customers. According to the stories, if Jacob and his clients couldn't quite see eye to eye on a matter of aesthetics, the situation usually resulted in loud, emotional Yiddish outbursts and wild gesticulations. This sometimes resulted in a hastily dressed digni-

**The spirit of entrepreneurship is deeply ingrained in my family for many generations and on both sides.**

tary fleeing the scene, unlikely to return for another fitting. Jacob had a temper.

Identical twins Al and Lou Stein were born on January 26, 1915, and because Al beat Lou into the world, he pretty much led the team. The phenomenon of identical twins is quite interesting; and from my own personal, highly unscientific perspective, these two guys together would have made up one balanced and complete personality. One exhibited domineering, take-charge, sometimes aggressive behavior, while the other had a subordinate, passive, and more accommodating personality. My father Al was clearly the former, and Lou the latter of the twins.

Growing up they were exceedingly close and virtually impossible to tell apart. My grandmother sent them off to kindergarten with long curly locks of hair, not having the heart to send them to a barber. They were immediately sent home with a note from the principal stating "their boys looked like girls" and that they needed haircuts before they would be allowed back in school. Always comedians, they often traded places in class, making sure the guy with the most information took the test. Later in life, they'd get waitresses completely flustered by pretending they had their orders mixed up just to mess with their heads and have a good laugh.

Al and Lou both helped out in the tailor shop in the late 1920s and 1930s, learning to run the pressing equipment as well as doing some sewing and alterations. Meeting Jacob's exceedingly high quality standards could not have been an easy task. The twins ultimately dropped out of North Division High School in 1933 (a half year short of graduation) as a result of Jacob's ill health. Dad took over duties at the tailor shop and Lou delivered potatoes for 25 cents a week to help feed the family.

## OFF TO WAR

The twins' only period of separation occurred during World War II when they both enlisted to fight in the European theatre. They both made promises to my grandmother, who naturally feared the worst, that neither boy would "shoot any guns" nor do anything to cause them bodily harm—quite a promise under the circumstances. But each kept his word. Lou left first in late 1941, and Al enlisted on March 31, 1942.

Dad's service began as a surgical technician assigned to Fitzsimmons General Hospital in Denver, Colorado. To this day, I'm not quite sure how he convinced his superiors that he was qualified for such service, but my dad could be quite persuasive when he needed to be. After completing eight weeks of training in the States, he went on to serve nearly two years of his three-and-a-half-year stint abroad ranked as a staff sergeant whose principle duty was as a surgical technician. But it was Dad's final year and a half of service that brought him the greatest satisfaction, and a small footnote in history.

Al Stein's final assignment was as Entertainment Director (army code 442), a role that included "the planning and organizing of entertainment for 14 general hospitals in the European Theater of operations." He booked and scheduled USO shows and touring entertainment units. This enabled him to brush elbows with many popular musicians and entertainers of the time who were either committed to the war effort or enlisted in a branch of the military. One such entertainment great was Glenn Miller, the American jazz musician, arranger, composer, and band leader of the swing era. Miller's "Big Band" made him the most popular recording artist of the day. His signature recordings included "In the Mood," "Moonlight Serenade," and "Chattanooga Choo Choo," to name just a

> The phenomenon of identical twins is quite interesting; and from my own personal, highly unscientific perspective, these two guys together would have made up one balanced and complete personality.

few. Miller played with the likes of The Dorsey Brothers, Benny Goodman, and Gene Krupa and starred in motion pictures in the 1930s for Paramount Pictures and Twentieth Century Fox. In 1942, at the height of his career, the thirty-eight-year-old Miller joined the war effort to entertain the troops.

In late December 1944, Dad arranged to have Miller fly from Britain to Paris to play for soldiers who had recently liberated the city. Regrettably, his plane disappeared over the English Channel, leaving no trace of the crew, plane, or passengers, shocking the nation and shortening his brilliant career. Dad never talked much about the incident to us; but in his final days, while being hospitalized with end-stage pancreatic cancer, visits from his many poker buddies included a healthy ribbing about the incident—Dad's own private *Glenn Miller Story*.

## MERE FORMALITY

The first department stores of the late 1800s and early 1900s were just massive, merchandise-filled halls. Elements of elegance and finery started to emerge in the late 1900s and early 1920s, only to be scaled back once again during the years of the Great Depression. The eras between the World Wars brought new levels of consumerism to American retailing that began to set the stage for the post World War II explosion of all things grand and glorious. Downtowns bustled with cars and electric buses, retailing chains grew, and shopping became high art, entertainment, and social event all in one. Chandeliers hung from grand ceilings, piano playing reverberated through departments, and well-dressed socialites mixed, sometimes uncomfortably, with the emerging middle class. Folks would meet for lunch, eating delicate little sandwiches in tearooms, which became a prerequisite of any properly outfitted department store.

By today's casual standards of dress and time-stressed mass consumerism it's hard to relate to the ceremonial nature of a trip downtown in the late 1940s or early 1950s. This was arguably the height of the department stores' reign and the pinnacle of the country's thriving downtowns. I vividly remember my sister and I dressing up in "good clothes" on a Saturday afternoon to venture downtown to see Dad. We'd hop in Mom's two-tone, salmon-and-gray '55 Chevy Bel Air four-door sedan and depart from our modest two-story home on Ardmore Avenue in suburban Whitefish Bay and head downtown. The familiar sound of the Chevy's straight six-cylinder motor revved repeatedly as it was being coaxed through the gears. Mom smoothly maneuvered the manual "three-on-the-tree" standard transmission as we made our way through the Bay into Shorewood, along Lincoln Memorial drive on the edge of Lake Michigan, and then to our destination in the central business district and the heart of Beer Town, U.S.A.

Milwaukee was a one-main-street downtown, which was to say most of the prime retail, movie theatres, department stores, and popular specialty chains were located on Wisconsin Avenue, what Dad referred to as the "main drag." Downtown was bisected by the Milwaukee River, which runs perpendicular to Wisconsin Avenue. East Wisconsin, which originated at the Lakefront, was originally devoted to the carriage trade, and West Wisconsin, running west from the river, was the heart of the shopping and theatre district. Ironically, due to a historical disagreement between land owners of the properties on both sides of the river, East and West Wisconsin Avenues were intentionally misaligned; which was ultimately rectified by an awkwardly angled bridge (which stands to this day) connecting East and West Wisconsin Avenue.

Gimbels Department Store was right at the river and the Boston Store, the other major downtown department store, was four blocks west, more or less bookending the prime downtown retail real estate. Between the two major department store anchors were various independent, specialty, and chain retailers similar to those that populated downtowns across the country. The specialties were generally divided into two categories: local or regional and national chains. As the term "specialties" implies, these retailers tended to specialize in a category of hard goods like shoes or appliances or soft goods like clothing, or they were segregated by value, such as off-price.

The pioneer of off-price retailing, just down the block from Jewelry and Toy Center, was the venerable F. W. Woolworth's "5 and 10 cent store"—arguably the forerunner of today's great discount chains. Founded by Frank Winfield Woolworth in 1878, Woolworth's, although considered a department store by some, sold discounted general merchandise. But what originally set them apart beyond price was that they were the first retailer to actually let customers mingle with and handle goods. It's hard to imagine by today's standards that nearly all general merchants prior to Woolworth's hired clerks to assist customers with their needs. Goods were separated from customers by glass-enclosed counters and clerks would fill customers' orders, one item at a time.

Woolworth's growth and success was monumental, brothers Frank and Charles soon began partnering with other groups to build similar store franchises, and by 1911 six different companies controlling nearly 600 stores in the U.S. and Canada were incorporated under the Woolworth name. In 1913 the Woolworth Building, then the world's tallest structure, was completed in New York to house the corporate headquarters. The complete construction project lasted three years and was paid for in cash. Another innovation in general merchandising that was uniquely Woolworth's was the lunch counter. This became a familiar gathering place, as well as a staple for business people and shoppers in need of a quick, inexpensive lunch.

In fact, it was a Greensboro, North Carolina, Woolworth lunch counter that played a pivotal role in the civil rights movement in the U.S. On February 1, 1960, four young, African-American students were denied service at the then-segregated lunch counter and they refused to leave. Word spread of their valiant actions and similar "sit in" demonstrations began to take place in other Woolworth's and competing chains throughout the country in support of the students and their push for equality and civil rights. On July 25, 1960, the first African American was finally served at the Woolworth's lunch counter in Greensboro where the first sit-ins began. The following day, the entire Woolworth's chain was desegregated. Today Greensboro Woolworth's is the home of the International Civil Rights Center and Museum.

Woolworth's clearly paved the way for four other major discount stores that can all trace their start back to the early 1960s. The other discount general merchandiser of the day, S. S. Kresge Company, opened its first Kmart in 1962, while Woolworth's opened Woolco (their full-line discount department store) at the same time. That same year in Rogers, Arkansas, Sam Walton opened his first Walmart and Minneapolis-based Dayton's department stores opened a similar concept called Target. These were by no means the only major discounters of the era, but they certainly became the central players in the huge trend toward off-price merchandising. Throughout modern retailing history there have been many stories of big against small, price against specialization, and the winners and losers have not been so predictable or obvious. Behind the battles for location, margins, brands, exclusivity, and commodity are people and families attempting to make a living and endure.

By the mid-1950s, downtowns nationally were already in de-

**The pioneer of off-price retailing, just down the block from Jewelry and Toy Center, was the venerable F. W. Woolworth's "5 and 10 cent store."**

cline. The popularity of the American automobile was driving a growing middle class from one car to two cars per family. At the same time, mass-transit ridership continued on the downturn that had begun two decades prior, as most "modern" American cities were proudly removing the last vestiges of the efficient and venerable streetcars that populated downtowns for over a half century.

## FOUR-WHEEL LOVE AFFAIR

The concept of mass transit had lost its appeal for mid-century Americans because they had fallen madly in love with Detroit iron and the independence that came with "See the U.S.A. in your Chevrolet," as Dinah Shore would croon every Sunday night on The *Dinah Shore Chevy Show*. Never before (and perhaps never since) had an actor or actress been so tied to a specific brand as was the case with Dinah and Chevrolet, which sponsored her huge hit NBC variety show that ran from the mid-1950s to the early 1960s. Today, the thought of a variety show's jingle being a blatant advertisement seems strange, but back then it merely signified the tightly woven ties between popular culture and consumerism, as well as the influence that advertising was beginning to have on consumer behavior.

Our new chrome-trimmed love affair was being playing out on ever-crowded streets, highways, driveways, garages, and parking lots. America was hooked. Detroit's Big Three were dishing out a good dose of planned obsolescence with the redesign of the cruisers on about a three-year cycle along with annual styling refreshment. But it was the New York mad men of advertising who were serving up the annual model change with a sense of ceremony and suspense that made the annual event something just short of a national holiday.

I am and always have been a "car guy" and, as I said before, in my family it's genetic, just like migraine headaches and high cholesterol. For me the excitement that came with the anticipation of the change of the model year each fall was monumental. By the time I was about eight, while most of my buddies were beginning to covet and collect comic books and baseball cards, I was anxiously anticipating the next issue of *Motor Trend* magazine, which Uncle Ivan (Mom's brother) got me hooked on. *Motor Trend* became my gateway drug to all things automobilia. By the late spring and early summer, those telephoto-lensed "spy shots" of the Big Three's new models were making their way into the car magazines and the previously published styling studio sketches began to manifest themselves into deliciously grainy images of the exciting new models. To further build suspense, by the second to third week in September, the dealerships would cover their big show windows with white paper to mask the changeover activity prior to the official date of the new model's unveiling. But the final suspenseful chapter came with the arrival of the massive car carriers, those great behemoth multiaxle, rolling skeletons packed solid with Motor City's newly minted offerings. Like great iron ghosts the vehicles were fully covered in white tarps to further heighten the suspense and prevent prying eyes from getting a premature glimpse of the new models—this was high theatre. And if that were not enough suspense for this prepubescent, geeky child, there would be excruciating teaser commercials on TV showing about a half-second shot of a new grill or fin to nearly drive me over the edge. Naturally, in 1956 there were no VCRs or TiVos to record and freeze the image; we were being teased and manipulated by the best in the business.

If the model year changeover was akin to the National League pennant race (we had the Milwaukee Braves, after all) than the annual auto show was my World Series. The excitement and antic-

**But it was the New York mad men of advertising who were serving up the annual model change with a sense of ceremony and suspense that made the annual event something just short of a national holiday.**

ipation of this annual November event would invariably be migraine producing; so I could only hope that the migraine would occur the day before or after, and not on *the* day itself. Anyone who gets migraines knows you have no control over when one will come. Then when one does, it's into a dark room with ice packs, interrupted by frequent mad dashes to the john to heave one's guts out, then back to the dark and quiet bedroom sanctuary to deal with the excruciating pain. Most years I was able to dodge the bullet and make the big show.

In the winter of 1956 (for the introduction of the new '57s) I had just turned nine, and when my parents asked me how I wanted to celebrate my birthday I decided what better way than to take a group of ten or twelve of my closest buds (guys and girls) to the auto show. Why not share the joy? You can imagine the response on the part of the kids' parents when my mom shared the news of the impending car party. Now, I had already seen the new '57 Chevys, which nearly brought me to my knees with excitement— so I was sure the rest of the kids were going to soon join my state of rapture. It was only a matter of time.

So the big Sunday arrived, headache-free, thank g-d. Our two used Chevys full of eight- and nine-year-olds departed for downtown Milwaukee and at the wheels were the cigarette-smoking parental team of "Steinie" and "Stein," as my parents irreverently referred to one another (at no time throughout my life had I ever heard either refer to the other by their given names). I was about to burst. Once we arrived downtown, parked the cars, and got the tickets, we entered the colossal Milwaukee Arena and Auditorium complex and I was transported to my nirvana. A barrage of color, sounds, and smells of newly minted Detroit iron mixed with tightly packed, milling Milwaukeeans (with the combined aroma of stale cigarette smoke, Old Spice aftershave, and Miller Highlife) and I was caught up in the annual celebration of all things "car-ific"; and on *my big day*! I remember turning around and looking into the eyes of nine of my buddies and seeing a combination of bedazzlement, confusion, and horror—and a lot of wide-open mouths. I was thinking, *yeah, ain't it great?*

I could soon tell that I was dealing with a group of newbies (sort of like sitting down on a first visit to a Chinese restaurant and not knowing what to do with the chopsticks), so I took the lead. "See kids, we go from model to model, stop and look at the girls on the big spinning platforms, and pick up two each of the car brochures. You'll want to make sure you take *two*—that way you can cut one apart to decorate your room and keep the other one neat and undamaged to page through." I was using my best sales technique, which I learned from my dad who carefully deconstructed the sale of any item by personalizing the product and emphasizing the benefits to the customer. Hmmmm.... There was not a lot of feedback from this crowd. "Then later we will get some hot dogs and pop!" "Yay!!!!!" Now, we were cookin'.

It turned out that while the hot dogs and pop probably saved the day for most, the kids really got excited at the Buick display, where we saw none other than Dale Robertson all dressed up in his TV western attire, including matching six shooters. Dale was one of the season's new stars being featured on *Tales of Wells Fargo,* which ran from 1957 to 1962. He was dressed completely in black and stood next to a brilliant blue Buick Roadmaster convertible that had to be a full twenty feet in length. With each revolution of the car turntable, he would pull out his six shooters and twirl them for the audience; Milwaukeeans really knew how to have a good time back then.

## DOWNTOWN IS GOING DOWN

For me and so many others in the middle of the twentieth century, our cars were stars. Certainly being able to pull up to the neighborhood Sinclair station and "fill 'er up" for about four dollars, and then get change back, made it pretty painless. But the traffic congestion caused by motorists clogging downtown streets was partly to blame for the deterioration of the downtown retail business. From the period immediately after World War II until about 1954, most major cities' downtowns had already experienced double-digit declines. As suburban flight began to take hold across the U.S., families were living farther and farther from the central business districts and retailers of all sizes and types were beginning to set up shop in the suburbs to cater to these new bedroom communities. With the moves came the population's desire for convenience, and their growing financial ability to pay for it.

The 1960s was a time of incredible optimism; powerful unions were responsible for wage increases that helped build and strengthen the American middle class. And the postwar Baby Boom that began in 1946 and culminated in 1964 was responsible for an unprecedented birth spurt totaling seventy-eight million children. We became a consumer nation. We also became a nation that had little respect for the heritage and preservation of our country's rich architectural fabric that was exhibited in many downtowns over the first half of the twentieth century. Land and building materials were cheap, labor was plentiful, and the merchants who were responsible for developing major downtown retailing were flush with cash and ready to clone the downtown department and specialty stores. So clone they did, but utilizing a new building vocabulary, that of the suburban shopping center and its big brother, the regional mall that would follow.

## RURAL AMERICANA

Standing in stark contrast to the urban population centers of the early 1900s was the country's vast rural population, who were still the majority of this country's seventy-six million people. Wisconsin became a state in 1848 and central Wisconsin became a popular source of hardwood and pine, which were actively being logged by East Coast lumber barons. In 1874 the town of Medford, Wisconsin, was founded—named after Medford, Massachusetts, where the Wisconsin Central Railroad hauled lumber to the East Coast. Medford became the county seat of Taylor County and by the turn of the century, it was beginning to prosper. As in thousands of other small farm-belt communities in the American heartland, the general store became the center of commerce, providing groceries and basic necessities for the communities' subsistence. In the fall of 1921 my maternal grandfather, Peter Bootzin, in partnership with his friend, Ben Semon, purchased the local Medford grocery store, and a year later Peter bought out Ben's interest.

My maternal grandfather was born March 26, 1896, in Rega, Russia. This was another time and place in history that was not very kind to the Jewish people. Throughout Russia there were waves of anti-Jewish atrocities known as pogroms. In 1905, the pogrom in Odessa, Russia was responsible for the death of 2,500 Jews. Similar sporadic attacks were taking place in towns and villages throughout the Northern Ukraine and word spread to distant Rega about the situation.

Around 1905, at the very young age of nine, with the help of a kind farmer, my grandfather was hidden in a horse-drawn cart under bales of hay and taken to a seaport; there he boarded an ocean-going vessel and made the long journey to the U.S. alone. Ultimately he was joined by an older sister in Milwaukee, where he had other relatives to live with. Peter eventually enrolled in night school to learn to speak English before making his way north to seek his fortune in Medford, Wisconsin with fellow immigrant and friend Ben Semon.

Peter Bootzin was a savvy retailer and businessman. By 1922 he had already begun to make a name for himself in Medford. He extended credit to farmers, who often subsisted on very little during planting season and got paid back at harvest time. While still in business with Ben, they ordered pottery mixing bowls from Red Wing Pottery in Red Wing, Minnesota, and had inscribed in the bottom "Compliments of Semon and Bootzin." In an early example of promotion and brand building, they gave the bowls away at Christmastime to appreciative customers.

In 1923, Peter married Bernice Braun, a second-generation American from one of the only Jewish families in Medford. In February 1925 they had the first of their two children, my mother Maxine. Then in August 1929, their son Ivan was born. Peter continued the tradition of offering his customers holiday gifts into the 1930s with even larger items: bean pots. By then, the inscription glazed onto the sides of the multicolor pots became a bit more poetic, "When you bake try me, When you buy try Peter Bootzin, The Corner Store, Medford, Wis."

Peter was a gentle and unassuming man who invested wisely in Medford and the surrounding towns. Building on the success of the Corner Store, he bought a grain mill, and then another, and before long he was supplying the farm families around Taylor County with not only the food for their families, but also the grain and fertilizer for their livestock and crops. He was always fair and took an interest in every family. People would come to him in need and unable to pay, and he would say in his broken English, "take what you need, you'll pay when you can," and almost all of them did. The week the stock market crashed in October 1929, and city folks who were heavily invested in the market lost nearly everything, Peter and Bernice took delivery of a new baby grand piano. Peter made prudent investments in "his people," the families of Medford and the surrounding communities. He knew something about sustainable business practices long before it became trendy.

**People would come to him in need and unable to pay, and he would say in his broken English, "take what you need, you'll pay when you can," and almost all of them did.**

# CHAPTER
# TWO

# FROM DOWNTOWN
# TO THE MALL

By late 1945, Al and Lou Stein were back from the war. They had turned thirty years old, and they were ready to settle down and start families. As with just about everything the twins did in life, they felt compelled to do it together or not at all. Lou had been seeing a girl from Athens, Wisconsin, who was living in a duplex above his married sister, but Al had not met "the right one" yet. Lou's sweetheart, Ruth Ann Semon, was the daughter of Ben Semon, Peter Bootzin's longtime friend and business partner.

Each year, the major Wisconsin feed dealers would gather for their annual convention, and in the summer of 1946 it took place in Milwaukee. Both Peter Bootzin and Ben Semon were planning to attend the gala along with their wives, and Ruth Ann asked Lou Stein to attend as her guest. This left Al dateless, which would never do. So Ruth Ann suggested that Peter's daughter Maxine should make the trip from Medford to Milwaukee to meet Lou's twin. For Maxine this was a mixed blessing; she was delighted to get a date with an available Jewish guy from Milwaukee, but she had mixed feelings about spending the weekend with Ruth Ann.

From the time both girls were quite young, the Semons and the Bootzins would visit one another, sometimes in Athens and sometimes in Medford. During one such visit to Medford, Ruth Ann took one of Maxine's dolls back to Athens, without Maxine's permission, and Maxine *never* got over it. I loved my mother dearly, but she really could carry a grudge. At the convention, Al's date with Maxine went swimmingly and within six months both couples were engaged and were soon married—in a *joint ceremony*. In addition, much to the anger and resentment of both brides, Maxine and Ruth were coerced into a joint honeymoon as well. Remember, they were dealing with two powerful and charming salesmen. Eleven months and change later, I was born and so was my cousin Suzy. We both got the same initials: SBS, but only one of us got circumcised.

## A SOLITARY GUY

I was an awkward kid, geeky long before it was fashionable. When it came to athletics, due to poor eye-hand coordination, I got picked near to last for games at recess, even after most of the girls got picked. "You get Stein," they'd say. "No fair. We got Stein the last time." You get the drift. Suffice it to say that growing up, I spent a lot of time alone—often in my room, building plastic car models or just listening to music. I had my Sony AM transistor radio (from Jewelry and Toy Center) permanently fixed to one of Milwaukee's two venerable rock stations; most of the time it was AM-920 WOKY ("WOKY in Milwaukee," as the jingle went). When not connected to the Sony via the single, tiny, white earphone (this was before stereo, remember), I was listening to long-play albums (LPs). I never really bought 45s like some of my friends. I didn't like to spend the money for singles, I preferred saving for albums.

Migraines were a constant and persistent problem for me growing up. They are often genetic—my grandmother, mother, and cousins all suffered from them. Some ENT doctor in Milwaukee (who shall remain nameless) convinced my parents that extensive nasal reconstructive surgery would curb the horrendous and frequent attacks. It seemed that many in my parents' generation looked upon doctors as gods and didn't question their veracity or the legitimacy of treatments like this. So I was put through two awful surgical procedures as a teenager, which contributed to other health issues later in life, but ultimately had no effect on the headaches. And to make matters (much) worse Milwaukee's Dr. Mengele felt it would stimulate my postoperative healing to give my thyroid gland some "harmless" radiation therapy.

I was a mediocre student at best, though I did excel at art in elementary school and mechanical drawing in high school. To this

> I got picked near to last for games at recess, even after most of the girls got picked. "You get Stein," they'd say. "No fair. We got Stein the last time."

day, I have nightmares about not receiving my high school diploma. I spent several weeks of every summer during elementary school in one type of remedial class or another, often reading. Had I grown up forty years later I would have probably been diagnosed with ADHD or some similar learning disability. I was a pretty intense kid.

A favorite childhood pastime was building plastic scale model cars, which proved to have very detrimental side effects. I would spend hours concentrating on complicated and detailed vehicles—a mix of American, foreign, and prewar hotrods. Copious amounts of time was spent studying illustrated directions (today, I'm a wiz with IKEA) and lovingly applying the Testors plastic cement, taking great care not to apply too much. Excess glue would quickly destroy a beautifully hand-painted finish that I had laboriously applied to the tiny unassembled pieces. It's fair to say I was fixated on achieving a higher level of quality in model making than most kids I knew. Sequestered in my small, eight-by-ten bedroom I can remember a sort of transcendence that would take place as the aroma of model enamel and plastic cement would permeate my brain and begin to affect my powers of concentration. Suddenly, the bedroom door would fly open, and my mother would emerge, uttering a shriek, "My God, Sandy. It smells *awful* in here," as she raced to open the window. "It does?" I would respond in my half-dazed state.

The creative energies I spent on those cars were indicative of my pursuit of other passions. Regrettably, schoolwork did not figure among them. I also had a very different approach to styling. AMT, Revell, and the other model manufacturers of the day provided endless pieces of trim and decals to customize the "rides" and most of my buddies would find ways to use all of them. My approach, on the other hand, was more Spartan. I was always wondering what a stylist would do to improve the design rather than just embellish it. Once finished with my most recent creation, I would labor for hours, carefully rearranging my entire plastic fleet to prominently feature my latest masterpiece. My model display looked more like a retail show window than a kid's car collection.

## THE CREATIVE CURSE

I've always felt that being a creative individual is a mixed blessing. The things that occupy the minds of most creative people are often less than footnotes in the lives of others. At some level, we live in a different world. We see, hear, and often feel things differently. Sensitivity can be both beautiful and nasty all at the same time. I believe most creative people are by nature highly observant. Visual artists and designers see and the musically inclined hear things differently or more intensely than others. I also believe there is a higher level of natural curiosity that often drives creative types to take the ordinary and do something extraordinary with it. It often starts with a mix of fascination and inspiration.

There are wonderful stories about what motivated certain creative individuals at a young age. The world-renowned architect Frank Gehry, whose stainless steel–clad buildings have become his iconic brand, was fascinated as a child by watching large carp swim in the bathtub of his grandmother's house, observing the way light played off their scales. That was before they were transformed into dinner, probably gefilte fish. The Spanish architect Santiago Calatrava, whose magnificent addition to the Milwaukee War Memorial Art Center virtually rebranded Milwaukee, has long been fascinated with skeletal structures of dogs and birds, and it's easy to see these manifestations in his brilliant architectural designs.

The creative process requires great discipline to yield a result worthy of recognition and capable of standing the test of time. Good design has an element of simplicity and purity that sepa-

**I've always felt that being a creative individual is a mixed blessing. The things that occupy the minds of most creative people are often less than footnotes in the lives of others.**

rates it from other products or solutions that have come before or after it. Great designers learn to balance form, function, processes, and materials in a manner that often results in something that exceeds the functional requirements or market intent of the product or building. The result is something soulful, even transformational. Whether it's an interior space, a car, or a chair, a well-designed object has the capacity to captivate and move its audience on an emotional level. I know my interest in design stemmed from my passion and love for the automobile. I can always remember the singularly outstanding cars whose designs spoke to me in ways that made deep and lasting impressions.

In late 1960, on a family trip to Detroit, we ended up spending the better part of a day at a Ford garage in Chicago because my dad's 1957 Ford Skyliner (retractable) hardtop would not open up to allow us to access our luggage. From 1957 to 1959, Ford produced a top-of-the-line hardtop convertible with a metal top that would fold up and store in the trunk. This was the precursor to many of today's hardtop convertibles, but long before the advent of microchips and computer-run servomotors. The Skyliner operated through a series of electric motors that would perform the following sequence: open the reverse-hinged trunk, unlock and raise the roof, fold the top and lower it into the trunk, and then close the trunk lid. When operating correctly, it had an almost ballet-like fluidity that was captivating, and I entertained the neighbors more than once with its Transformer-like robotics. But the trip from Milwaukee to Detroit was too much for the three-year-old Ford and when we attempted to access our luggage near Chicago, we couldn't get the electric motors to budge. Our possessions were held captive in its great rear deck.

We ended up at the venerable Courtesy Motors in Chicago, which was at that time the largest Ford dealership in the world, to get our electric circuits uncrossed. It wasn't a quick fix, so we ended up spending much of the day waiting for a diagnosis and repair. Mom, Dad, and my sister Debbie (three and a half years my junior) were pretty cranky and out of sorts, but I had the chance to spend several hours just nosing around this really big car dealership—it was cool. In fact, Courtesy Motors and its owner/founder "Jim Moran the Courtesy Man," as he was known in Chicago, was the first auto dealer in the nation to advertise on TV, and the only automobile dealer ever to appear on the cover of *Time* magazine. At the time of his death in 2007 he had a net worth in excess of two billion and was ranked among Forbes 400 wealthiest people.

Now 1960 was not exactly a banner year for design at the Ford Motor Company, so I wasn't expecting any big surprises as I was perusing the massive service bay on my own guided tour—until I saw in a dark and distant corner of the service area an unidentified vehicle that required further investigation. The closer I got, the more mysterious, unfamiliar, and out of place the vehicle seemed. It was clearly not American; its diminutive size and shape was definitely European. It had sculpted lines, at once long and low with a fluid appearance. It sat poised on great, chromed spoke wheels, with genuine knock-off wheel hubs, common to only British and Italian sports cars of the era. This was the fastest-looking, most splendid automobile shape I'd ever laid eyes on. Marilyn Monroe in the flesh (whose scantily dressed photo in *Life* magazine graced the inside of my bedroom closet door) would not have gotten this twelve-year-old more jazzed. My heart was racing and my throat got dry—what was I freaking looking at?

Completely devoid of side markings or chrome trim that Detroit would customarily lavish its vehicles with, I couldn't yet identify the mystery car even at close range. The car was wedged into a corner, which made getting around the rear to attempt to identify

**Good design has an element of simplicity and purity that separates it from other products or solutions that have come before it or after.**

it difficult. But from an oblique angle I could read the small inscription on the trunk lid: E-Type Jaguar. "Oh my God," I whispered, "it's the new XK-E." They weren't even on the market in the U.S. yet, and maybe not even in Great Britain, and I was staring at (and touching) one in a Ford garage in Chicago! The E-Type Jaguar, or XK-E as it was referred to, was introduced in early 1961 and ran until 1975, and became one of the most famous sports cars in the world—and one of the most iconic shapes in the history of automotive design. It also became synonymous with design purity and elegant execution.

## EARLY INSPIRATION

While it was undeniable that automotive design was my passion, I was also gaining an early appreciation for contemporary architecture and interior design. The Milwaukee War Memorial Center building designed by Finnish architect and designer Eero Saarinen was completed in 1957 (decades prior to Calatrava's addition) on Milwaukee's lakefront. It represented a strong and important break from Milwaukee's traditional neoclassical approach to public buildings. Its magnificent and imposing cantilevered design made it appear to float over Lake Michigan, and was breathtaking in its strength, simplicity, and tendency to defy gravitational forces. I remember the first time my family drove past the newly completed building. My dad, not an advocate of contemporary art, architecture, or almost anything avant-garde, commented, "There's a guy who had a bad dream." Meaning Saarinen. I chuckled, because I knew I was supposed to, but I still looked on with amazement.

Unfortunately for Saarinen, the design appeared so shocking and visually unnerving to Milwaukeeans' sensibilities that shortly after the building's completion his firm was forced to design additional faux supports to visually "anchor" the building to its base before the public would dare to send their children there for art classes. Saarinen begrudgingly gave in to the blind demands of Milwaukee's uninspired, but he also had the last laugh. The additional structural wedge-shaped supports that were designed and added don't actually touch the ground. They float about an inch off their base and people used to jam gum and wads of paper underneath, maybe because they got the joke. The added elements that made the building appear "safe" for occupancy had compromised the purity of the original design.

I distinctly remember the first time I entered the lobby of the War Memorial Center and saw Mies van der Rohe's beautiful Barcelona chairs poised majestically in the sparsely furnished open lobby. The curvature of the chromed steel frames both contrasted with and visually complemented the simple leather upholstery. More sculpture than furniture, but functional nonetheless. I was quite taken by their elegant shape and simplicity. Years later, in an art history course, I learned these were first designed for the German Pavilion at the 1929 Barcelona exposition. Mies, whose popular aphorisms "less is more" and "God is in the details," would later become one of my design heroes during my Bauhaus-influenced college design curriculum. While the art center certainly made an impression on me, I was all about cars and I was sure my future was going to involve designing them.

## THE END OF JEWELRY AND TOY CENTER

By 1963 things were starting to change at Jewelry and Toy Center as Dad and Uncle Lou started experimenting with some new products that a jobber had brought in. Jobbers were the lifeblood of small independent retailers back then. They were the intermediaries who would buy and sell goods to small retailers like Dad and Lou, who were generally too small to establish direct relationships

Mies, whose popular aphorisms "less is more" and "God is in the details," would later become one of my design heroes during my Bauhaus-influenced college design curriculum.

37

with factories or larger distributors. Because these middlemen needed to make a living, the margins or profit that the twins ended up with were never very good. One jobber convinced them that he could take an unproductive area in the store and show them how to merchandise a new category that could "turn product like never before."

In retailing, besides profit margins, turning product is one of the keys to financial success. The more turns the better. If something stays on the shelf too long, it's not making money. This new category of goods that the jobber was talking about were health and beauty aids: toothpaste, deodorant, and the kind of stuff you would normally buy at the drugstore. Now Dad and Lou heard lots of pitches from all kinds of characters and through the years they hit on some winners. They sold some of the earliest transistor radios from Japan and one of the first "portable" TVs (both from Sony), which ran on batteries no less. But there were plenty of losers as well, stuff they couldn't *give* away; I think the clocks that *ran backward* were among them. An essential part of this guy's pitch had to do with discounting the product below what the drugstores were selling the goods for; this concept the twins understood pretty well.

They figured it might be a worthwhile experiment, so they took the jobber up on his offer and it worked. Before long, a twenty-foot section on the far west wall of the store morphed into a whole wall. Then they started clearing out old floor displays and soon about a third of the store area was devoted to this new category of product, producing more than sixty percent of the gross revenue of the entire store. And while the twins could begin to see the makings of a new business, other fates were at work.

In 1964, after a decade at the corner of Second Street and Wisconsin Avenue, the twins lost their lease. The site had been purchased and was set to be gutted and remodeled into the headquarters of a new regional bank. Al and Lou had a big going-out-of-business sale. This ended an important chapter, but the last years of Jewelry and Toy Center proved transformative for the Steins. The accidental product mix and haphazard merchandising approaches that embodied most of their ten-year retail existence at the corner of Second and Wisconsin Avenue was replaced by a new, more disciplined approach to product mix, merchandising, and the evolution of a *concept*. A pure category was emerging and they were experiencing the first signs of what would evolve into a future success and a bona fide *brand*. They were learning.

Clearly, things in the retail world were changing and the days of accidental retailing like that of Jewelry and Toy Center were about over. Specialty retailing was emerging as a dominant force in both the downtowns and newly emerging suburban shopping centers. Major players in every specialty category were materializing. In footwear Thom McAn had grown from some 850 stores in the mid-1950s to 1,400 stores by the mid-1970s. The venerable St. Louis-based Edison Brothers Stores was arguably one of the most successful specialty groups, developing retail brands with clear price points and core customer focus. Edison's brands included Baker's, Burt's, Leed's, and Chandler's; they had over 500 stores open by the mid-1960s and 1,000 units a decade later. This phenomenal growth in the specialty retail sector was fueled by the postwar economic boom and suburban sprawl.

What followed over the next several years proved life-changing for our two families and defining, career-wise, for me. After the twins closed the store, Mom and Dad took a brief vacation to the Orient. Once they returned, they began to contemplate what to do to support the family. I remember these were pretty tense times as neither family was flush with savings. I even recall Dad studying the classified section of *The Milwaukee Journal* and writing a resume,

**In retailing, besides profit margins, turning product is one of the keys to financial success. The more turns the better.**

something I don't believe he had ever done in his near fifty years. One time, he asked me to proofread a letter he had written to a potential employer. I was a high school junior (and hardly a stellar student), but I had at that moment as much formal education as he did, so I guess he figured he had little to lose. After I read the letter and his attached résumé, I remember thinking the family was in trouble if he thought he could make it in the corporate world. I got a migraine and went to bed.

It was not unusual for Dad to ask my opinion about business matters. The family was always a sounding board for business decisions both large and small, and dinner conversations were mostly focused on what had happened at the store. In fact, it was pretty much business matters that defined the limits of our father-son relationship. Suffice it to say, we had an unusual parent-child bond. It was always much easier for Dad to throw me the car keys (even at ten years old) so I could "practice" driving in the driveway than to commit emotional energy to more conventional child-rearing or father-son bonding. I actually thought it was pretty melodramatic when neighborhood parents would quickly emerge from their homes up and down the block (like a flock of geese) to retrieve their youngsters as I was maneuvering one of the family cars in the driveway. What's all the fuss I thought? Years later, I had a better sense of what was *different* about our relationship.

In the movie *Field of Dreams* there is a particularly moving scene (for me at least) in which Kevin Costner's character talks to his son about "having catch" together. The level of intimacy implied by the term was so profound to me that it made me sob the first time I saw it, and every time since then. Dad did not have that capacity in our relationship. Being the adaptable fellow that I was, I acquired many surrogate fathers growing up. A number of my buddies' dads provided the kind of nurturing that was missing at home and I was pretty OK with that arrangement.

## A BONA FIDE BRAND IS BORN

It was only a matter of weeks before there was serious talk around the kitchen table about Al and Lou getting back into retail. But the words used to describe the endeavor were different in every way from what had preceded it. I remember them talking about a clean slate, a new approach, something simple and straightforward, a clearly defined retail concept. Their little experiment with health and beauty aids in the last year of Jewelry and Toy Center was about to be resurrected—but on steroids. They envisioned the "cleanliness" of a pharmacy but with greater product depth. They were going to carry *all* the brands, not just what a jobber could get on closeout. If a particular deodorant came in three sizes, or two different scents, they were going to shelve all of them, rather than the most popular "flavor" (as Dad would refer to it) that you'd likely find in most pharmacies or grocery stores. And, naturally, the key was going to still be discounting, what they started calling "everyday low prices." This sounds pretty pedestrian today (and rather like Walmart), but it was revolutionary in 1965. Variety, product depth, and price were going to become their brand differentiators.

They knew how much space the average pharmacy devoted to health and beauty aids, and they were going to beat it two- or threefold. They were contemplating stores in the 2,000- to 3,000-square foot range, which would give them a strategic category depth advantage. They also knew they needed a catchy and memorable name. I can remember hours spent in informal family brainstorming sessions for names that would be memorable and descriptive of the product category. Everyone agreed that shorter was better and after several weeks the preferred name was "Puff & Pill" for the new venture. That is until my thirteen-year-old sister

Debbie said "Pill & Puff" sounded better, and we all agreed. I had just experienced the first of many identity development sessions that I would participate in or administrate in the coming decades. But as I always tell my clients: "Really, don't try this at home!"

Things got busy fast. Homes were refinanced and locations were sought. Then in 1965 the first two stores opened, one on Wisconsin Avenue just two blocks from the old Jewelry and Toy Center and the other in suburban Whitefish Bay, where both families resided. Just as my sister was the "identity consultant," I was asked to offer my opinions on the look of the stores. By my junior year in high school I had demonstrated some space-planning prowess in my architectural drawing class, so Dad and Lou allowed me to assist with store layout, materials, and color selection for the stores. My bedroom drafting table became an early meeting place for those decisions for the initial and subsequent stores. It's fair to say that none of us knew much about what we were doing at the time, but we all agreed that the stores needed to be clean and bright, and they all needed to look similar and be recognizable to a customer. We even established what would now be called plan-a-grams, depicting how the product layout and category adjacencies would work in each store so there would be little difference from store to store, regardless of the store configuration. Essentially, we were creating a branded concept and we didn't know it. In fact Pill & Puff became a defining brand in a niche category that hadn't yet emerged anywhere else in the entire country at the time.

The experience of watching my father and uncle reinvent themselves from accidental retailers to brand builders was formidable—like going from the Model T to the Mustang. I was paying close attention to what was going on, perhaps because I could tell there was so much at stake. I was also getting some strokes from my family for making a small contribution, which was uplifting. For the first time in my life I was using some formative creative skills to make a difference. I had discovered what would ultimately become a career path as an interior designer with a unique specialty in retail.

Besides creating what would become a defining brand in the marketplace, it was becoming apparent that the twins were also creating new "personal brands" for themselves, as well. While they were always entrepreneurial in business, they also functioned within a fairly safe and limited comfort zone, in part because there was never much money around to take significant "managed risks." Perhaps it was also because they were never truly dissatisfied with what they had. It had taken a major kick in the pants brought on by losing their ten-year lease, combined with the small, yet significant, success with the new health-and-beauty category to motivate them to go to the next level of personal and professional development. At the same time that they were strategizing this new endeavor, they were smart enough to look beyond their own limitations to find some key personnel to help stack the deck in their favor. This meant looking to established retail institutions for available talent, a notion that up to now had been anathema to their "our way or the highway" style of doing business—an approach that had been passed on from their father, Jacob. But they were learning.

## STYLISH REINVENTION

A small yet significant component of the personal reinvention came from Cal Schildkraut, their new operations manager, who suggested that they should "look like" executives in their new business. Cal had seen the twins working the floor at Jewelry and Toy, attired in casual sport shirts and slacks. This was no longer good enough, because their new lives would include bankers, manufacturers reps, and other business types and it was time they dressed the part.

> Essentially, we were creating a branded concept and we didn't know it. In fact Pill & Puff became a defining brand in a niche category that hadn't yet emerged anywhere else in the entire country at the time.

Given the gregarious personalities of the twins, plus the desire to be noticed, this new "brand extension" was pursued with gusto and unique style. Deep inside both Al and Lou was more than a little bit of Jacob the tailor, and given that they were just directed to address their dress...*dress they did*. Initially, the selections were defined by the limited budget of the start-up business, but as success came their way so too did the suits, of many colors. First, off the rack, and then custom tailored. They all had silk linings that appeared to have come right out of the photo from the *Sgt. Pepper's Lonely Hearts Club Band* album, along with ties to match the neon-hued internals. A mid-morning phone call (neither rose before 9:00 a.m.) took place between the boys as they choreographed their attires. They needed to make sure that they would complement one another and not cause any unnecessary traffic accidents while crossing Wisconsin Avenue on their way to their office. Their wardrobes became legendary along with the cars that complemented the ensembles. Even Dad's casual wear had to make a statement beyond the conventional cuts and colors found in the more established menswear shops. The go-to spot for the urban hip and pro athletes of the day was Johnny Walker's in downtown Milwaukee, which attracted my dad like a moth to a polyester flame. During our frequent visits, Dad appeared as at home in that environment as he'd be in a Jewish deli, regardless of being the only white patron in the store.

## ENTERING AN EVOLVING DESIGN FIELD

The launch of Pill & Puff in 1965 came just a year before my high school graduation, and as much as I wanted to "get out of Dodge," it was not to be. I received my interior design education in Milwaukee at the Layton School of Art and Design, the predecessor to the Milwaukee Institute of Art and Design (MIAD). Layton was a small, private college that featured both fine arts and degrees in graphic, industrial, and interior designs. I think there were only about a hundred students in my entire class. Several of the Layton instructors were students of the Bauhaus School both in Germany and the U.S., which influenced the curriculum in a profound way. The other major attribute of the design program at the time was the number of significant local design practitioners who taught part-time at the school.

It's fair to say that in the 1960s the field of interior design was evolving from its historical roots in interior decoration to more evolved practice levels. Driven in part by the booming economy and the exploding corporate workplace, there was also a new focus—away from residential design and toward commercial or contract interiors, considered by some to be an extension of the architectural discipline. This was a period in which every major metropolitan area of the country had hundreds of thousands of square feet of commercial space being built or renovated annually to house America's booming corporate workforce. There were also new vernaculars and disciplines being introduced to both plan and more effectively operate within these spaces.

Half-century-old notions of how the corporate workplace ought to look and function were being challenged. New interests in productivity and efficiency were beginning to change all aspects of corporate office design. Moreover, there was new research being done on how the design of the working environment could actually affect the workers' productivity, health, and welfare. This gave rise to the entirely new field of ergonomics: the science of designing based on user interaction with the workplace's elements. Some of the Bauhaus's early twentieth-century dogma "form follows function" was being taken to new and more highly developed levels by designers including Robert Propst, George Nelson, and Charles

**Several of the Layton instructors were students of the Bauhaus School both in Germany and the U.S., which influenced the curriculum in a profound way.**

and Ray Eames, to name just a few.

This new focus, along with the introduction of new modern materials and technologies, had a profound effect on all aspects of planning, design, and space utilization. The term "office landscape" came to describe the new systems being pioneered and developed. The first and arguably most important of these systems was Action Office designed by Propst for furniture manufacturer Herman Miller in 1964. This breakthrough design introduced a highly flexible, componentized approach to the layout of the new corporate office. Inherent in the design was the notion that workspaces should be highly functional, efficient, and readily reconfigured. This drove the development of a whole vocabulary of panels, work surfaces, and storage elements, while at the same time introducing an entirely new functional aesthetic driven by new attention to the ergonomics of the humans using these often downsized spaces.

Gone were the heavy dark woods ("walnetto," as we laughingly called it) and sharp edges of the past, replaced by lighter colors (easy-eye green) and soft radius surfaces that were more user friendly. These systems promoted greater efficiency for the design and the installation as well as readily adapting to the rapidly growing corporations that drove their evolution. With them came new levels of complexity and specialty in their application beyond the basic office interiors of the past. This evolving field was becoming the territory of commercial or "contract" interior designers, a distinctly new breed. I was becoming one such practitioner.

Interior design programs at universities and private colleges were also recognizing the evolving field and were creating curriculums to meet the new rigors of the practice. One of the leading programs at the time was at the University of Cincinnati, which recognized the importance of having the interior design education aligned with its school of architecture. While I had applied to

UC, my marginal high school grades (and worse standardized test scores) prevented me from getting into the program.

It's also fair to say that in the eyes of many architects back then, interior designers were, shall we say, second-class citizens. There were also few architectural firms back in the mid-1960s that recognized the discipline for what it was becoming. There were even fewer that sought out young professionals from degree programs for interior design. Fortunately for me, however, I was about to be introduced to one of them.

## AN EYE-OPENING INTERNSHIP

Getting an internship in those days wasn't that common for interior designers. Getting an interior design internship in an architectural firm was even rarer, so I jumped at the chance when one of my architectural design instructors, Gary Zimmerman, gave me the name of the principal of a Milwaukee firm to contact for a possible internship opportunity. I will always remember the thrill I felt when I first spoke to Dick Blake, one of the founders of Blake Wirth and Associates Architects. After making that initial phone call, I received an invitation to interview for a summer internship.

At the time, I was sitting in the studio of my small, ninety-dollar-a-month apartment on Milwaukee's "bohemian" lower east side. To be clear, the so-called studio was a converted Murphy bed alcove (large closet) that was just big enough for my drafting table (moved from my bedroom in Whitefish Bay) and the rest of the paraphernalia that design students acquire for their various studio courses. A considerable amount of stuff was shoehorned into the alcove. The good part was I could close the accordion door on the occasional (read: rare) weekend night when the stars aligned and I was graced by the presence of a female. A few actually succumbed to the heady aroma of English Leather, the ambience created by the

Some of the Bauhaus's early twentieth-century dogma "form follows function" was being taken to new and more highly developed levels by designers including Robert Propst, George Nelson, and Charles and Ray Eames, to name just a few.

properly premelted candles, the Harvey's Bristol Cream Sherry (a significant discovery of the day), and the sounds of Simon and Garfunkel. Unlike similar settings of the era, no pot was involved. I was too square, and I couldn't stand the smell of the stuff. At the conclusion of that phone conversation, after receiving an offer for what was to become my first foray into design, I promised myself that if I was ever in the position of offering other students a similar opportunity, I would return the gesture. And fortunately for me (and dozens of young design students), I have been able to make good on that promise.

There was a bit of irony connected to my starting at that particular firm. It turned out that Blake Wirth's new foray into corporate design began with the successful renovation of what had become the Midland Bank Building in 1966, the structural shell of which had formerly housed Jewelry and Toy Center on the corner of Second Street and Wisconsin Avenue. This became one of the first major karmic coincidences of my adult life. That summer I also became the only intern in the firm's history with his or her own client. Given that Pill & Puff was taking off, and Dad needed help planning the new stores, he reluctantly agreed to hire his own son—though he objected strenuously to the "outrageous" ten dollar-per-hour rate that the firm was charging for my time. Nonetheless, he seemed pleased that I was able to practice my skills in the real world, even if I was only making two dollars an hour (the going rate for a paid internship back then). It was, however, twice what I made pumping gas in high school.

From its inception in 1965 to when it was sold in 1978, the Pill & Puff chain quickly grew from two to twelve stores, was taken public, and then bought back. Between college classes and other firm assignments, I was laying out new stores as new locations were being considered. I was also dealing with landlord criteria, emerging signage ordinances, contractors, and remodeling budgets. I sat in on lease negotiations with major landlords and made contributions where I could, and I was validated for them, which felt very nice. Now that the product library of an architectural firm was at my disposal, I was able to experiment with neat new products. As an example, track lighting was in its infancy and was only being used in high-end residential and commercial applications at the time. But I convinced my dad that it would be beneficial to incorporate in the stores to "get the goods to pop," as he used to say.

Back then the quality of even the best fluorescent lighting was really bad. There were only two lamp colors available (warm and cool) and the "color rendering," or the actual color that reflected off the lighted surfaces, was horrendous. The mad men of Madison Avenue were beginning to package products using decent, high-impact colors, but the fluorescent lighting in most stores at the time would pretty much kill the packaging. Track lighting afforded the opportunity to use incandescent lamps that had better, more balanced color rendering to highlight the product and create the punch I know Dad sought. I was also learning that multi-light sourcing is critical in retail because the type of lighting that is efficient for ambient or general illumination is usually different than the systems that work to highlight the specific product and create definition.

Probably the most important early lesson I learned was how to "sell" design, which has served me well for over forty years—and believe me, Dad could be a pretty tough sell. I learned that when presenting almost any new idea or concept that if I could simply relate the recommendation to a clear benefit, I would usually prevail. In retailing, then and now, those benefits have to do with one of two factors: building the brand, selling the product, or both.

In 1966 the Stein twins were presented with an opportunity to secure a second downtown site through the acquisition of a small, two-tenant infill building about four blocks west of the first store. It would ultimately become the most financially successful location. The building in question was located halfway between Boston Store and Gimbels department store on the south side of Wisconsin Avenue, which was generally considered more advantageous to retailers. The bonus in the deal was that the other existing tenant was Baker's shoe store, one of Edison Brothers Stores' flagship brands and the long-term lease with Baker's convinced the bankers to give the boys financing to make the deal.

The twins were quite troubled by the store's bowling-alley layout. I remember walking the long and narrow space with Dad and Lou, and I suggested that if we painted the store white and introduced a deep orange hue on the back wall (one of the P&P colors) the store would not appear as tunnel-like. They looked at each other as if they were just told the true meaning of life by an ancient mystical seer. "Really?" they both responded. "I think so," I said with newfound authority. The store went on to become the first million-plus grossing store in their chain; and they started referring to me as "the maven" which in Yiddish means "expert." Pill & Puff was rockin' downtown Milwaukee, but after that it would be back to the suburbs for continued growth.

## A MODEL RETAIL PLAN

While the downtowns were certainly the origins of mass-market retailing for the first half of the twentieth century, the suburban shopping centers and regional malls dominated the second half. It was this new retailing form that became the engine of growth for both the department stores and the specialty retailers like Edison Brothers Stores. But the origin of the suburban shopping center, at least in the U.S., goes back to year 1907 when J. C. Nichols began purchasing land in what was then suburban Kansas City for what would ultimately become Country Club Plaza when it opened in 1923. The fifty-five acre site was the first retail development in the U.S. designed to accommodate customers arriving by car. Architect Edward Buehler Delk approached this new community development with a strong urban-planning sensibility clearly lacking in most shopping center developments fifty years hence. Roadways, pedestrian walkways, buildings, and parking were carefully integrated. Parking was distributed throughout the site, hidden beneath and on top of buildings, resulting in a development that was both pedestrian and vehicular friendly. This stands in marked contrast to the model that would later dominate, which featured acres of massive, unsightly (but more efficient) grade-level parking surrounding America's ubiquitous shopping centers and malls.

Not only was this the nation's first planned retail center of its nature and size, but it has also been the most enduring. The design of Country Club Plaza reflected classic Spanish influences incorporating many statues, murals, fountains, and public sculptures. Its location and scale made it almost prototypical of today's fashionable and preferred open-air lifestyle centers, as it integrated shopping, entertainment, and pedestrian walkways with neighborhood housing close by. Its thoughtful urban design has helped it endure aesthetically and economically for nearly seven decades. The Plaza was unique in another way—it was the first development to charge its tenants percentage rents, based on the gross income of the stores. This has become standard practice for landlords in commercial leases for the last half century.

In stark contrast to the elegant, pedestrian-friendly Country Club Plaza were the more ubiquitous open-air shopping centers that were beginning to punctuate suburban America. Arguably, the prototype of the open-air shopping center was Northland Center

**But the origin of the suburban shopping center, at least in the U.S., goes back to year 1907 when J. C. Nichols began purchasing land in what was then suburban Kansas City for what would ultimately become Country Club Plaza.**

in Detroit, which opened in 1954. Northland was the first major U.S. work of Austrian-born architect Victor Gruen three years after the founding of his Los Angeles-based firm, Victor Gruen Associates. Initially the Detroit mall was anchored by a four-story Hudson's department store that was surrounded by a ring of specialty retail stores. Victor Gruen is probably most famous, however, for his next and more significant contribution to shopping center design—Southdale Center in Edina, Minnesota, a first-ring suburb of Minneapolis. Southdale is generally recognized as the first fully enclosed, climate-controlled shopping mall in the nation, and while that was certainly significant, its ultimate form fell far short of Gruen's original vision.

Gruen, like many planners of his day, felt that the ubiquitous suburbs were compromising quality of life for Americans. He felt that cities no longer had central meeting places that were so vital to life and socialization in European cities. It was Gruen's original plan to literally remake downtown Minneapolis *in* Edina. Starting with a nearly 500-acre tract of land, Gruen planned for the enclosed shopping center to be surrounded by housing, apartment buildings, schools, and medical facilities as well as natural amenities such as a lake and a park. The project was funded by the Dayton Development Company with ties to Minneapolis-based Dayton's department stores. Dayton's went on to later launch Target, for which the company was ultimately renamed. Although Gruen's concept for Southdale (modeled after the arcades of many European cities) didn't fully manifest itself in the way he had imagined, it certainly became the prototype for suburban malls nationwide for the next fifty years.

The original Southdale Center featured the massive, multistory, central Garden Court, the nation's largest indoor public area, seen as the communal gathering space. It featured an indoor fountain, which became a signature mall feature. The department store anchors, in this case Dayton's and Donaldson's, did just that. They anchored the corners of the center and generally created the impetus for the specialty retailers that filled in on two levels between the major department stores. Woolworth's and Walgreen's were also among the larger initial tenants.

Southdale was immediately deemed a huge success and for decades to follow (through many expansions and facelifts) was a consistently high-grossing mall by national standards. The Center had the distinct advantage of being developed in an economically vital and healthy area (later considered upscale) at a time when area shoppers were looking for convenience and a fresh alternative to tired-looking urban shopping districts. No longer did a shopper have to make the twenty-minute drive downtown and then search and pay for parking. The mall provided over 5,000 parking spaces for free, even though it could mean a twenty-minute search for the car after the trip.

Soon department store owners would begin to partner with developers and city governments to identify demographically desirable tracts of land to build their own Southdales and this new form of destination retail was off and running. Financially speaking, the anchor department stores would become the economic lynchpin that would get the projects underway, but it was generally the specialty stores that ended up paying the freight. The department stores soon learned that they could cut great deals for lease agreements, construction, and tenant improvement contributions from the developer because their participation was often the impetus for getting the deals financed and the motivator to bring the specialty retailers along. The specialties would often spend more dollars per square foot for their occupancy and a percentage of gross revenues. And the department store would be able to dictate

**Southdale is generally recognized as the first fully enclosed, climate-controlled shopping mall in the nation, and while that was certainly significant, its ultimate form fell far short of Gruen's original vision.**

many terms of the specialties' leases, including what type of re-tailing would be allowed within the mall or within certain distances from its entrances and how big the specialties' signage could be in comparison to their dominating logos. The anchor stores basically called the shots.

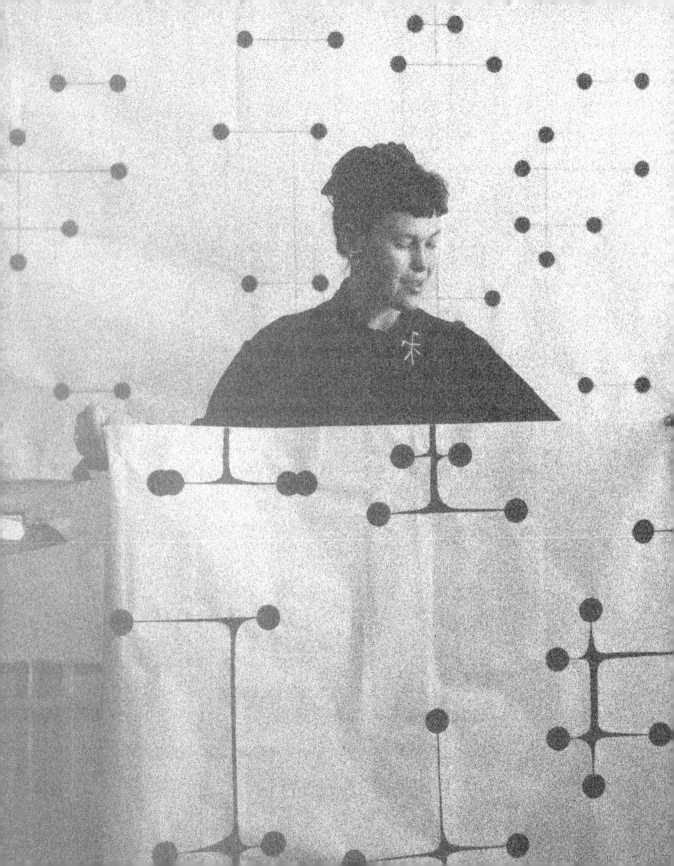

# CHAPTER THREE

# HEROES AND MENTORS

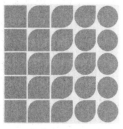

Like most teenagers, music was very important to me, and I consider myself lucky to have grown up in what is believed by many to be the golden era of rock 'n' roll. In the early 1960s I got heavily into the Beach Boys for their harmonies, as well as their early affinity for cars ("Little Deuce Coupe," "Fun, Fun, Fun," and "409") along with the teen stuff ("In My Room" and "Don't Worry Baby"). And like remembering where I was when I learned John Kennedy was shot (high school physics class), equally as indelible is the memory of when I first heard the Beach Boys' *Pet Sounds* album in the summer of 1966. Many rock 'n' roll aficionados consider this the most influential rock album of all time. Even Paul McCartney has been quoted saying that it was Brian Wilson's transformational work in *Pet Sounds* that motivated the Beatles to make *Sgt. Pepper*. Most of my most vivid high school memories are paired with a corresponding Beatles single or album and I feel fortunate to have those unforgettable sounds as the backdrop of my adolescence.

As I moved on to college, my taste for music began to expand to include folk rock and jazz rock, including Joni Mitchell, James Taylor, Steely Dan, and Simon and Garfunkel. I was dealing with the standard identity stuff that comes with late adolescence: Who am I? Why am I here? Why did my parents screw me up? One time, I was listening to Simon and Garfunkel's *Bookends* when the lyrics to the song, "Fakin' It" spoke to me with unusual clarity. In the fourth stanza Simon describes himself as owning... and being... the face and hands of the tailor. And I thought to myself: Jacob the tailor, sure enough. My need for perfection in what I do. My almost anal attention to small details others didn't seem to see or care about. I'm him, and he was me, a mixed blessing indeed. One could argue that Jacob suffered from what some behavioral scientists refer to as the Rolls-Royce syndrome, a tendency to want to do all things too well. This is something I've identified and struggled with all of my life, often trying to balance getting things done with getting things right—and, like Jacob, sometimes at my own peril. Suffice it to say, it was important for me to begin to come to terms with my own personal identity.

My college experience was as challenging and uplifting as high school was miserable and defeating. For the first time in my life I was learning things that really mattered to me from instructors who were passionate and informed. Because most of my classes were studio in nature, I didn't feel limited by some of the learning disabilities that had often paralyzed me throughout elementary and secondary schools. Layton had a number of full-time professors who lived double lives as practicing designers in the community and the course work reflected real-world points of view. As in all good design programs, we worked hard unlearning, relearning, and developing new skills. Since my college education (from 1966–70) predated the personal computer, we were drawing a lot in every media, free hand and mechanically, as well as learning basic design principles and their applications. Learning how to see, as strange as that sounds, really becomes an important part of any design education. I remember looking at one chair and drawing it over and over for an entire semester. The chair (and I can still draw it pretty well forty years later) was the classic "Potato Chip" molded plywood dining chair designed by Charles and Ray Eames.

The Eameses were as inspirational to me during their active careers as they continue to be today. Their design legacy includes nearly every imaginable discipline, including furniture, architecture, exhibitions, and film. All were approached with a freshness and level of innovation that has kept their signature designs timeless. What enabled Charles and Ray to take on such diverse work and succeed at such a high level was their highly disciplined design process, which was tailored to the media and methods of the project at hand. The products changed, the process didn't. Another Eames hallmark was their insatiable, almost childlike, curiosity that drove them to look at even the most mundane things in new ways, always going beyond the status quo.

I was fortunate to see and hear Charles give a wonderful lecture at the Walker Art Center in conjunction with the Walker's exhibition entitled *The Design Process at Herman Miller*, which opened in November 1975 in Minneapolis. The exhibit featured the works of George Nelson, Alexander Girard, Robert Propst, and Charles and Ray Eames. A highlight of the exhibit was an address by Charles, and it featured a number of their miraculous films. As was always the case, the demure Ray was present but in the shadows of the theater stage.

Almost exactly a decade later, nearly eight years after Charles's passing, I was honored to actually meet Ray Eames when she was among a group of distinguished guests invited to jury a Minnesota AIA Interior Design Awards competition. Coincidentally, it took place in the very same auditorium at the Walker Art Center. To my complete delight, she and her fellow judges recognized my young firm's design work, awarding us three of the evening's five top honors. The only thing more miraculous and memorable was to hear the diminutive Ray's commentary about my work through her nearly inaudible but carefully chosen words. I'm not sure what she said about it, because I was dumbfounded trying to grasp the notion that her utterances were directed at my creative efforts. This was truly a singular moment in my early design career, and a memory I will always cherish. Ray passed away just two years later, exactly ten years to the day after Charles's passing. In 1985 the Industrial Design Society of America recognized Charles and Ray as the most influential designers of the twentieth century.

## ORIGIN OF DIS-EASE

My internship at Blake Wirth and Associates went quite well and I was kept on part-time after school when I started my senior year. But as my Aunt Betty (the twins' sister and bookkeeper) used to say, "I was burning the candle from both ends." Like many college students, I would attend classes during the day and go to work afterward. I'd grab a bite and then spend much of the evening on class assignments—and if I was lucky, I'd catch some sleep before the next morning's classes. I wore myself down to the point that I got a rather severe case of mononucleosis, which had me on my back for several weeks. After recuperating at home, I was able to rejoin my classmates but things were never quite the same for me after that virus. I've been told that for some Epstein-Barr–type viruses (often associated with mono) never completely leave their host, and my body must have been particularly accommodating. Decades later, I've come to believe that the combination of the latent virus, the unnecessary childhood surgeries (and treatments), and exposure to countless carcinogens from the model cement to the rather toxic art supplies, conspired to compromise my immune system and set the stage for a lifetime of chronic illness.

At first it was chronic sore throats, accompanied by swollen glands. A doctor at the University of Wisconsin, Madison, removed the tonsils but no relief followed. I'd be fine, even quite function-al, but virus-like symptoms were never far away. The symptoms would clear up, but a profound lethargy would haunt me. The ep-isodes were sometimes weeks apart, sometimes months apart; it didn't **seem** normal, and it certainly got in the way of "normality" for a young adult, whatever that was supposed to be. The psy-chological component was as frustrating as the symptoms. I am by nature a very busy guy and I have always been that way. Even

**Another Eames hallmark was their insatiable, almost childlike, curiosity that drove them to look at even the most mundane things in new ways, always going beyond the status quo.**

61

my morning kindergarten teacher noted, "Sandy's a very busy little guy," on my 1952 report card from Lake Bluff Elementary School. I had little time and less patience for these symptoms then or during subsequent decades. It wasn't until the 1990s that I learned to make time to get much better.

I remember sitting in a chair in my parents' very burnt orange-and-brown-vinyl couched family room at a holiday family gathering in 1970 or '71. The lethargy and heaviness of my body made it feel like all 122 pounds of me was being swallowed by the pumpkin-toned vinyl—as if the chair and I were both being absorbed by the also orange-and-brown shag carpet. A whole room full of smiling Jews ate, talked, and carried on around me, but I felt like I was somewhere else entirely, strangely different, and very, very tired.

## GETTIN' INTO PLASTICS

The 1970s were a tremendous time of transition for me, for U.S. retailing, and for the political and cultural landscape of the entire country. I got married and divorced, got laid off from my second architectural design firm, and left Milwaukee for the promising and more progressive Twin Cities of Minneapolis and St. Paul. Before doing so, however, I made a life-altering career detour. Throughout my experience as a Layton design student, I secretly admired the work of the fine art students. They were never constrained by function, economies, and the overarching notion of having to practice one's craft, based largely on the needs and direction of an eventual client (the Jacob in me). It seemed to me as if the painters, sculptors and printmakers were having all the fun—also demonstrated by the pot smoke that occasionally permeated the fine art floors at Layton (it was the late 1960s after all). However, I knew that even the mere mention of such a secret yearning to my father (and financier) would send him into a near ballistic tirade about making a living and thinking just like him—or else.

It's safe to say that for the first twenty-five years of my life, I was preoccupied by trying to win my father's approval (and love) in ways both big and small. Acknowledgments were few and far between. In 1971, I was about to take on a personal growth journey that I knew would be controversial at best. My then wife, Doris, and I both had a passion for fine arts—for me it was sculpture, for her it was jewelry design. We devised a plan to spend a year following these unfulfilled passions and we used our small wedding fund to finance the plan. We rented a forty-dollar-a-month studio and went to work. However, unlike the Eames partnership, we ultimately could not make the two designers in one household dynamic work.

I had always been fascinated by the acrylic plastic sheet material that is often used for sign faces: Plexiglas. Plexiglas is an interesting example of one of the few brand-name products, like Kleenex, where the brand is so powerful, and commands so much market share, that the brand name is often used as a default descriptor for the generic product. The transparent thermoplastic material was first brought to market in 1933 by Rohm and Haas Company. Its lightweight and shatterproof characteristics, combined with the inherent ease of fabrication, made it a desirable replacement for glass. One of its early large-scale uses was during World War II for the massive bubbles of the clear bombardier nose compartment on fighter planes.

The postwar commercial sign industry was one of the greatest volume users of Plexiglas once the phenomenon of the illuminated box-sign format began to replace the more labor-intensive neon signs of the first half century. I, like many other designers, would argue that America's roadsides did not become more handsome when these more efficient, high-impact, and ugly transilluminated signs replaced the artfully hand-bent neon signs of the first half of

**Plexiglas is an interesting example of one of the few brand-name products, like Kleenex, where the brand is so powerful, the brand name is often used as a default descriptor for the generic product.**

the twentieth century. Though there is no denying that they provided an effective and efficient way to get a company's name noticed, these signs also became the virtual signature of both urban and suburban blight when they became overused, which was most of the time. Regrettably, I was a minor offender early in my career.

My earliest introduction to Plexi, as it's often called, was while working on the signage for the first Pill & Puff stores in high school. I would visit the 20th Century Sign company to watch them fabricate the signs, and they would offer me the cutoff wastes that were too small for them to use. I would generally take as much as I could carry out of the place at one time. What attracted me to the stuff (besides the price) was the color, translucency, and the ability to easily and precisely cut it by merely scoring it by hand with a sharp blade and breaking the pieces into the desired shapes. Throughout college, I was often teased by classmates when some of my model-making assignments resulted in a couple dozen well-executed matte-board constructions, and one of polished Plexiglas. "Oh boy, it's Stein the Plexi-king," was often voiced in a well-deserved, sarcastic tone.

Our new studio digs were located in a rather tired urban Milwaukee neighborhood, amidst a group of rundown, nondescript storefronts next to a corner bar, which are as ubiquitous in Milwaukee as beer and baseball. By now (thanks to a commission) I was able to replace hand-scoring and breaking the Plexiglas with the buzz of a table saw. I was capable of fabricating nearly identical plastic cubic volumes that formed the basis for my minimalist constructions—very 1970s. The carefully cut pieces morphed into three-dimensional volumes through the use of a powerful, over-the-counter solvent, ethylene dichloride (EDC). This clear liquid was applied with a syringe and almost magically (through capillary action) was drawn between two pieces of acrylic and melted and fused two planes into one form.

I know now that much of what I did while handling and applying this toxic substance was not careful or appropriate. Unfortunately for me, the Environmental Protection Agency (EPA) had only just been founded in 1970, when corporate America's arrogance and indiscriminate pollution had reached its zenith. (Lake Erie, for example, had erupted in flames.) At that point the EPA's first priority was not focused on preventing idiots like me from accessing and misusing such toxic chemicals. This probably proved to be the final, and maybe pivotal, toxic cocktail that became the tipping point for my immune system and led to the onset of what would later be diagnosed as chronic fatigue syndrome (CFS).

During my year-long sabbatical from the interior design profession, I became a man with a mission and immersed myself in the new and challenging medium of sculpture. I entered numerous exhibits and showed many pieces, and a few sold. However, this brief yet inspiring career detour did culminate in my participation in a statewide competition, and I also gained some profound insights that have shaped me as a designer and a person. The competition, and associated commission, was to design and build a monumental piece for St. Norbert's College in De Pere, Wisconsin, not far from Green Bay. The site of the sculpture was a new plaza, which was next to one of the oldest and most noteworthy administration buildings on the campus, built in the late 1800s. A five-thousand-dollar award for the design and fabrication was established and it was open to all Wisconsin sculptors.

The criteria had been clearly established, with the medium quite open, but the part that intrigued me the most was the challenge of complementing the diverse architecture of the campus. This naturally led me to visit and thoroughly photograph the campus. I focused on all the buildings adjacent to the plaza, taking

**During my year-long sabbatical from the interior design profession, I became a man with a mission and immersed myself in the new and challenging medium of sculpture.**

note of the coloration of the brick as well as the architectural diversity. I started with sketches that quickly led to cardboard mock-ups and then to small-scale models made from Plexiglas. Using my training as a designer and strategic problem solver, I put myself in the place of the judging committee and started thinking about their likely concerns and issues that might weigh heavily in their decision process. Of course, I could not possibly know how style, materials, or sculptor's background would be viewed. But the one thing I knew I could do was give the committee a very good idea of how the campus would look with my piece in place—eliminating some of the unknowns and creating a more predictable outcome for the judges. This was a tactical approach that I thought would differentiate how I would "tell the story" versus the way I thought a fine arts–trained sculptor might approach the situation.

I photographed my small-scale model from every possible angle, even playing with lighting to create convincing shadows. I blew up the campus photos and cut in images of the eight-inch-tall model of the sculpture that appeared about twelve feet tall in the enlarged photo and prominently positioned in front of the admissions building. Today we do this sort of thing in minutes using Photoshop, but this was a half dozen years before the invention of the personal computer, so it was a bit out of the ordinary. I'll be the first to admit that my design may or may not have been as timeless or relevant as the other submissions, but the committee knew exactly what to expect and what it would look like once in place. I won the competition and commission ten months into my career as a fine artist.

The installation and dedication took place on a cold and wet fall day. I made the long drive to the campus and watched as a huge crane lifted the vibrantly colored cubic assemblage off the flat-bed truck and carefully lowered it onto the concrete base, which had been made especially for my piece that I had nicknamed "Norby." It was a bittersweet experience, at once highly satisfying, the culmination of a short yet intense dream, but also sad. Besides the well-wishers, college administrators, and local media, I was the sole member of my entourage. I suspect my folks felt it was either not important enough, or that their presence would be a tacit gesture of support for something pretty much alien to them. To make matters worse, we were out of money and it was time to go back and get a "real job" which I did. As it turned out, deciding to pursue another direction that year proved to be one of the most uplifting and liberating things I had ever done. I proved something important to myself and would soon discover that the whole episode would play a significant role in the next chapter of my story.

**Today we do this sort of thing in minutes using Photoshop, but this was a half dozen years before the invention of the personal computer, so it was a bit out of the ordinary.**

## FRESH START AND A NEW MENTOR

With the 1973 OPEC oil embargo and its block-long gas lines, Milwaukee was feeling the effects of a major recession. I was feeling it was time for a fresh start in a more progressive design environment. I had read an article in one of the architectural magazines, about a Minneapolis-based "interdisciplinary design" firm as they referred to it called InterDesign. I freshened up my small resumé and got an interview with the graphic design partner, Peter Seitz. After a quick trip to the Cities, I had a new job, a new home, and a renewed purpose.

At the time, InterDesign was beginning the planning and design phases of a huge new zoo, Minnesota Zoological Garden, for which the very young group had worked several years to secure. The firm had four principals at the time covering the disciplines of architecture, landscape architecture, graphic design, and of all things, computer programming (remember, this was 1974). The principals were all quite young, and the staff was even younger. I was considered senior staff at twenty-seven, and I was paid more than twice what I had been making at the premier Milwaukee architectural firm that had fired me, along with about six others at the time.

Minneapolis is a mere 330 miles north and west of Milwaukee, but culturally speaking they were light-years apart, at least back then. Minneapolis was as progressive as Milwaukee was provincial. Contemporary arts and design were thriving with terrific support from the business community, and my new boss and mentor was, in part, responsible. Peter Seitz was schooled in Germany at the Ulm School, which continued the modernist teachings of the Bauhaus (after it was closed down by the Nazis) under the direction of Max Bill, a Swiss architect, designer, painter, and former student of Walter Gropius, the founder of the Bauhaus. Peter came to Minneapolis in 1964 to become the design curator at the Walker Art Center and brought with him the seeds of modernism and design sensibilities that flourished in the upper Midwest. Peter became a catalyst in uniting the business and arts communities and enlightening business leaders about the benefits of good design, decades before it became a mainstream idea.

What was curious and interesting about the position I had assumed was that despite the fact that the firm had never practiced interior design, they were offering me a chance to do contract interiors as well as become involved in three-dimensional "environmental graphics," starting with the interpretive display program at the zoo. While clearly outside of my comfort zone, I took it as a challenge to expand my design portfolio, while working with some incredibly talented people. In another interesting coincidence, the initial sketches of the interpretive displays, which were to be used throughout the zoo to aid in educating the public, looked very much like Norby. The designs were based on multiple cubic forms with a similar module size. Peter needed a team member who could develop this three-dimensional "family" of forms, and work with his staff to integrate the necessary graphics and interpretive materials into them. This provided me the unique opportunity to interact with architects, graphic designers, and landscape architects on a very large scale.

Peter's work in the Twin Cities had already become somewhat legendary. Before the mid-1960s, graphic design in the U.S. was still considered an offshoot of what was termed commercial art. In fact, when Peter first set up his practice in the Cities there had not yet been a listing in the phone book for graphic designers and he initiated it. By the time I joined the staff, Peter had already been doing some very important and recognized corporate identity work for some of the Cities' leading arts and corporate entities. By working with and for some of the best graphic designers, I developed a strong understanding and awareness for brand thinking, which would ultimately become a key component in my eventual thirty-plus years in the practice of designing branded environments.

One of the key shared attributes of the Bauhaus, the work of the Eameses, and the philosophy behind InterDesign was the holistic approach to any project, regardless of its size and or nature. At the Bauhaus, every element was thought about contextually. The architecture, interior space, furnishings, graphic design, and even fabrics were developed in a unified fashion, and often by the same people. It's for that reason that some of the twentieth century's most enduring and highly regarded furniture designs are the work of architects, many from the Bauhaus. While few of the signature building designs from that era still exist, original furniture designs from Marcel Breuer, Mies, Corbusier, and others are commonplace in today's contemporary environments.

**Minneapolis is a mere 330 miles north and west of Milwaukee, but culturally speaking they were light-years apart, at least back then. Minneapolis was as progressive as Milwaukee was provincial.**

69

## MEDITATION

My new home in Minneapolis was fulfilling on every level. Career, friendships, and new interests all contributed to a feeling of satisfaction and self-esteem. This was somewhat marred by increasingly frequent and troublesome viral-like infections similar to my previous experiences, but now accompanied by a combination of symptoms that made even simple tasks quite difficult. Even after the most acute manifestations had passed, the lethargy remained. I was also beginning to understand that there seemed to be a correlation between stressful periods and these outbreaks and the more I attempted to just work through them, the worse they got and the longer they lasted. My doctor, who was attentive and sympathetic, referred them as "my viruses" (as if I had invented a disease) because the blood work always made the events appear to be viral. The only recommendations were to rest, something that I had little time for.

In 1976, after two years in my new city, a designer friend was diagnosed with what the doctors were describing as early-stage multiple sclerosis, and she was advised by her doctor to find a way to better manage stress. It was at this time that transcendental meditation (TM) was becoming a phenomenon, particularly on university and college campuses around the country, where TM clinics had become commonplace. The founder and principal proponent of TM was the Indian guru, Maharishi Mahesh Yogi, who had become something of a cultural phenomenon at the time due to the Beatles and other celebrities traveling to India to learn the TM techniques in search of "peace, love, and higher consciousness." The Maharishi's work had begun back in the mid-1950s and by the 1970s he was well on his way to teaching the TM technique to over forty thousand teachers, who in turn would ultimately share it with between seven and ten million individuals before his passing in 2008.

Suffice it to say, I was more than a little skeptical of the whole idea. What did intrigue me was the fact that by the mid-1970s there had already been hundreds of credible studies on the effects of meditation. Published papers from both UCLA and Harvard noted clear physiological changes in brain and heart function that suggested the technique could, in fact, help manage stress for regular practitioners. Given that both my friend and I were looking outside the norms of conventional medicine for help with our conditions, we figured the initial, free orientation couldn't hurt. The process was taught in a seven-step course by teachers certified in the training. It begins with two introductory lectures, including theory. Once a commitment is made (and fee paid) there is a personal interview and "initiation" in which one receives his or her mantra. After that, the basic technique is taught, and then there are subsequent follow-ups to ensure the technique is being properly applied.

We both completed the training and while I had a difficult time with some of the pseudo-religious overtones of the initiation ceremony, I consciously separated that from the possible benefits that the technique might ultimately provide. I also took some comfort knowing that some form of this mantra repetition and "transcendence" to an altered state of awareness has been part of nearly every form of organized religion for at least five thousand years. I had very clear images as a young boy attending my grandmother's orthodox synagogue of primarily old Jewish men *davening* (the Yiddish word for prayer). This ritual repetition of passages, with eyes closed, appeared to induce an almost hypnotic state through the barely audible chants—not much different than what I was learning. Hence, I felt I wasn't really going too far to the dark side.

The first several weeks to a month were the most difficult because it took a concerted effort to begin to integrate this practice into my lifestyle. The practice took between fifteen and twenty minutes in the morning and again in the early evening, but I stayed with it largely because I was really starting to feel different during and after meditation. I knew I was experiencing something moderately remarkable when I was able to slip away to "the place between thoughts" (as Dr. Deepak Chopra refers to it) and automatically bring myself back and feel not only rejuvenated but with a profound sense of calm. (And no, I never fell asleep.)

I attribute my now thirty-six-year practice of meditation to be the single most significant factor in my managing CFS and being able to conduct a relatively normal and productive life. It wasn't until the mid-1980s that the Centers for Disease Control in Atlanta first recognized CFS as bona fide chronic disease, and I wasn't officially diagnosed with the condition until 1991. For those unfortunate souls who must manage CFS, and its associated condition of fibromyalgia, I believe meditation has become one of the accepted and recognized management regimens for these treatable but incurable maladies. As strange as this may seem, over the course of the three and a half decades I have probably missed only thirty days of meditation in total. I have managed primarily with a single, late-afternoon "deep-dive." Although, if my body tells me I need it, I will do a morning session as well. While a quiet, relatively dark room is optimal, I have meditated in cars, taxis, airports, airplanes, beaches, park benches, and hotel lobbies. In fact, I was once booted out of an exclusive Midtown New York hotel lobby while "caught in the act" because they thought I must have been a vagrant.

# THE DESIGN PROCESS

4

Throughout this book I talk about the consistent design process practiced by many of my design heroes and mentors whose work has been recognized as being exceptional over the decades. There are some misconceptions about the nature of design when compared to the fine arts. Anyone who has read about or studied the great masters (whether they are from music, visual art, or the performing arts) knows that exceptional creative work springs from a combination of innate talent, inspiration, and dedication to one's craft. While all of these elements are also necessary in the design idioms of architecture, interior design, graphic design, and product design, it has been my observation that exceptional practitioners use an objective process or road map to get where they are going. I refer to this as the design process. While the specific components of this process may vary from one discipline to another, the overarching methods and procedures do not. I believe there are five key elements to this process, and while undertaking each in the appropriate order will not necessarily guarantee success, design excellence requires keeping them in mind. The five components common to the creation of exceptional design outcomes are: immersion, context, openness, style, and communication.

## IMMERSION

### Getting Dirty

Becoming immersed is essential when approaching any design problem; this is something one of my professors referred to as "getting dirty." In my design practice we call it getting into the client's bloodstream. One cannot design anything for any person or company unless he or she understands all aspects of the product's or the space's use. Frank Lloyd Wright was famous for literally moving in and living with a client before he would even begin designing a house for them. In the context of retail design, becoming immersed means understanding the nature and objectives of the client and their particular brand (which I explore further in chapter five). This means understanding both short- and long-range objectives, and developing a healthy skepticism for what you are told. In fact, sometimes the designer's biggest challenge has very little to do with design and a lot to do with careful listening and thoughtful observation to go beyond the stated or obvious in order to make meaningful changes.

When my design practice began in the early 1980s, my first clients were small specialty retailers with equally small budgets. As things progressed and the firm started making a name for itself, we began to attract the first in a series of national clients. The first such client was Wild Pair, one of the ten or so brands owned by St. Louis–based Edison Brothers Stores (EBS). Their brands included Burt's, Baker's, Chandler's, 5-7-9, Jeans West, Oak Tree, and many more. Their 3,000 stores made them one of the single biggest non-department-store tenants in the rapidly growing number of shopping centers and regional malls. I first attracted the attention of EBS as a result of a mass mailing of the first promotional color brochure we ever produced (which was financed by selling my near-classic 1968 Mercedes Benz 250SE sedan).

Even in the early days of dealing with small local or regional chains, I always made sure to visit as many of my clients' stores as possible. I took copious amounts of photos and spent time observing how the customers behaved in the store and how they interacted with sales personnel. I would also get to know some of the salespeople to get the scoop on what worked and what didn't. This was always a valuable reality check against what the business owners thought were the priorities. My research almost always generated insights into issues that had not yet surfaced. Working

**The five components common to the creation of exceptional design outcomes are: immersion, context, openness, style, and communication.**

77

with EBS brought a whole layer of corporate structure to our firm that added new challenges to what we today call the "analysis of existing conditions."

Once I was briefed by the president of the Wild Pair division, a lovely man by the name of Les Cherry, I conducted multiple store visits and the associated observations. During my reconnaissance I saw something "in the field" that looked very wrong—and counter-productive from an operational point of view—that would influence the design of the new retail prototype. When I asked someone at the store about it I was told that "it came down from corporate." With my initial field work complete, I asked to meet with a very broad representation of folks ranging from Mr. Cherry to the heads of marketing, buying, and store operations. I also wanted to have at least one store manager and a floor sales person present. I could tell by the response that I received (and the activity in the conference room once everyone was assembled) that this level of sharing was not common at EBS.

As I listened to everyone in the meeting express their thoughts regarding the new retail prototype, it became apparent there was no consensus on the overall objectives for the new design. This realization ultimately influenced the initial programming phase of all of our work for the next twenty-five years. It became our fundamental predesign objective to establish initial consensus (through a brief white paper) on the key objectives for the retail design. This included key brand positioning and points of differentiation, core customer profiles, product/SKU (shelf keeping unit) counts, operating requirements/concerns, budgets, and timing. As the meeting neared completion, I made a passing mention of the operational hang-up I'd witnessed, and I saw the manager of the store nod his head at my observation. Much to everyone's surprise, Mr. Cherry jumped out of his chair and asked, "Why in the world are we doing that? It makes no sense." That taught me to always listen to my gut if something seems wrong—maybe it is.

Our work with EBS was transformative for us and I think for them. I remember receiving a call from Mr. Cherry when our first Wild Pair prototype store opened in the late 1980s. He told me that people in the mall were lining up to enter the new store and the fire marshal was monitoring access because the store had exceeded its legal occupancy capacity. This had never happened to a Wild Pair store before, and he was delighted. Years later when EBS began to unravel, it wasn't due to any single factor but to the cumulative effects of undifferentiated brands, corporate silo thinking, losing a connection to its customer, and a race-to-the-bottom price/quality factor. These elements, along with unbridled overexpansion, contributed to their undoing and the demise of their once-heralded brands. Starbucks's Howard Schultz was explaining his company's recent restructuring in terms that in all probability were relevant to the EBS undoing decades earlier by stating that, "Growth must never be a strategy but rather a tactic for success."

## CONTEXT

### The Use and the User

While many built environments are designed to be celebrated and used for generations, this is not the case in the complex world of branded retail environments. As I've often said: store design is the architectural equivalent of fast food. One of the most interesting characteristics of its practice is that the designs are never intended to be enduring. In fact, they rarely have a style life of more than five years. This is, in part, influenced by the leases store owners engage in with landlords, which nearly always contain a remodeling clause after a designated period of time. Another feature of these evolving, even chameleon-like, environments is that they are an expression of both the product that resides within and a reflection of the consumer who is intended to be drawn into the space. To understand the complexities of the contextual component of store design we have to address the overall objective of what the spaces are intended to do, as well as how both the product and the consumer influences its shaping. I learned very early on that the fundamental objective of the retail designer is to "create a predictable sales outcome" for our clients—in other words, drive sales.

I found myself at a distinct advantage early on when talking to my clients about their past experiences with other design practitioners, and often it was not pretty. Over and over I would hear things like "all the designers wanted to do was create a pretty space, so they could take some pictures before we messed things up with our product." My retail indoctrination, which arguably began almost immediately after my mother's C-section, enabled me to converse with these retailers in their language regarding: ROI (return on investment), margins (profits), and product turns (numbers of times the product will be restocked).

There is a triad of forces at work within the context of store design. In order to create a successful retail environment and a predictable outcome, the designer must engage and balance three factors: the space, the product, and the customer interface. My clients typically have been quite astute when it comes to what they were selling along with the functional and spatial requirements of their new or remodeled stores. They have been frequently less insightful about who their customers are. More often than not they make broad, sweeping generalizations about age and gender; or sometimes allude to a very narrow audience toward whom they are focusing their brand and concept. In both cases, I feel they are compromising their own brands by not being in touch with who their real customers are; as well as what group of potential customers are being excluded by virtue of product mix, presentation, or brand positioning. We will dive deeply into the whole issue of brand positioning in a later chapter.

Over four decades of working with retailers and manufacturers locally, regionally, and nationally, much has changed and evolved regarding all aspects of the space/product/customer triad, but none more than the science and metrics related to understanding, identifying, and grouping the "target customer." Since 1903, the U.S. Census Bureau has been collecting census data every ten years to understand the rapidly changing characteristics of the U.S. population. The original purpose of the surveys was to keep track of the number of citizens and where they lived, largely to properly allocate seats in the House of Representatives. With the rise of postwar consumerism guided by the savvy mad men of Madison Avenue, these data were beginning to be used to better understand and predict changes in consumer behavior and marketing patterns. Consumer demographics has emerged as a study and grouping of people by gender, age, race, disabilities, home ownership, etc., in order to define purchasing trends.

The subject of demographics has always interested me. As a member of the Baby Boom generation (class of 1947), I'm conscious of the attention that marketers have focused on us throughout our lifetimes. I often compared the Boomer phenomenon's effect on the marketplace as being akin to a snake digesting a Volkswagen. The post-WWII generation (born from 1946 to 1964) totaled over seventy-eight million individuals, whose arrival coincided with the growth of the most prosperous middle-class society of modern times, and as a result we have had an outsized influence on the consumer marketplace for the past sixty-five years. Today, every seven seconds a Boomer turns fifty, which equates to

> Over and over I would hear things like "all the designers wanted to do was create a pretty space, so they could take some pictures before we messed things up with our product."

4.5 million per year. That's a lot of candles. At the front end of the group, ten thousand of us are turning sixty-five every day. (Hence all the Viagra ads.)

My initial interest in correlating design and demographic trending was largely anecdotal and from the gut, which was complemented by a near obsession with *American Demographics* magazine. On a very intuitive level, I've always been building a case for design as a differentiator, rather than an additive or stylized embellishment. This process of discovery is intriguing and it also builds genuine trust with one's client, something the design business isn't always known for. The other component of digging deep (not unlike unearthing artifacts in an ancient archeological site) reveals that sometimes the smallest discoveries yield the biggest dividends.

As a designer, I have always worked to develop a culture of understanding with my clients—giving primary attention to their brands, products, core customers, competition, and marketing trends, as opposed to passing fads. This emphasis has enabled us to support and often defend our design direction, and ultimately to become more influential throughout the entire process. It became the highest priority to always justify proposed design solutions based on the objective (brand positioning, psychographics, human behavior, style, and endurance) rather than the subjective (style for style's sake). I suspect some of this sprang from my early observation of the twins' evolution from the anti-brand Jewelry and Toy Center to the branded (though extremely basic) Pill & Puff.

*The First Chain Store Client*

My first significant attempt to move the needle from a style and trend standpoint came with my first local chain store client, Goodman Jewelers, in 1978. Goodman's was a second-generation, family-owned, independent jeweler in the Twin Cities and a very successful and reputable one at that. They were considered "popular priced" and had stores located throughout Minneapolis and St. Paul. Suffice it to say, the stores were "none too pretty," as my dad would have said, even by late 1970s mall standards. I received a call from Arthur Goodman to come out to their Southdale store because he felt their windows weren't as attractive as they could be. Nothing about that call made feel particularly excited or optimistic because, A) I knew how ugly the store was, and B) thinking about "trimming a window" at a Goodman's store made my teeth hurt. I almost declined the invitation and to this day I play that tape back in my head whenever I'm about to dismiss an opportunity before really checking out the situation.

I met Arthur at the store and listened to the issues that they were having with the "dead" windows. I continued to listen as he took me around the space explaining his business and how they became such a successful jeweler. I remember that he spoke about his clientele in a manner that I thought was respectful but limited, since they were undercutting their own market reach due to the look of the stores and the way they were merchandised. In our initial meeting, I challenged some of Arthur's marketing assumptions, which was either very bold or very stupid, but I recall that at some level he enjoyed the challenge, and we had a healthy discussion about my views. I liked Arthur immediately and was soon invited to their St. Paul offices for some additional discussions.

What I did not know at the time of the initial "window dressing" meeting is that Arthur was being pressured by the owners of Southdale and the other key Minneapolis-based "Dales" (Southdale, Rosedale, and Ridgedale were still owned by the Dayton family) to improve the look of his stores in the malls. While I was assuming that the discussion in St. Paul was going to be about

**I almost declined the invitation and to this day I play that tape back in my head whenever I'm about to dismiss an opportunity before really checking out the situation.**

83

windows, it turned out to be about the remodeling of their biggest and most profitable store. We were about to embark on what Humphrey Bogart's character refers to at the end of *Casablanca* as the "beginning of a beautiful friendship."

Over the course of the next ten years we would design and/or remodel all ten of the Goodman's stores in the Twin Cities. In the process, I managed to test virtually every store design standard previously held by the company. This started with my conviction that elevating the look, feel, and quality of the store would broaden the appeal, and engage a higher-level customer than the less affluent demographic that they focused on. We raised the standard showcases so customers could view products within them in a more upright and relaxed manner. We broke away from the age-old jewelry store paradigm of prohibiting customers from being able to actually walk up to a wall case and get close to the product. The strong yet simple architecture reinforced key product display areas, and was punctuated with light coves, creating a comfortable ambient (background) illumination. We were one of the first designers in the upper Midwest to utilize halogen lighting to highlight the gold and diamonds throughout the stores and in show windows. The signature touch—which became iconic for the brand—was tossing out the tired, faux walnut showcases and replacing them with brushed stainless steel. The storefronts featured linear, horizontal cases that emphasized fewer products while creating greater visual impact. Non-glass areas were sheathed in brushed stainless steel panels, giving the stores themselves a jewel-like quality.

None of this was easy or occurred without a challenge. Arthur was a brilliant and passionate man and a terrific negotiator. We had some very interesting dialogues throughout our decade-long association. They were always respectful and often humorous exchanges that were usually punctuated by a slightly devilish gleam in Arthur's eye. The conversation was almost always followed by a sarcastic comment from Arthur about when we could expect to get paid. But with each project we undertook, the sales results exceeded projections and they were finding (as I had first suspected) that not only did their core customers appreciate the look and feel of the new stores, but that they had been able to draw in new customers to add to the mix. Goodman's was sold to a major national group (Sterling Jewelers) in the late 1980s and Arthur credited our work involving my initial "psychographic endeavors" and repositioning of the chain as being influential in the sale.

*Psychographics Evolves*

In 1978, social scientist and futurist Arnold Mitchell and his colleagues at Stanford Research Institute introduced a new and more evolved concept for evaluating consumer behavior known as VALS (values, attitudes, and lifestyles). This was a huge step in the direction of today's psychographic market segmentation, the basis of most product development and modern-day marketing. VALS was the first "attitudinal" metric developed to look at lifestyle types that transcend issues of gender, age, race, and location. This work takes into account that a thirtysomething, middle-class, single women living in the San Francisco Bay area is likely to have a very different world outlook than a middle-class, married, thirtysomething mother living in, say, rural Wisconsin. VALS divided the American consumer into nine lifestyle types: survivors (4%), sustainers (7%), belongers (35%), emulators (9%), achievers (22%), I-am-me (5%), experiential (7%), society conscious (9%), and integrated (2%). This new way of looking at the population was immediately embraced by marketers and advertisers as a more effective means of defining, separating, and connecting to consumers.

The next and perhaps most important breakthrough occurred

> **This was a huge step in the direction of today's psychographic market segmentation, the basis of most product development and modern-day marketing.**

in the 1990s when Claritas (now NielsenClaritas) developed a system for geodemographic segmentation called PRISM. It uses census-data analysis and categorizes the U.S. population into various lifestyle, life-stage, and social groups. PRISM defines sixty-six demographically and behaviorally distinct segments. Each segment (or bucket, as it's often called) has very specific age, income, geographic, ethnic, educational, and family makeup. What makes the system so brilliant and useful is that Claritas takes every zip code in the country and determines the relative existence and density of each of the sixty-six different and distinct lifestyle groups. On a practical level, this enables marketing groups to determine in exactly which area of the country to test a specific product. It enables chain retailers such as Target to adjust product mix not only by geographic region and state, but also by consumer preferences throughout a given metropolitan area. Commercial real estate developers can market a property to a retailer based on an exact match for the retailer's or brand's core customer base and conversely every good retailer knows exactly which buckets their highest-value customers occupy.

We have been able to use this data in a variety of ways that have helped us become better acquainted with our clients and has helped our clients understand their customers. In 2007, we were retained by Good Feet, a San Diego-based manufacturer of arch supports, to develop a new retail prototype for a national roll out to their franchisees. During programming we received general and somewhat vague demographics regarding their core customers. To clarify who their highest-value customers were, I requested a list of their best-performing stores in the U.S. With the help of Claritas's PRISM, we did a geographic analysis of two-, five-, and ten-mile radiuses of these top-performing stores. In less than week (with a very small investment) I was able to tell the principals the exact mix of customers that made the high-performing stores so successful. These high-indexing lifestyle groups (from about twenty of the sixty-six buckets) demonstrated and confirmed a younger and more affluent shopper than the company had previously thought was its core customer.

## OPENNESS

It's been my experience that good designers, like most creative people, have an openness and innate curiosity about the world around them that is almost childlike in nature. We know that the working environment at the Eames studio contributed to playful, unbridled discovery. Their studio looked like a cross between a circus, a theater, and a laboratory. Likewise the modern-day work environments at companies like Google, Facebook, and Apple are the antitheses of the traditional corporate work environments of just a couple of decades ago. This movement to unstructured, nurturing, and playful space planning may indeed help creative people escape to their inner child—and therefore influence the process of discovery itself. In the design profession this process can indeed be double-edged, because this unrestrained creative energy must ultimately be merged with the overarching requirements of function, purpose, timing, and budgets—definitely the stuff of grown-ups.

It is this essence of openness and discovery that has long driven creative people to play in a really big sandbox. Think of the diversity of such renowned creators as da Vinci, Michelangelo, and Edison. One of the most exceptional design minds of our time was R. Buckminster Fuller, known to students and admirers as "Bucky." Fuller's range of creative genius included systems theory, architecture, engineering, and industrial design. He was a prolific author of more than thirty books, an inventor who held over two dozen

One of the most exceptional design minds of our time was R. Buckminster Fuller, known to students and admirers as "Bucky."

patents spanning fifty years, and a noted futurist. He was arguably one of the first and most passionate proponents of sustainability, coining the phrase "spaceship Earth," though he died before the green movement ever got started.

Fuller is probably most famous for the design and engineering behind lattice shell structures, or geodesic domes, and planned, large-scale, sustainable domed cities. His interest in safety and aerodynamics led to his designing the Dymaxion car in the 1930s, which remains one of the most iconic vehicular designs of all time. Ironically for Fuller, his creative energy and intense curiosity made him hard to categorize, and during the height of his influence he was shunned by the architectural community for being too diverse and not focused enough. It's only been in recent years that the breadth of his creative contribution is being recognized.

In the early 1970s, while Bucky was on a promotional tour in Milwaukee, I had the distinct pleasure of listening to him give an over-two-hour lecture. Already in his late seventies, he covered an almost-unimaginable amount of information. He spoke at a rapid, almost frenetic, pace at times and for the entire speech he never referred to a single note, nor was there a disjointed thought. His presence (complete with the iconic eyeglasses) was spellbinding and left an indelible mark on me, and probably the rest of the audience. I still have the "Bucky 71" pin that was distributed at the event, which I suspect was a parody on the upcoming 1972 presidential election.

*Feelers Up*

Even with the demanding client needs and challenging time constraints that are ever-present in retail, I have always attempted to remain as open and free of preconceived notions as possible. This is particularly important during the observational predesign phase. Designers are often so anxious to dig into the visual and conceptual process that they sometimes don't give the informational process time to gel, or in the cooking vernacular, a chance to marinate. (I may get flack for that analogy.) We always try to make sure we're picking up on all the signals our clients are giving while maintaining a healthy skepticism for what we're hearing, which means watching for out for industry dogma or preconceptions. A terrific example of this occurred when my firm was first engaged by Brunswick Corporation to help reposition and manage their valuable billiards brand at point of sale.

Brunswick, founded in 1845, is the longest continuing brand of billiard tables in the U.S. Through the years, the Brunswick name has been on a vast array of consumer products, ranging from refrigerators and tires, to phonograph records and toilet seats. In 1999, we were invited to the headquarters of the Brunswick billiards' division, located in Bristol, Wisconsin, population 4,500, a "village" in Kenosha County that's midway between Chicago and Milwaukee. It seemed rather strange at first, approaching the warehouse headquarters that was standing in a cornfield, but the image became quite familiar to us over the next ten years.

Brunswick's issues at the time were typical of many brands and manufacturers—erosion of profits due to cheaper, low-quality imports; challenges to the age-old independent distribution channel from the big boxes; and loss of control of their valued brand. Even though Brunswick had the greatest name recognition in the industry, their brand was being commoditized in the marketplace. Many of their dealers felt compelled to feature multiple brands and, unfortunately for Brunswick, price was often the only apparent differentiator, which is the essence of brand commoditization. Brunswick recognized that they needed to take control of their brand within the multibrand environment if they had any hope of preserving brand value. A classic example of brand management getting out of control came up during my very first meeting with the division president, John Stansky. It seemed that the independent dealers actually had gotten in the habit of stacking the billiard tables, one on top of another to jam more products onto the floor (not unlike stacking wood.) John had formed an opinion on this approach and he wanted to see how I felt about it (a test question). My response was that my father-in-law and I had just visited a new Lexus dealership over the past weekend and I did not see the Lexi (plural) stacked. Apparently I passed the first test. This turned out to be the beginning of an ongoing, fifteen-year relationship with John, who I consider a gifted leader and visionary, in four different corporate leadership positions in and out of Brunswick Corporation.

## STYLE

Style is a tricky thing to talk about when addressing the aesthetic component of the design process. Style can be intensely personal, it's often an expression of one's very being. We all dress ourselves in the morning and some of us do a better job than others. We change our hairstyles to make us feel and look different—that is, for those of us who still have those options. We live in houses that often offer tacit references to iconic architectural periods and each year we spend billions of dollars to change, update, design, decorate, or otherwise alter its style. Style influences the cars we drive, the places we dine, the people we are attracted to—or put off by. Sounds shallow, but it's true, nonetheless.

Style can be very confusing and sometimes emotionally charged when related to the idiom of design. Architects, industrial designers, graphic designers, and fashion designers are motivated and influenced by the times in which they live, as well as the period of time that preceded them. It could be argued that the most influential among them presented a unique point of view that resulted in a strong, enduring style, sometimes even defining. We know that Wright used natural materials to reinterpret nature and his command of form, shape, and proportion led to a style that is uniquely his. In strong contrast, Mies van der Rohe, who worked at the same time, recognized the simplistic beauty of expressed structure, steel and glass, "skin and bones" architecture, as he called it—creating a new architectural style to reflect the modern times.

In the early half of the twentieth century, automotive style was largely an expression of what the engineering departments dictated. During that period, size played perhaps the biggest role in differentiating what the middle and upper classes drove. The exception being that for the very rich there were "coach builders," whose mission it was to take factory-made chassis from a myriad of manufacturers and adorn them with one-off body styles, custom designed and fabricated for the dukes of industry and their duchesses, not to mention Hollywood stars and starlets. Some of these surviving Packards, Auburns, and Duesenbergs (origin of the term "Duesy") with one-off coach work are among the most valued of the prewar collector cars. That changed radically when designers including Harley Earl at GM and Virgil Exner at Chrysler began to reinterpret the era of flight through their finned fantasies of the 1950s and 1960s. The success of these designs, along with Detroit's new era of planned obsolescence, gave the newly mobile middle-class Americans a new means of personal expression. It also heralded a new era of design for consumer products of every imaginable kind, fueling Madison Avenue with the "stuff of dreams" for which they became expert weavers.

> **That changed radically when designers including Harley Earl at GM and Virgil Exner at Chrysler began to reinterpret the era of flight through their finned fantasies of the 1950s and 1960s.**

*Classic versus Plastic*

Ultimately, the design practitioners whose bodies of work are recognized as revolutionary, iconic, and enduring carry with them styles that transcend mere decoration or ornament. They are often an outgrowth of pivotal issues regarding the user, evolving technology, or a reevaluation of the status quo. The Bauhaus designers developed a highly functional aesthetic that evoked the materials and shapes of the machine age. Their designs are an expression of efficiency and simplicity. Rather than hiding or masking methods of joinery (as had been the custom) connections were expressed in an honest and direct fashion. Similarly, the transcendent work of Charles and Ray Eames came from the dedication to and deep understanding of the materials and manufacturing processes that informed and influenced their designs. The famed "Potato Chip" chair, which was introduced in 1946 (and which I spent hours drawing at Layton), grew out of intense experimentation in bending and laminating plywood that was not initially connected to furniture design. Charles was working in Los Angeles at the time, developing molded plywood traction splints for the U.S. Air Force during World War II. The necessity of the curved shape (modeled after Charles own leg) drove the development of new techniques for molding plywood into complex curves. This ultimately informed and contributed to the design and manufacturing of their iconic chair, arguably the most noteworthy piece of furniture of the twentieth century. Perhaps the ultimate expression of honesty in its design was in exposing the laminated plies of the chair, something unheard of up to that time.

Like most artists and designers, I have confronted the challenges of and engaged in the ever-changing issues of style and trends throughout my career. I used to take quite a bit of pride in hearing that friends and fellow designers could recognize one of our styles in a newly opened store, back when much of our work was concentrated in the Twin Cities. It then occurred to me that if the purpose of our work was to support an expression of a particular brand or customer demographic, then our aim had to become less about our style and more about the brand and the customer experience; it was a career wake-up call.

*His or Hers*

The issues of style and the intended audience for the product came up very early on as we were developing the store-in-store, branded environment known as the Brunswick Pavilion. Both the manufacturer and the retailers were fixated on the perception that the massive tables were (excuse the expression) a "guy thing" and that the selling environments needed to reflect this. After spending several weeks visiting stores and watching sales take place—and many that didn't—I went back to the corporate offices with some of my initial observations. The folks at corporate were both somewhat taken back and enlightened when I told them that their dealers were not selling a guy's toy at all, but instead were selling a very large piece of furniture, and more often than not, a women was the gatekeeper for the sale. Moreover, all of the selling environments I visited had two things in common: the first was that the manufacturer's brand was being commoditized badly; the second was that the spaces were anything but female-friendly, let alone stylish.

This insight helped to properly position and inform the Pavilion's design. It inspired the development of signature four-by-eight-foot photographic scrims depicting images of the billiard tables in aspirational environments of many different styles. The images enabled the customers to visualize and get a feel for the product in their

> **I told them that their dealers were not selling a guy's toy at all, but instead were selling a very large piece of furniture, and more often than not, a women was the gatekeeper for the sale.**

home environments, which resulted in many more guys getting their big-boy toys after all. Another important insight came from witnessing dozens of salespeople interacting with the customers, with each one telling a different brand and product story. Not only was there no consistent approach, salesperson to salesperson or store to store, but nothing in the store helped the customer understand the features and benefits, brand heritage, or the level to which the customers could personalize their tables. After considerable research, we developed what came to be known as the "selling wall," a kiosk-like structure, featuring individual images of every Brunswick table along with a simple key that enabled the customer to understand the process of making a choice through assisted discovery. This accomplished two key selling initiatives. First, it allowed the customer to form questions that would help them make a selection. This is particularly important for any brand or manufacturer who sells items with a long purchase cycle (i.e., something we purchase infrequently). Some customers are uncomfortable asking questions and any tools that begin to educate and empower will lower the resistance to engaging with a sales assistant. The second benefit of the selling wall was that now the salespeople had a device that could be used for assisted selling— and it had the added advantage of getting them all singing from the same hymnal.

I will explore this concept further in a later chapter when I touch on the radical changes that technology brings to store-based retailing along with the disruptive effects the Internet is having on all aspects of retail. As the Internet becomes the initial brand touchpoint in so many purchases, stores must learn to behave in a very different manner than in past.

## COMMUNICATION

After covering four key components of the design process—immersion, context, openness, and style—we are left to tackle what may be the single most important attribute: communication. There is a duality to the issue of communication that has made it one of the single biggest challenges to the design community in the U.S.

There are two aspects of communication that influence the success or failure of the design process. The first is the practitioner's interest and ability to understand the needs of the client. The second is that the designer has to be able to clearly and succinctly communicate how a particular design solution can meet those needs and become a value-enhancing proposition. Unless the design solution directly addresses the client's issues (which can be articulated in a manner that is objective, focused, and persuasive), it won't matter how great the solution is or how passionate the designer may be about his or her "baby." I personally believe that over the course of the last millennium, the design industry has had a PR problem. We have too often been perceived by businesses, communities, and the general public as being arrogant, out of touch, or not relevant. I suspect the personalities of some of our star practitioners may have had an effect, but I also believe that some higher-education institutions have contributed to this perception.

The greatest design concepts in the world may never see the light of day if the practitioner can't communicate their ideas in a meaningful and effective way. For the designer, this means that he or she must sell him or herself along with their ideas. For example, both advertising and the motion picture industry have, at their core, the communications cornerstone of the pitch. Each industry understands that regardless of how much time is spent on the

**Unless the design solution directly addresses the client's issues it won't matter how great the solution is or how passionate the designer may be about his or her "baby." I personally believe that over the course of the last millennium, the design industry has had a PR problem.**

development of an ad campaign or a movie script, if the essence cannot be communicated succinctly it doesn't matter how good it really is. We've all seen the (somewhat exaggerated) portrayals of hungry scriptwriters or ad execs pitching ideas where the proper setup, turn of phrase, or eye contact was the difference between success and failure. While I don't think design can or should be distilled down to this level of pitching, I do feel that much can be gained by developing excellent marketing and communication skills and including basic business courses in design programs. I have witnessed many talented students, graduates, and young practitioners in portfolio reviews, charrettes, critiques, and presentations so passionate about their designs, but unable to make a coherent connection between a well-stated problem and how their design resolves it. This immediately compromises the credibility and integrity of the presentation, if not the firm's brand.

These basic communication skills are fundamental not only to being able to sell an idea or concept, but also to maintain proper influence and control throughout the project. When the designer is unable to get out "in front" of a client in a genuine leadership capacity, the design outcome can fall prey to the whims and arbitrary decision-making of the client. One of the key differentiators between outstanding design practitioners and those who don't rise to greatness is less about sheer talent and more about the ability to communicate a shared vision with the client and maintain a position of strong leadership. Trust me, this is not easy.

*Proactive versus Reactive*

The process of learning to communicate effectively through the input/output duality has played out in many ways in the course of my career. There is an old business adage that says the best and easiest source of new work is not in searching out a new client but pursuing new opportunities within an existing one. This has never been a more timely and appropriate notion than in post-downsized America when everyone wants to do more business with established relationships and trusted partners, rather than troll for new, untested talent. One of the greatest dividends of working extremely hard for a client and maintaining the trust that often comes as a result is when a new opportunity presents itself and you are the presenter. Deepak Chopra often says, "When preparedness and opportunity meet, the result is good luck."

Such was the case with another of our projects with John Stransky at Brunswick Corporation—and communication and preparedness played a key role in how the opportunity unfolded. One of my biggest issues early on with the Brunswick product line was the fact that virtually all of the table designs were neoclassical and pretty much derivative of one another. I felt strongly that America's tastes were changing and that companies like Target, IKEA, and Crate & Barrel were reaching an ever larger audience of people who admire clean lines and contemporary designs. While I was certainly building a sense of trust at Brunswick, I felt it wasn't enough to just make my case on consumer trending and expect them to simply buy in.

So we began doing our homework on building a very cogent case for creating better product diversity within the line. We shared statistics on contemporary trends, and provided their product planners (who were already convinced) with the ammunition to build the case internally. While I felt we were gaining some traction with this approach, we took it upon ourselves to design what we felt would be a great entry-level, contemporary billiard table. In 2003, Brunswick introduced three new contemporary billiard tables including the Apollo billiard table that we designed. The Apollo entered the line at a very affordable price point and looked like nothing else on

**When the designer is unable to get out "in front" of a client in a genuine leadership capacity, the design outcome can fall prey to the whims and arbitrary decision-making of the client.**

the market.

Shortly after its launch, the table appeared on two network TV reality shows where set designers needed a billiard table to finish out two very different, but both highly modern, sets. One appeared in a very upscale L.A. "bachelor pad" the other in the training area of NBC's boxing reality series *The Contender*. I remember the feeling of watching both series to catch fleeting two- to five-second glimpses of "our child" with great satisfaction. I knew that if I had waited for the assignment to design a modern billiard table for Brunswick, I'd probably still be waiting. I believe our proactive determination and ability to communicate a shared vision brought the sketches to life and the table to market.

# CHAPTER
# FIVE

# BRANDING
# 101

For successful retailers the issue of identity is of paramount importance to their relevance and viability. One of the ad hoc lectures
that Dad often gave at the dinner table, after their brand enlightening experience with Pill & Puff, had to do with successful retailers
staying consistent with their message: "If they [unfocused retailers]
think they're one thing on Tuesday and something else on Friday,
how is the customer supposed to know what they stand for?"
Rhetorical question, of course. Dad was right. Most successful
retailers that do things well over the long haul are all about consistency. They achieve initial success by having a concept and
establishing a benchmark for who they are and what their company stands for. Call it their core values or brand differentiators.
It can't be too complex or it will be too hard to enforce, but it must
be unique and well defined. Great retailers hone their identities with
great care to establish their particular value proposition and differentiated market position. Once this benchmark is well established,
all decisions can be referenced against it and all brand extensions
or touchpoints are aligned.

## A PERSONAL BRAND STAND

While the terms brand, branding, and branded environments will
occur throughout this book, it was never my intention to write a
book about branding. It could be argued that the term may be
among the most overused of our time. In looking at the evolution of
retailing over the past hundred years, it's impossible not to spend
time talking about this five-letter word. To explore some of the key
components that make up enduring retail concepts or brands, I'm
going to borrow from one of this country's preeminent brand builders, Scott Bedbury. In the late 1980s he helped Nike "Just Do It" —
and when "It" got done, he moved over to help make Starbucks
one of the fastest-growing brands and retail sensations of our time.

I've taken some of Bedbury's lessons of great brand building, and personalized and adapted them to the realm of retailing and branded environments. Given our culture's love of acronyms and the apparent requirement that there be at least one in any quasi-business book, my acronym to define the essential components of an exceptional brand is INTERDES (with a nod to my first Minneapolis employer, InterDesign). These vital elements are: *identity* (knowing who you are); *nuance* (subtle points of differentiation); *transcendence* (going beyond boundaries); *emotion* (connecting on a primal level); *relevance* (what people want); *design* (the key differentiator); *endurance* (being in it for the long haul); and *soul* (the whole is greater than the sum of its parts).

## IDENTITY

Any good retail concept must start with insight into market conditions, competitive set, and demographics; these all shape the fundamentals of identity. The Stein twins knew there was a void in the Milwaukee market for discount health and beauty aids back in the 1960s and they leveraged the opportunity. Their identity was clear from the start, and their elevator speech (had they had one) would have been: Unmatched choice in name-brand health and beauty aids at discount prices in pleasant, convenient locations. And they executed that identity from day one, never veering from it. Today, that hardly sounds like a market differentiator, but in the early 1960s most consumers had only three choices in where to buy their health and beauty aids. The first was the pharmacy, which would have been full price and often without full product lines. The second was the grocery store, also at full price and with an even more limited selection. The third choice for Milwaukeeans looking to save money on their toothpaste and deodorant was one of the few general merchandise discounters, an option that did not

> "If they [unfocused retailers] think they're one thing on Tuesday and something else on Friday, how is the customer supposed to know what they stand for?"

provide a pleasant shopping experience. In those days, discount merchants were just about price, with cluttered, dark, dirty stores in bad locations—or as Dad would put it, "the second floor over a vacant lot." Pill & Puff presented a better choice, so it became a defining brand in the Milwaukee market and a pioneer in the new and emerging segment of discount mass merchandising.

## Unformed Giants

At just about the same time in Minneapolis, Minnesota, and Bentonville, Arkansas, two other discount mass-market retailers were emerging. They shared a similar focus but each had a distinctly different core identity. Target and Walmart had their origins in 1962 as the highly fractured, regional, off-price warehouse retailers were gaining traction around the country. Walmart started out in rural America and throughout their formative years remained rooted strictly in secondary markets, mostly in the south. Meanwhile, Target built its brand concentrating on large urban major markets beginning in the Northwest. Both saw the opportunity to provide customers with great value as well as taking the concept of off-price merchandising to new heights. I vividly remember visiting the first Target store that opened in Minneapolis; though it was a long way from today's highly evolved Target prototypes, it was a quantum leap beyond its major competitors at the time.

The origin of Target's core identity lies in the successful overlay of the highly developed merchandising skills of the Dayton's department stores onto a fairly conventional big-box format. Their insight at the time, and one that has continued over the last half century, was to bring the style, sensitivity, attention to detail, and merchandising display execution from the upscale department store and introduce it to the then anything-goes world of off-price mass merchandising. The aisles were wider, the stores were brighter, product adjacencies made sense (e.g., the toilet paper wasn't next to light bulbs) and the facings (how the products are lined up on the shelves) were managed in a way not seen in a discount store before. The public loved it, and continues to do so, fifty years and nearly 1,800 stores later.

## NUANCE

People who may know little or nothing about architecture can freely quote Mies van der Rohe's well-known "God is in the details" mantra. In the world of brand building, every little thing counts. A great concept executed poorly will not survive. Even good brands that may execute well across several brand touchpoints will suffer when one of the key elements is not properly executed. Today, more than at any time in history, for a brand or concept to survive it requires laser-like attention to even the most nuanced details to maintain brand value and market dominance.

Not surprisingly, as we look to the true retail innovators and highly successful retail brand builders in the second half of the twentieth century, these agents of change were and are detail driven, often to the point of obsession. Urban Outfitters' Richard Hayne understands the subtlety of visual merchandising and has made store display evolve to a high art that merges product and lifestyle in a way that is emotional and engaging. His stores control every aspect of the holistic storytelling that takes place between product and display. As a result, he has built one of the most successful specialty retail empires of our time with the Urban Outfitters, Anthropologie, and Free People brands, and in the process has become one of the 400 wealthiest men in the U.S., according to *Forbes* magazine.

> Today, more than at any time in history, for a brand or concept to survive it requires laser-like attention to even the most nuanced details to maintain brand value and market dominance.

## Costco Phenomenon

I've learned that this attention to detail among successful retail brand builders succeeds only when it is woven into and throughout the culture of a company, as has been the case with Costco's founder and CEO Jim Sinegal. To quote Sinegal, "Culture is not the most important thing, it's the only thing." Costco has become a puzzling phenomenon in the world of retailing. It has broken many rules and established norms on the way to becoming the most successful retail membership club, and one of the most successful big-box retailers, period.

Why do three million customers a day clog the parking lots of their 600 stores to buy everything from televisions to tires to tuna fish—and in the process generate ninety-three billion in revenue for Costco? The answer: the shopping experience is primal. Sinegal refers to it as "wonder and stumble" with a feeling of random discovery not unlike a garage sale. But in strong contrast to a garage sale, nothing about the customer experience at Costco is remotely arbitrary or accidental.

A half century ago, Walt Disney taught us about the concept of a managed experience with the manner in which Disneyland was laid out. Disney pioneered what came to be known as "experiential sequence," the art and science of managing a visitor's experience through a carefully engineered multisensory planning process. Disney understood that it took more than just building a large-scale fantasyland to achieve the transformational experience he sought. The Disney planners, under Walt's watchful eye, thought about every visitor movement to build the proper sense of wonder with planned surprises that would ultimately create the desired emotions and outcome. Disney would be quite impressed with the immersive, engaging experience that Costco delivers through disciplined planning and execution. Digging a bit deeper reveals Costco's points of brand differentiation.

First, unlike most other grocery or general merchandising stores, the choices are intentionally limited at Costco. While Walmart may stock 100,000 varieties of goods, Costco stocks about 4,000 items. In a later chapter in a section titled "The Dichotomy of Choice," I discuss the fact that too much choice can be as formidable a barrier to success as too little choice. It can easily become overwhelming for today's time-strapped and stressed-out customer and lead to indecision. Sinegal and his team learned early on that when a customer has the opportunity to buy three times as much of a popular brand of laundry detergent for what they would ordinarily spend for less than half the quantity, the lack of brand choice doesn't matter so much. With less than ten percent of the SKUs of today's leading retailers, and the massive volumes that Costco sells, you can bet they're spending less and getting more from the few select brands and suppliers that make the cut.

Second, there is the "secret sauce" behind the product mix in the stores that Costco refers to as "triggers and treasures." This is Costco-speak for the careful and enticing 75/25 mix of the incredibly priced staples or "triggers" that dominate the inventory, contrasted against the here-today-and-gone-tomorrow "treasures" that play an outsized role in bringing their sixty-four million members into their stores. And while the obsessed Costcoanians are there again and again to save money, their demographics are in sharp contrast to budget-minded Walmart customers. Costco customers boast an average yearly family income in excess of $100,000, twice the national average. So why does this work so well? Certainly the discovery aspect pulls folks in the door, but it is their attention to detail and amazing values that translate to the $1.5 billion a year profit and customer loyalty that is off the charts.

To quote Sinegal, "Culture is not the most important thing, it's the only thing."

The truly surprising piece to the equation, that is not at all obvious, is the extent to which Costco's buyers and product managers sweat the details, truly demonstrating Jim's mantra about culture.

A great example, though not a very romantic one is TP—yes, toilet paper. They sell a lot of it: $400,000,000 a year, which equates to one billion rolls. It's their single biggest seller at over 1.6 million roles sold per store. What is so incredible, besides these numbers, is the degree of testing, assessing, and obsessing they go through to make sure that their customers are getting the best roll available. And they do this by testing every imaginable performance factor in laboratories that you'd expect to find only in the hallowed halls of Charmin. This kind of attention to detail has made Costco's Kirkland brand so highly trusted that they're now bottling their own private label wines. And unlike Trader Joe's venerable Three Buck Chuck (which I mention with great fondness and memories of my late father-in-law, who would attempt to rebottle Chuck in an effort to fool me), these wines are being selected and sourced from some of the finest growers and bottlers in Europe and the U.S.

## TRANSCENDENCE

A great brand transcends boundaries, it can be anything. One of the most thoughtful and influential business magazines of our time, *Fast Company*, did a cover article in 1997 called "The Brand Called You." This was one of the pivotal articles on the concept of personal branding, and I developed a seminar presentation around the topic. One of the most outrageous out-of-the-box demonstrations of the power and flexibility of branding came via one of my most influential mentors, Ken Walker. Ken is an industry pioneer who blended his architectural training with an innate understanding of marketing and brand strategy to create one of the first and largest retail planning and design firms. Ken founded the Walker Group in

New York in 1970 and helped many of the world's largest department stores, mass market, and specialty store chains achieve their marketing objectives with highly memorable and successful retail designs. Ken coined the term "retail theater," which emphasizes the importance of a branded environment to transcend a "box filled with product" and establish a high-level, memorable interaction between the customer and the product to elevate brand value.

I was first introduced to Ken in 1987 when he was on the jury for the American Institute of Architects Minnesota interior design awards. That year we had submitted the first completed prototype for the Edison Brothers Stores Wild Pair division. Our entry was the only retail design project submitted that year and I had a suspicion that it would get Ken's attention. It did, but not necessarily in the way I had hoped. It should be noted that Ken possesses many of the traits we often associate with New Yorkers—he's not a bit bashful, and you usually know where he stands on an issue.

Our project did get recognized but only with an honorable mention. During the jury's review of the works there was a designated judge for each project and when it came to ours, Ken shared his thoughts: the good, the bad, and the very colorful. Not willing to be demoralized by the experience, I made it a point to introduce myself to Ken afterward and found him charming and engaging. He asked for my card and gave me his in return. He also made an offhand comment about how I might feel about working in New York, and immediately my heart began to race.

What transpired over the course of the next six months was a huge ego boost and a potentially career-altering experience for me. It started with phone calls from Ken's secretary, flights to the Walker Group's impressive New York headquarters, and visits to our studio by Ken and his associates. Ken made it quite clear that he thought I could be a significant addition to his senior staff. Ulti-

> He asked for my card and gave me his in return. He also made an offhand comment about how I might feel about working in New York, and immediately my heart began to race.

mately, I felt that the pace of the New York design lifestyle was not a match, but I was flattered and we promised to stay connected nonetheless.

In 1987, Ken sold his firm to the London-based media giant, the WPP group, where he remained at the helm until starting his own consultancy in 1993 called Retail Options Inc. (ROI). During this period Ken was restricted from doing retail interiors based on his buy-sell agreement, and as fortune would have it, he reached out to us to develop a collaboration that lasted for nearly a decade. Our work with Ken during this time brought with it national and international travel, including occasional visits to his New York office and, more interestingly, to his spectacular penthouse apartment. Ken is a huge art collector and was incredibly smart in procuring architectural drawings produced by the hands of some of the most renowned architects of our time. He bought many of them long before they were thought to have intrinsic value beyond that of communicating a concept to a client. Many were done by some of his instructors at Harvard and others by his design contemporaries. Today, with the prolific use of computer-aided drafting, these hand-drawn sketches and detailed renderings have become extremely valuable. A trip through his apartment is like a chronological architectural history tour of the works of many of the twentieth century's architectural masters; it was simply breathtaking.

Ken's charismatic personality, business prowess, and innate sense of marketing combined with an imagination that knows no limits has enabled him to become one of the most successful architects and interior designers of the twentieth century. But it was the almost-outrageous notion that he came up with in 1998 that will forever define him as a cutting-edge, innovative thinker who knows how to transcend the perceived limits of a brand.

## Branding the Millennium

During one of my New York visits, Ken said he had something "interesting" to share with me. I was instructed to wait in the library while he went to fetch the item of interest. Ken walked back in the room adorned with a baseball cap placed securely upon his signature domed cranium. He looked at me with a sly grin on his face and said, "Well, what do you think?" I stared at the stark black hat bearing bold, white Helvetica numerals 01-01-00, and I was at a complete loss. At first, I thought it had to be some kind of computer code. I kept staring hoping to be struck by some cosmic insight to delight my friend and mentor, but nothing came to me. Finally, Ken burst out: "It's the *millennium. I've branded the new millennium!*" And sure enough, here we were sitting in Ken's New York apartment in mid-1998 and he was about to undertake one of the shrewdest branding efforts since Coke. And with this stroke of brilliance (and audacity), came the monetization of our planet's impending birthday, which would become the preoccupation of its nearly seven billion inhabitants. To say that the scheme worked would be an understatement. Ken secured the rights to the Millennium brand and had literally hundreds of products created bearing the simple, elegant logo, in black on white and white on black. He produced everything from wearables to mugs and magnets; there was even a book. The products were distributed to department stores and specialty retailers around the world in time for the big celebration. The financial success of this venture was astronomical, but the real message is transcendence. There are no limits to a brand—if it's conceived and managed correctly, it can surpass any predefined boundary.

> I stared at the stark black hat bearing bold, white Helvetica numerals 01-01-00, and I was at a complete loss. "It's the millennium. I've branded the new millennium!"

## EMOTION

When someone contemplates the purchase of a product, ranging from a cup of coffee to a car, it involves both emotional (right brain) and intellectual (left brain) decision-making. This frequently manifests itself in a subconscious fight between wants and needs and often results in a certain level of rationalization. For example, one needs transportation (an efficient Honda Civic would adequately provide it) but one wants the "ultimate driving machine" at the BMW dealership. It is the goal of media and marketing mavens to create messaging that results in our emotions winning over our intellect.

Great brands have a story that is woven so deeply into their DNA that the brand and the stories are subconsciously merged, not unlike mythology. These brands connect a very emotional message to their offerings that resonates with its target customer, and their products become highly differentiated in the marketplace. A story is infinitely more memorable than a product purchase because for as long as people have been able to communicate, stories have been created and passed down from generation to generation. The moment a child is born we begin to tell him or her stories, and those stories become deeply engrained in the culture. Nike uses the powerful images of sports and the stories indelibly linked to champions to sell its shoes. Porsche's racing heritage is deeply linked to its coveted sports cars and to those who own them. In some small, visceral way when you join the Porsche brand by buying one you become a part of its culture and lifestyle. Undoubtedly the most effective brand stories are based on authentic roots and origins, and I was introduced to such a brand and its originator at the very moment of its inception.

*A Lifestyle Brand*

In 1985, I received a call from a man speaking in a delicate German accent, who identified himself as Horst Rechelbacher. I knew him as the founder of a chain of upscale hair salons in Minneapolis. Rechelbacher explained that he wanted to talk with me about a new retail concept he had. He arrived at my office toting a large briefcase which he gently placed on my conference table and proceeded to launch into a speech that sounded like one he had given numerous times. Not five minutes into his dissertation, the briefcase began to ring. I was both shocked and dumbfounded as Horst opened the case and withdrew a large-handheld device that appeared to be a cross between a telephone and a *M\*A\*S\*H*-era walkie-talkie. He immediately began to give whoever was at the receiving end loud and firm instructions in a mixture of German and English. He then jammed the device back in the case and reestablished eye contact as if nothing had happened. I had just been introduced to the father of all cell phones by an early adapter to the technology. The meeting only got more interesting from there.

With great passion, Horst shared with me his Austrian origins and the influence that his mother, an herbalist, had on his formative years. She taught him an understanding and appreciation for the power of plants in creating remedies and the benefits of essential oils derived from plants and flowers. I'll admit it all sounded quite strange at the time, but I could tell he was a man with a mission. Horst spoke about the harsh chemicals the cosmetic industry uses in many beauty products and the damage associated to both people and the planet. With ever-increasing emotion he shared his vision for a new brand of products with plant-based nutrients and essential oils that would work in harmony with our bodies and the planet and bring to fruition the work his mother had started years

**Great brands have a story that is woven so deeply into their DNA that the brand and the stories are subconsciously merged, not unlike mythology.**

before.

At that point he paused and looked at me with laser-like intensity (which was admittedly a bit intimidating) as he began to talk about his image for the environments that would embody the new brand. He envisioned a multisensory, otherworld-like experience for the customer. He knew instinctively that everything about the brand, from the scents of the products to the design of the packaging and every aspect of the stores' aesthetic had to feel natural, unique, uplifting, and holistic. I didn't know it at the time, but I was getting an important lesson in brand touchpoint integration from a pioneer brand builder. This was about two decades before behavioral scientists embarked on a field of study that defined neurological connectivity, which recognizes the ways well-conceived and well-executed brands (i.e., Apple) influence consumer behavior.

The name of Horst's revolutionary new brand, Aveda, had its origins in Ayurveda, the ancient Hindu holistic system of medicine. This alternative to Western medicine recognizes the powerful mind/body connection and seeks to create balance, because according to its philosophy, the source of all disease stems from imbalance. Horst shortened Ayurveda to the name Aveda, which reflected the same principles. Like many visionaries and entrepreneurs, Horst melded his passion with an awareness of market trends and was at the forefront of the emerging "wellness" mind-set. The Aveda brand addressed the public's growing demand for natural products and sustainable business practices. Its popularity was a result of its authentic nature combined with the seamless execution regarding every brand extension or touchpoint of the customer experience. Aveda became a defining brand in the cosmetic industry. Horst's passions stirred the passions of his many customers.

In 1997, Horst sold Aveda to Estee Lauder Companies for $300 million. While we were not ultimately hired to design the new Aveda prototype, I was grateful to be given a peek inside the mind of an agent of change. His insights on the value of connecting brand touchpoints inspired me and became fundamental to our work for decades to come.

## RELEVANCE

A great brand makes a connection to people and provides what they want. While I ordinarily don't like to use a negative experience or challenged brand to illustrate an important concept, I'm going to make an exception. In 1997, Sony introduced its new Vaio brand of personal computers, and it was arguably the first breakout in laptop PC designs. Vaio featured slimmer profiles and handsome lighter units, along with faster processors and a relatively longer battery life. It was right about then that my laptop died and I was anxious to see one of the new Sony Vaios up close, while comparing them to the major competition. My exploration took me to CompUSA, which was then the well-known, big-box destination for all things computer. Fifteen years ago there had not yet been a shakeout in the segment—HP, Dell, Gateway, and Sony dominated. Apple was still a niche player, though one with a very devoted following.

My CompUSA shopping experience became a memorable one for all the wrong reasons, though it did produce a bit of enlightenment at the same time. What I discovered that day should be of no great surprise to many. The store was essentially crammed full of stuff. It lacked order, brands were commingled and there was no good way for a customer to begin the process of making a choice or editing the offerings. The only obvious product differentiator was price (the very definition of brand commoditization). And when it came to trying to find someone with any knowledge (or a heartbeat) there was simply no sign of intelligent life. After spend-

**And when it came to trying to find someone with any knowledge (or a heartbeat) there was simply no sign of intelligent life.**

ing nearly forty minutes in the store trying to get noticed, I walked out. To my great disappointment there was no Vaio in sight; even though Sony was running a marketing campaign and CompUSA was a Sony retailer.

I sat down in my car and began to make some notes for an address I was scheduled to give in the coming months on retail trends. I thought, if the major brands are expecting the retailer to manage their brand story at point of sale, they are delusional. And if that retailer thinks they can stay in business with that kind of customer experience, they are kidding themselves. But it was what was about to transpire for the three companies in question (Sony, Apple, and CompUSA) that made that day quite memorable for me.

*Sony's Big Blast*

The electronics giant Sony recognized that they had a brand-management problem and they decided to make a striking statement to the world in their own backyard in downtown San Francisco. In June 1999, Sony's $85 million Metreon opened. With 350,000 square feet, it was to be the first of a proposed chain of urban entertainment centers. Metreon was a combination theme park and gallery for all things Sony, and what corporate leadership thought would be the antidote to the CompUSAs of the world when it came to managing their brand. I hopped aboard a westbound plane to be one of the first to become immersed in the brand experience, and I'll have to say that at first I was blown away by it. The interior architecture was a thrilling tech heaven, and the product was staged more like Tiffany's than Best Buy (particularly of the day). There was an IMAX theatre and multimedia interactions were everywhere, and for a short time Metreon was a sensation, bringing in six million visitors the first year.

Not surprisingly, however, despite the huge initial turnout, Metreon failed to turn a profit; in time, it became a gang hangout and was ultimately shuttered. Unfortunately, there was never a serious attempt by Sony to take some of the experiential approach and brand-management thinking behind Metreon and incorporate it into the national retail store level, which could have had a more meaningful outcome for the Sony brand.

## Apple: To the Core of the Issue

Being relevant to the consumer is Apple's stock in trade—so relevant, in fact, that Apple prides itself on developing products that customers want even before they know they want them. And while many marketing departments pay homage to focus groups, Steve Jobs knew better. "Customers don't know what they want until we show them," Jobs often remarked. This is akin to the famous Henry Ford line, "If I'd asked customers what they wanted they would have told me 'a faster horse.'" Jobs cofounded Apple in the garage of his parents' home in 1976. He was ousted from the firm in 1985, leaving with about $70 million worth of Apple stock (of which he sold all but one share). Jobs returned as interim CEO (iCEO) in 1997 to rescue the company from the brink of bankruptcy. He planned to rebuild the company from the ground up, never imagining that by the time of his unfortunate death in 2011 it would be the most valuable company on the planet. But it was his collaboration with retail guru Ron Johnson, whom Apple hired away from Target in 2000, that turned the retail world on its head. Johnson had been Target's senior vice president in charge of retail operations and was responsible for launching the Michael Graves line of products at Target.

By late 2000, the media had gotten word of Apple's plans to become its own retailer along with its strategy for managing the

> **"Customers don't know what they want until we show them," Jobs often remarked.**

customer experience—a move that stood in stark contrast to Sony's mega Metreon launch a year earlier. To quote the late Steve Jobs, "deciding what not to do is as important as deciding what to do." As the details of a single Apple prototype store to be opened in Tysons Corner Center in Virginia started surfacing, articles began appearing written by the who's who of retaildom. Each article was more critical than the previous, saying the last thing Apple should be doing now is opening stores that could undermine (even cannibalize) its selling channel, referencing the legions of electronics stores and chain retailers that sold their products. Mind you, this was after Apple had pulled the product from most every big box, with the exception of CompUSA, who would also ultimately lose the line. Apple had been introducing new and inspired products, but the brand suffered immeasurably at point of sale in these large entities. Customers continued to experience comingled brands amidst a sea of PCs and poorly trained sales teams often less knowledgeable than the Mac customers who came to worship at an untidy brand altar.

But the move to becoming its own retailer had a cool reception among many within Apple as well. With Gateway in the midst of closing its once successful, customer-friendly stores, it did not seem to the board of directors to be a logical and prudent move. The exception to that was from board member Millard (Mickey) Drexler, the former CEO of GAP Jobs brought on board in 1999. Drexler understood the importance of "owning" each and every brand touchpoint to ensure high brand value as well as giving the small but avid legions of MacFolk a retail experience that was truly "brand-centric" and relevant.

As was the case with everything Jobs did, no layout or design detail of the stores' development was too small or insignificant to be overlooked. At Drexler's recommendation, Ron Johnson had a full-sized prototype built in a Cupertino warehouse not far from Apple's headquarters. With the prototype complete and the launch slated, everything was put on hold. The project was delayed for a few months so the layout could be revisited. For Jobs and Johnson, everything that was known about electronics retailing (even specialty retailing) was being challenged and reconsidered in pursuit of brand relevance and the delivery of a superior customer experience.

**To say that Jobs was right about Apple's need to control the brand at point of sale in order to own and protect every brand touchpoint would be like saying Michelangelo was "gifted."**

The rest as they say is (ever-evolving) history! To say that Jobs was right about Apple's need to control the brand at point of sale in order to own and protect every brand touchpoint would be like saying Michelangelo was "gifted." The new Apple store did more than properly feature and display the celebrated product—it further enhanced the brand's "halo effect" in much the same way a vintage cabernet can make a good dinner an excellent one. Every item in the store became "staged," to quote Ken Walker, in such a manner that the product was patiently waiting for the customer to initiate engagement: a virtual and actual interplay. This act served to further cement the relationship with the legions of Applephiles and coax many millions more to join the brand.

We must not, however, understate the degree to which the sheer numbers of the staff and the devoted "geniuses" tending bar facilitated the entire retail act in a way not seen before in modern retailing. But the bottom line was, and is, the bottom line. Despite the cost of the build-out that exceeded anything previously seen in the retailing of electronics; the grosses have been equally astounding. In an industry that respects gross revenues of $350 to $375 per square foot for healthy regional malls (the overall average is about $340), Apple stores are averaging numbers north of $5,600 per square foot.

## CompUSA—R.I.P.

I will not attempt to fully understand or explain the trajectory of CompUSA. I can only guess that my highly unsatisfactory shopping experience might not have been an exception. From the company's inception as a single store in 1984, its early successes and accelerated growth occurred under the direction of big-box veteran Nathan P. Morton, who was hired in 1988. By 1991, the chain had surpassed two billion dollars in sales and with its category-killer status it was taken public on the New York Stock Exchange. Morton was ousted by the board in 1993.

A deal was struck with Apple in 1997 to open short-lived, store-within-store concepts. I can only imagine that Mr. Jobs did not find the marriage synergistic, given the nature of the customer experience. The combination of Internet pricing competition, low experience warehouse environments, and the lack of expertise by its minimum-wage employees was starting to take its toll. In 2000, the company was taken private by the Mexican retailer Grupo Sanborns, controlled by Carlos Slims. Slims gained status as the world's wealthiest individual (2007, 2010–13). There was no shortage of money or ideas thrown at the CompUSA brand after it was purchased at the onset of new millennium. Loyalty programs were initiated and terminated; multiple slogans were devised and changed; home entertainment centers were tested (à la Best Buy's Magnolia Home Theater). In 2007, a final effort was made to save the ailing brand with the closing of 126 stores, over half of the remaining units. Slim then invested another $440 million into it. In 2008, Systemax Inc. purchased the CompUSA brand and e-commerce business. As I've noted, the definition of brand commodization is when price is the only differentiating factor, and if that's a company's position (as it appeared to be with CompUSA) then the Internet wins.

## DESIGN, ENDURANCE, SOUL

The last three letters of our acronym blend the last three components of a holistic brand: design, endurance, and soul. While I defined the first five points of brand differentiation (identity, nuance, transcendence, emotion, and relevance) individually, I wish to treat the last three as one. I do this to make an overarching point that design has in modern times become a key differentiator in the creation of enduring brands. Yet without the presence of endurance (built-to-last factor) and soul (the whole being greater than the sum of its parts) the design itself will fall short of excellence.

For as long as I can remember, I have been seduced and influenced by great design. In the 1950s and 1960s it all revolved around cars, for me back then it was the new model introductions, the Detroit stylist's infatuation with speed, and the winged wonders that were born of the era. The 1970s turned me on to the Bauhaus, the Eameses, and leading manufacturers whose work symbolized the best of the modernist movement from Knoll and Herman Miller, to the work of Milan-born Massimo Vignelli (graphic designer, industrial designer, interior designer, and architect) along with his wife and design partner Lella Vignelli.

A significant design awakening came in 1968, when I was fortunate enough to spend the summer touring Europe. Over that short, but intense, seven weeks I began to understand how so much good design emanated from places like Denmark, Italy, and Germany. I came to appreciate the influences that thousands of years of history, steeped in the celebration of arts, crafts, music, and culture, had on the generations of people who shaped the many magnificent cities I visited. I was also struck by the obvious difference in scale of all things when compared to the U.S. I was impressed by the efficiency of homes, stores, cars, and cafés, and I began to understand how many of the fine European design traditions were born of the need to be creative and resourceful with space and resource limitations. I became aware of products and brands that were new and exciting, many bearing an attention to design and detail not seen in the U.S., and I felt envious of the folks whose lives were touched by these objects. I also remember immediately upon my return to the U.S. how odd it seemed to see people driving our supersized Detroit iron with front seats the length of a three-piece sofa after my aesthetic sensibilities had become accustomed to small and efficient European cars.

## From Embellishment to Design

I am now, and always have been, a huge fan of mid-twentieth century American design. I believe it is authentic and expresses an era of optimism, an exploration of new materials, and a fascination with speed and motion that makes much of it unique and sought-after a half century later. However, in post-WWII America, consumer product manufacturer's priorities focused on meeting the rapidly growing demand for consumer goods. And while some young industrial designers were beginning to make their mark in the U.S. in the 1950s and 1960s (Richard Teague and Raymond Lowey, for example), most product development and design was being overly influenced, if not driven by, engineers and marketers. With a few rare exceptions, design was more about styling and often at the "back end" or after the fact. New lines or design "refreshments" often took on an appliqué approach of how much faux wood-grain vinyl was necessary to embellish the product to meet the taste level of the average American consumer—whoever that was.

Thoughtful and functional design has long been a cornerstone of European manufacturing companies, but I believe it was the foreign car that was first responsible for Americans getting a taste of European design sensibility and liking it. By mid-century Volkswagen, Mercedes, Porsche, Jaguar, Austin-Healey, Saab, Volvo, Citroën, and Peugeot were beginning to make their mark in the U.S. for being purposeful, safe, well designed, and (mostly) well engineered, and for largely avoiding the finned-fantasy approach that was Detroit's signature. These European brands that demonstrated design innovation hardly made a dent in our marketplace and were no doubt being laughed at by the impenetrable Big Three. That was until the gas stopped flowing in the early 1970s and Detroit received its first wake-up call.

In the meantime, with the import of the Japanese electronics making significant inroads in the 1960s, Americans were getting a taste of what would ultimately become the undoing of many of our consumer electronics manufacturers. While these imported products were initially considered cheap and shoddy, it wasn't long before they were seen as equal to or superior to what was being made in the States, and they were usually less expensive. I distinctly remember the first Sony transistor radios and the first battery-operated Sony TV (products I mention in chapter two) that occupied podium positions at Jewelry and Toy Center and made comparable U.S. products look stunningly behind the times.

## Shining a New Light on Home Furnishings

A young Chicago-based couple having seen the exquisitely designed and economical housewares and furnishings in the European markets, decided that Americans would welcome these inspired products if they were available. In December 1962, Gordon and Carole Segal opened a small 1,700-square-foot store in the bohemian Old Town area of Chicago and named it Crate & Barrel. The name was almost a literal description of how they first displayed

> **I believe it was the foreign car that was first responsible for Americans getting a taste of European design sensibility and liking it.**

the colorful and tastefully designed articles, which were simply removed from the shipping crates and placed on top of them for display, often with the packing materials still present. They sourced their products through small European craftspeople who didn't yet have representation in the U.S. markets. This enabled them to buy direct without a middleman, and to feature unique products not yet seen by consumers in the U.S. The growth of the chain was slow but measured, with three stores opened in Chicago by 1971 and their first outside of Illinois in Boston in 1977. While their chain's early growth was not significant, its impact in the marketplace was. Department stores and specialty retailers were beginning to take notice and, as is often the case with industry pioneers, the things they were doing were being emulated. At the same time, America was getting one of its first good doses of inspired contemporary home furnishing designs at affordable prices.

The Segals were bona fide tastemakers who understood the power of design as a brand differentiator. From the brand's inception fifty years ago until today, every brand extension and touchpoint bears a consistent and well-executed design sensibility. Their products, store designs, fixtures, visual merchandising, and marketing maintain a consistency, attention to detail, and excellence in execution that has led to the company's success (170 stores and counting) and high-brand value, the hallmark of a great brand. In 1998 the Segals sold a majority stake to a German company, the Otto Group.

*The Tide Has Changed*

It's fair to say that the tide has turned in America from design being an afterthought to becoming a defining advantage and brand differentiator for nearly every successful consumer products and manufacturing company in the U.S. One of the champions and observers of this movement has been the business magazine, *Fast Company*, whose writers have recognized and artfully reported on this trend since the magazine's beginning in 1995. One cannot write about this subject without recognizing the impact that Apple and Steve Jobs had in moving the design needle and influencing the taste and sensibilities of our culture and our time. We are all also indebted to author Walter Isaacson, whose best-selling biography of Steve Jobs offers insights into how he "changed the world."

During Jobs's eleven-year hiatus from Apple he accomplished more than most high achievers might in several lifetimes. With the proceeds from his $70 million worth of Apple stock he was able to launch NeXT, a computer startup that he would ultimately sell to Apple for $400 million. He then moved on to found Pixar Animation Studios, which single-handedly reinvented animation and in the process created some of the most enduring movies of our time including *Toy Story, Monsters, Inc., Finding Nemo, The Incredibles, WALL-E, and UP*. While at NeXT and Pixar, Jobs gained, among other things, an even deeper appreciation and respect for the creative process and design purity. His regard for understated simplicity may have been influenced by conferences he first attended at the Aspen Institute in the 1970s in a Bauhaus-style environment. This clearly became the prevailing aesthetic at his computer start-up NeXT, which embodied a neo-Apple Store sensibility and attention to detail.

At Pixar, Jobs collaborated with the creative genius John Lasseter, and became ever more immersed in the creative, collaborative process. Jobs's design identity was clearly cemented while working with Apple's industrial designer Jony Ive, who many called his soul mate. This collaboration resulted in the most astonishing run of product hits of modern times: iMac, iPod, iPod nano, iTunes Store, MacBook, iPhone, iPad, and the AppStore.

**The Segals were bona fide tastemakers who understood the power of design as a brand differentiator.**

As has been stated many times, good design is the result of a cohesive process that melds the needs of the consumer, a high degree of functionality, a respect and awareness of history, and the ability of the participants to look with fresh eyes and reimagine what was, what is, and contemplating what could be. While respecting the interdisciplinary nature of the design process, visionary designers and motivated industry leaders can often collaborate in creating products and environments that are soulful and enduring; much more than the sum of their parts. I'm often reminded of a conversation that took place between me and my oldest daughter Ariel, who in 2007 was preparing to begin her college education at Brandeis University and she needed to shop for a laptop computer (by then a prerequisite for any incoming freshman). Being mindful of the enormous cost of her impending four-year education (not to mention the likelihood of graduate school) and the fact that her dad had managed quite well with many PCs, I suggested that we go out and look at the state of the PC-based laptop market. I so clearly remember the look on her face and the assertive body language that was unmistakable when she declared, "But Dad, I'm an Apple." Thus with one emotional declaration she stated what should have been obvious to me by then, that she so associated with Apple that she basically took on the brand as part of her identity. It was at that moment that I truly began to appreciate the power of a brand that so completely and effectively transcended a product and a category and took on almost a religious embodiment. That's great design meeting endurance, wrapped in soul.

# CHAPTER
# SIX

# RETAIL
# MATURES

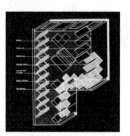

Through the late 1960s and 1970s the Stein twins managed to build Pill & Puff into the single largest independent health and beauty aids retailer in Milwaukee and a defining brand in the segment. They pioneered many things that today seem quite commonplace. They were the first Milwaukee retailer to actually publish weekly coupons in the two major Milwaukee papers (in color, no less), and the numbers of individual coupons redeemed on any given weekday were astronomical. This gave them additional clout with the manufacturers, as well as greater pricing and benefits. One of the quirkiest of the perks they received was the opportunity to have the 1973 Miss America, Terry Anne Meeuwsen, make a public appearance at one of their stores. (Her visit was sponsored by Gillette, I think.) Watching the twins prepare for this occasion was similar to watching a sixteen-year-old girl preparing for her first high-school prom. Suits were ordered, tailored, and modeled for family members. Much time and attention was spent selecting and reselecting matching shirts and ties. When the big day came and the requisite photos were taken—at that moment they achieved a sense of personal pride and accomplishment that came from their hard work, properly managed risk, and unwavering focus that was required to reach this zenith.

While the visit from Miss America may have been the symbolic culmination of a decade of achievement for my dad and uncle, it was not the only such milestone. My personal favorite story of "makin' it" came a mere two-plus years after Pill & Puff's founding, when there were three successful stores in operation. For many of Dad's generation, the symbol of professional achievement was to own and drive a Cadillac. And because Dad was never one to be subtle or understated about anything in life (his motto might very well have been "nothing exceeds like excess"), it couldn't be just any Cadillac. In 1967, Dad arrived home with a spanking new Cadillac Fleetwood Brougham sedan, the largest vehicle in the fleet, with the exception of the presidential limousines of the era. To give you some sense of how very large this vehicle was by today's standards, at 227.5 inches in length it was comparable to the size of any long bed, quad crew cab pickup truck produced today by Chrysler, Ford, or Chevy—it was ginormous. Naturally, it was metallic gold, with a gold brocade interior. It even had fold-out ebony wood tables in the back seat, which was large enough to comfortably seat four rather zaftig individuals. But much to my dad's utter surprise (and I think perverse delight) the caddy wouldn't fit in the garage of our modest suburban colonial. For the first several weeks, the car sat parked with its hindquarters hanging out from under the partially closed garage door. This was until the family carpenter, Elmer Zerngable, was able to attach a doghouse-like appendage to the front of the garage, thus giving the Caddy's massive nose its own mini enclosure so it would be fully protected from the elements. Unfortunately, for the Caddy (and me) its life was to be short.

In late 1967, less than a year after its purchase, the car was driven down to Miami Beach where Dad and Mom had rented a condo for an extended stay. I was on break from college, and one evening I was out driving on Collins Avenue in North Miami when a speeding black Plymouth Valiant full of young teens crossed over the median into my lane and struck the Caddy head on. The enormous force of the collision (the Valiant was estimated to be moving at fifty miles per hour) totaled both cars and critically injured a number of the passengers in the smaller compact. I lunged forward, breaking the windshield with my head, but I didn't sustain life-altering injuries. It was the last time I ever drove a car without seatbelts properly fastened. The Caddy was replaced.

The last chapter for Pill & Puff came in 1978. After building up to twelve stores throughout Milwaukee, taking the company public,

> **But much to my dad's utter surprise (and I think perverse delight) the Caddy wouldn't fit in the garage of our modest suburban colonial.**

and then buying it back again, the twins found a New York–based investor who became interested in the business and offered Al and Lou what they needed to close the successful business chapter and retire.

## OUT AND BACK

In the late 1970s, retailing continued to evolve as shopping centers expanded and multiplied. Suburban flight had been an ongoing dynamic for almost two decades and the construction brought about by the prosperous middle class was spawning second-ring suburbs, many of which had been farms and pasture-land only a handful of years earlier. At the same time, the nature of the nation's shopping centers was beginning to change in several ways. Many of the first open-air centers were "getting malled" as customers were spending more time (and money) shopping as it evolved from just a means of attaining goods to an American pastime. With the downtowns of so many of the great cities in decline and the interstates growing like out-of-control weeds, each population center now had a default town center that for many communities became a favorite place to hang out for many teens and preteens. Unfortunately, unlike the rich urban city centers of the past that had distinctive DNA, the new malltopia lacked a sense of character or context that would differentiate itself from mall to mall and city to city. But hey, you could visit twenty different shoe stores in an hour without breaking a sweat.

Besides the fact that many of the drive-up-and-shop outdoor centers were being turned "outside-in," the tenant mix was also changing and not necessarily for the better. While the earliest shopping centers offered a mix of local, regional, and national tenants, the rapidly escalating costs both in rent, common area expenses (CAM), and build-out were pricing many of the local retailers out of the game, leaving only the larger regional and national chains able to bear the increasing financial burden. This further contributed to the growing uniformity of many of the malls and the similarity of the products they held.

As the costs were rising and more and more of the players were large corporations and publically held companies, the forces of margins, profitability, and quarterly reporting were also beginning to have a race-to-the-bottom, commoditizing effect on many of the brands. It is fair to say that this resulted in a lack of differentiated product that probably led to the demise of a number of these entities. By the late 1980s and early 1990s my client Edison Brothers was one of the bigger players to succumb. Fortunately for specialty retailing, this was not the case across the board. One player, arguably America's pioneer of specialty retailing, Les Wexner, took a very different tack, and created of one of the greatest specialty retailing empires of the latter half of the twentieth century.

In 1963, Leslie Wexner, whose parents ran a general merchandising store in suburban Columbus, Ohio, borrowed $5,000 from his aunt to start The Limited. Named for the fact that he planned to limit the clothing what would appeal specifically to younger women rather than taking the more common general merchandising approach that his Russian immigrant parents had taken. And thus began one of the single most successful retail stories of our time. While Wexner majored in business administration at Ohio State (and spent a brief time in law school), it is his innate marketing genius and almost obsessive attention to the smallest detail that made it possible for him to launch and grow one of the America's largest retail empires, and in the process amass great personal wealth.

While most fashion retailers were building very conventional stores on fairly modest budgets, Wexner knew that if his stores offered a unique style statement that extended from his fashion-forward product to all aspects of the customer experience, he could begin to differentiate The Limited brand while building a loyal following. From the 1970s on, Limited stores would regularly spend more per square foot for build-out than any of their competitors and the stores' designs were always way ahead of other apparel retailers. This strategy did not go unnoticed. As soon as a new Limited prototype was launched and rolled out, it wasn't long before other fashion retailers were taking note and copying the "Limited look." However, as is often the case with most knock-offs, the imitators never performed as well as the original. And just about the time the look-alikes were starting to get traction, a new Limited prototype would be launched that was completely different and distinctive, and the cycle would continue.

But The Limited's success went far beyond just creating unique offerings and a terrific shopping experience, it literally reinvented fashion retailing. Wexner changed the game by controlling the entire supply chain, designing and sourcing their product on a scale that no other retailer had done to date. The brand was differentiated further with unique styles, improved margins, and shortened design-to-market times, the result made it a marketing juggernaut. Each new brand and product segment that Wexner introduced virtually reinvented the category and almost immediately become the defining brand within it. Limited Brand's Victoria's Secret was the first brand to "legitimize" the intimates category and bring it out of the shadows of the department stores. Bath & Body Works took an equally clean-slate approach to its unique category, making it the defining brand in a new niche segment that was soon copied everywhere.

What has differentiated each of the Limited Brand companies is the degree of research and development behind each brand's launch and evolution. Wexner probably wrote the book on touch-point connectivity. He understood the influence that a holistic approach has on creating brand value and longevity in a world that sees great concepts come and go for a lack of proper execution at every level of the brand's embodiment. Today, at seventy-five years old (as this chapter was being written), though he is among the top 100 wealthiest individuals in the U.S., he is still actively involved in the day-to-day operations of his retail empire. Wexner will sit through staff design presentations and worry through the details of new store concepts and prototype revisions. And one cannot comment on Mr. Wexner's amazing career without recognizing the philanthropic contributions the Wexner family and its associated foundations have made to the greater good of society. He has been, and continues to be, one of the greatest givers of our time.

While I have never had the opportunity to meet Mr. Wexner, a story connects us that (if it's true) gives me particular joy and satisfaction. Back in the early to mid-1990s when the Mall of America was still rather new, the then-head of leasing was giving Wexner a tour of some of the mall's newer fashion retailers. My firm had by then completed designs for a dozen or so of the specialty stores in the 450-store megamall. The most outrageous and fun project, without a doubt, was a store that featured a "grunge" fashion concept called Junkyard. We took great pains in creating a fashion experience that was long on irreverence and theatrical shock value, and in the process we broke about every design criteria that the mall had established. The theming of such a concept had to be very legitimate and authentic to avoid looking cheap. I personally spent the better part of a day at a massive junkyard outside of the Twin Cities walking for miles, sorting through eight decades of dead cars, and then selecting "artifacts." The stars of the design show were three complete junk cars that were to be stacked on

**Wexner changed the game by controlling the entire supply chain, designing and sourcing their product on a scale that no other retailer had done to date.**

top of one another at the storefront lease line; the aim was to stop even the most jaded shoppers in their tracks. In the process, we had to figure out a way to cut each car in half in order to get them up a freight elevator in the mall and then subsequently reassemble them in the store. We created the Junkyard logo to look as if we had used a broom and a bucket of black paint to draw the letters in the name to maintain the theme of haphazard grunginess. Anyway, as the story was told to me, when Wexner was escorted to the Junkyard store he stopped and slowly took it all in, and then he remarked to the leasing agent, "I was that good once." Funny, I find myself feeling the same way these days about the work of many other younger designers.

## THE OLD IS NEW

The new malls and remodeled centers were not the only retailing story of the late 1960s and early 1970s, there were converging trend forces at work that conspired to create a new/old type of retail that America was hungry to discover through adaptive reuse. Sadly, some of the greatest architectural accomplishments of the late nineteenth and first half of the twentieth century were lost and much of the urban fabric was shredded by bulldozers to make way for bigger-newer-better buildings. Fortunately, in 1966 the first national policy for historic preservation was enacted with the National Historic Preservation Act. The act led to the creation of the National Register of Historic Places and the associated list of National Historic Landmarks. Perhaps of equal importance, it established a new dialogue and a heightened awareness in America over the need to preserve our rich architectural heritage.

In 1962 (four years before the act passed), San Franciscan William Roth and his mother, in a move to prevent the demolition of an important piece of California's past, purchased the land and buildings formerly housing the Ghirardelli Chocolate Company in the historic Fisherman's Wharf district. The Roth family retained landscape architect Lawrence Halpern and the architectural firm of Wurster, Bernardi & Emmons to convert the late-nineteenth-century buildings and property into a restaurant and retail complex, making it the first major adaptive reuse project in the U.S., and the model for similar projects in nearly every major urban center in the country for decades to come.

This synergy or convergence of forces combined the awareness of new uses for old, often decrepit, buildings (many occupying the edges of major downtown areas) with a growing interest in preserving what remained of our historical urban centers. Ironically, many of these vintage buildings exist today because they were far enough away from urban epicenters that they were considered to be of little value and were consequently overlooked by developers. This adaptive reuse created new opportunities for small retailers, who either could not afford the major malls or simply sought a more authentic, urban environment, along with a young, "culturally creative" consumer who was hungering for unique products, emerging brands, and an imaginative environment in which to spend their time and money.

The newly renovated Ghirardelli Square featured over forty shops and restaurants and it opened its doors in 1964. One year later, the Minnesota-born architect Benjamin Thompson, co-founder of The Architects Collaborative, opened a Design Research (D/R) store in the renovated clock tower of the square. Along with many other young designers and architects, I read the many feature articles about Ghirardelli Square with great interest, and made a pilgrimage to San Francisco in 1970 to take it all in. Seeing the new palette that combined half-century-old brick and stone with contemporary colors and architectural detailing was a

**Many of these vintage buildings exist today because they were far enough away from urban epicenters that they were considered to be of little value and were consequently overlooked by developers.**

joy. And while the architecture and urban design were compelling, I'll have to admit that everything about the D/R store was completely eye-opening. Benjamin Thompson had opened the first D/R store in Boston in the early 1950s, giving America its first taste of international design and the first such contemporary lifestyle store. Its products represented the works of many renowned architects and designers whose furnishings and housewares are considered revolutionary and timeless in terms of design. Designers such as Hungarian architect and designer Marcel Breuer, Finnish architect Alvar Alto, and Italian designer Jo Colombo were represented. D/R featured the iconic Heller Designs stacking dishware, as well as the creations of Massimo and Lella Vignelli, whose work for Bloomingdales, Saks Fifth Avenue, and Knoll International brought them international acclaim. Many of the designs first seen at D/R are featured to this day in the permanent collection of the Museum of Modern Art, and in private residences worldwide. The D/R store was also the first importer of the Finnish line of Marimekko fabrics, which featured bright geometric prints that were stunningly different from anything I had ever seen before. (Jackie Kennedy appeared on the cover of Life magazine in the early 1960s wearing a Marimekko dress from the Boston D/R store). For me, the visit to Ghirardelli Square and particularly to the D/R store was a transformational experience and one that had a huge influence on my career path from that point forward.

## GREENER PASTURES

By 1978 I had gotten what I had wanted out of InterDesign and was ready for a new challenge and more independence. One of my nearest and dearest friends, landscape architect Damon Farber, had left InterDesign to join with architectural designer, Tim Geisler in launching a new firm called Design Consortium Inc., DCI for short. Unlike many young start-ups, they chose not to rent some innocuous space in a warehouse building somewhere because they were out to brand the new business in a way that would get them noticed. Geisler was an early advocate of what was known in the 1970s as "high-tech," taking industrial-like materials and forms and utilizing them in new ways. He was also a consummate student and devotee of the work of architect Richard Meier. The group scraped together enough money to lease a storefront in downtown Minneapolis and Geisler designed an absolute gem of a stainless steel-clad space that made its way to the cover of *Architectural Record*, the pinnacle of architectural design achievement. This was an almost unheard of feat of recognition for a firm that had only been in existence for a few months.

The energy and enthusiasm of these young entrepreneurs (along with the shiny new digs) was seductive and ultimately irresistible, and I managed to leverage my new work with Goodman Jewelers as a bargaining chip to become the firm's fourth partner, after architect Tim McCoy was added. The subsequent three-plus years were a whirlwind professionally, emotionally, and financially. As is often the case when four young creative individuals get together, there can be a lot of energy and dynamics at play, and it's not always accompanied by harmony or compromise. Such was the case with DCI. Geisler was without question one of the most talented individuals I have ever had the opportunity to work with; his grasp of space, form, and the third dimension are incomparable. The man also had (as we used to say in the precomputer days) quite a hand. Tim could draw like none other, and he did it day and night, just as long as there were cigarettes, coffee, and other substances around to keep the machine stoked.

In the DCI days virtually every drawing created was by hand, in ink, on velum. It was arduous, labor-intensive, and in Geisler's

**Benjamin Thompson had opened the first D/R store in Boston in the early 1950s, giving America its first taste of international design and the first such contemporary life-style store.**

hands, a thing of great beauty. The design work the firm was putting out was consistently being recognized, winning awards, and for the most part, losing money. The awards and recognition in the community were very heady and my association with the group gave me a sense of self-worth that I dearly needed. Regrettably, within three years and change, the banks wanted to terminate the line of credit that we all had guaranteed. Farber had the intelligence to get out early, and he started his own landscape architectural practice that became very successful. That left the three of us on the hook for the dough—and, unfortunately, I had the deepest pocket at the time (though trust me it wasn't that deep). Thus ended the first painful step to my entrepreneurial independence, and the sense of failure overshadowed the highs of the journey. Many days were spent in bed, the depression quite profound. I remember turning on David Lettermen's new morning show and trying to make sense of my life as Lettermen was launching himself against a wall wearing a uniform covered with Velcro. It was time to get out of bed.

My days became occupied by some small real estate investments I had made with my friend Cotty Lowry. The two of us had begun purchasing small-income properties at the onset of one of the greatest real estate booms in modern history. One of my dearest surrogates and mentors was my Uncle Irv (known to his nieces and nephews as Uffy), the twins' youngest brother, who was a well-known and highly respected realtor in Madison, Wisconsin. Dad had dissuaded me from getting into real estate, but fortunately Uncle Uffy assisted Cotty and me by helping us write "bulletproof" purchase agreements with all the vital contingencies to protect our interests. While the properties we purchased were rapidly appreciating, there was little cash flow to actually convert to food, and I really needed to concentrate on finding a new source of income.

And even though the design firm debacle was still very fresh, I was really missing the creative outlet I had known for a decade.

Back in Milwaukee, my dad had been recently diagnosed with pancreatic cancer, and he was spending much of his last year receiving treatments for an advanced stage of one of the worst forms of the dreaded disease. Final hopes hinged on a very experimental, high-dose radiation procedure being done at Mayo Clinic in Rochester, Minnesota. Because it was close to the Twin Cities, I was commuting to Rochester, mostly on weekends, to be with my mother and father. On one of my trips, I told Dad I was thinking of starting my own firm and specializing in retail planning and design. I had carefully fashioned a rationale for the decision, stressing that his tutoring had been of great help in my being able to speak to retailers in a way that few designers could. I further stressed the notion that if I specialized in retail design it would add credibility to how I positioned myself and my firm. Not being one to hold back or sugarcoat his thoughts, his response was, "And how are you going to eat?" I should have seen that one coming.

## STEINDESIGN: RHYME, RHYME

Late in 1981 came the official start of my firm's first incarnation and the second act in my movement to independence. I felt I needed to brand myself in a way that would stick, keep it simple and memorable, and linking Stein and design seemed obvious. I had purchased a turn-of-the-century, brick fourplex apartment building in Minneapolis's trendy Uptown area. Selling the idea of the twenty thousand-dollar down payment I needed to borrow had been pretty tough, because in my father's eyes no four-unit apartment building in the world could be worth $92,000. I'm quite sure it was my mom who closed the deal. I devoted the front half of my apartment to my new office and lived in the recently renovated back half.

**I remember turning on David Lettermen's new morning show and trying to make sense of my life as Lettermen was launching himself against a wall wearing a uniform covered with Velcro.**

As good fortune would have it, a mere four blocks from my apartment in the heart of Uptown, local developer Ray Harris had purchased a square block of vintage buildings on the corner of Hennepin Avenue and Lake Street. It was one of the busiest inter-sections in the Twin Cities and a stone's throw (light stone, good arm) from Lake Calhoun in a demographically rich and culturally creative area. His plan for his Calhoun Square project was to cre-ate one of the largest adaptive reuse projects ever undertaken in the Twin Cities by retrofitting the buildings' old shells and filling them with trendy shops and restaurants. I knew the leasing agent Ted Schuster, and made it a point to let him know I really wanted to design some of the stores for what would become the hottest new lifestyle center in the Upper Midwest. Ted came through in a big way and SteinDesign was off to the races. One of the first in-troductions that Ted made to me was the husband-and-wife team of Mort Gerber and Mary Ann Levitt. Mort and Mary Ann had re-cently taken over a small, family-held group of record stores that were in financial trouble in an attempt to save the company. Mary Ann was a smart, Harvard Business School–educated woman who had spent much of her career in the music industry. Mort was a New York–born-and-raised lawyer, and they made a formidable pair. Mort was the charming, laidback, Yiddish-speaking voice of reason and Mary Ann was the all-guns-blazing powerhouse who drove the team. I fell in love with them both almost immediately.

Over the course of the next ten years, beginning with the pro-totype for the Calhoun Square Record Shop, we would do forty projects for them—first throughout the Twin Cities, and then even-tually up and down the West Coast. Working with the two of them was like a graduate course in business wrapped up in Borscht Belt stand-up comedy. The three of us had our roles down pat. I natu-rally played the part of the headstrong concept guy always arguing for investing in the brand. Mary Anne played the part of the tough and assertive, financially grounded client, forever pulling me back from the edge, and Morty played the part of the referee. Design presentations were a hoot and Mary Ann and I often got into heated debates. One such presentation occurred at a fine restaurant (a familiar backdrop for us three foodies). I was being particularly passionate about a point that I felt was not negotiable, and Mary Ann was stubbornly standing her ground, at which point I asked, "What do I have to do to bring this point home to you, *stand on the table*?" So I did, right in the middle of the appetizer course. I had made my point.

The period from the early 1980s through the early 1990s, the music industry and specialty retail in general were in their heyday. The evolution of music formats from vinyl and 8-track, to cassette, and ultimately to CD, kept the firm busy with store updates. The signature look we developed for the chain became easy and inexpensive to replicate, and working on the store's image was helping in the highly intricate dance that would take place between store owner and mall developer. I became privy to the inside financial negotiations that took place between lessor (landlord) and lessee (tenant). These included base and percentage rents, common area expenses, and build-out contributions that were integral to cutting a lease deal. While it was a seller's market for the mall developers, Mort was a cunning negotiator and was able to get great concessions and locations in terrific new malls. I was getting a terrific chance to learn much more about the financial underpinnings of the retail world.

In the late 1980s their decision to move the Record Shop headquarters out to San Francisco, California brought the couple great joy and further prosperity as they sought to expand the chain throughout California. They bought a lovely home overlooking Sau-

> "What do I have to do to bring this point home to you, *stand on the table*?" So I did, right in the middle of the appetizer course

salito Bay, and rented office space and a slip for Morty's lovely new sailboat, appropriately named *The Manhattan Transfer*, after the recording group. With each new California store that we opened came one or two trips. I had a lovely room to stay in overlooking the bay and there would always be terrific restaurants, and often an afternoon would be spent on the sailboat. I was riding high both professionally and personally.

By 1992, the couple could see the handwriting on the wall for the industry. The smaller independents were being swallowed up by the bigger players and Record Shop was in prime position to be taken out. The duo negotiated a very nice purchase by one of the larger players, Warehouse Records, and they received their big and well-earned payday. Ironically, within eighteen months of the sale, Warehouse filed for bankruptcy.

## BEST FOOT FORWARD

Adaptive reuse was not the only story of the late twentieth century to run counter to the malling of America. Big-box retailers were becoming a phenomenon unto themselves, and certainly not in a very elegant way. There was, however, one significant outlier bucking the trend of ubiquitous faceless boxes, catalog retailer BEST Products. In 1957, Sydney Lewis, son of an encyclopedia salesman, started a retailing catalog and sales showroom in Richmond, Virginia, in a manner similar to what Sears and Montgomery Ward had done a half generation before. Sydney was a lawyer and a Harvard Business School graduate with a strong passion and appreciation for modern art—so much so that in artistic circles he would trade the company's merchandise for art, which ultimately led to a significant twentieth-century collection. However, unlike other big-box formats, these 40,000-square-foot outlets were considered catalog showrooms rather than stores. Best Products customers would roam the aisles viewing and testing products and then take a product tear sheet to a service counter. Then a sales associate would retrieve the item from the large stockroom at the rear of the showroom. The concept was an efficient, low overhead, retail/catalog hybrid. At the height of the company's operation it had 169 stores nationwide.

What distinguished BEST from other retail operators was Lewis's unique approach to branding the company. In 1972, Lewis commissioned James Wines's architectural firm SITE to design nine unique and highly unorthodox stores, actually they were the façades of stores, which the firm looked upon as a "built commentary" on the ubiquitous boxes the facades were attached to. This resulting tongue-in-cheek tweak to big-box architecture became for a time the most-talked-about and photographed buildings in the country. What made the SITE approach so significant and noteworthy was the outrageousness with which they approached the simple materials, and doing so without actually engaging with each building's architectural shell. They created a sense of retail theater that every approaching customer would interact with.

The first building in Houston, Texas, was an existing structure onto which SITE applied a new brick veneer with the front edges strangely appearing to be "peeling away" from the structure behind. It looked as if it were an architectural model that had been left in the rain. One couldn't help but be amused by the sleight of hand employed to make the statement which implied there was something a bit off-kilter, in a nice way, about the company, and this was only the beginning. With each subsequent store, the retail theater of the absurd became ever more interesting and amazing. The next project in 1974, also in Houston, involved what Wines referred to as the "de-architecturization" of the facade. The top edge of the building appears to rise at one end way beyond reason while the

> **With each subsequent store, the retail theater of the absurd became ever more interesting and amazing.**

145

rest of the façade appears to be under demolition, almost as if King Kong had a major hankering for brick and began to chow down on the face of the building, and then was chased away before he could finish leaving a giant pile of brick cascading down the face onto the storefront canopy.

With each successive joke played on the architecture, new and more provocative notions were devised and executed, each more inventive than the one before. 1977's Notch Project in Sacramento, California, appeared to once again employ the talents of King Kong, although this time the ape appears to have successfully torn away and slid the corner of the building from its foundation, revealing the storefront entry nicely tucked-in to the gaping hole that resulted. And the experiments continued from there, each more dramatic and highly anticipated by the architectural community.

To add to the visual conversation and architectural commentary, in 1979 architect Philip Johnson, in collaboration with the Museum of Modern Art (MoMA), asked six architectural stars of the late twentieth century to engage in BEST's architectural tomfoolery and to take a whack at the "problem." The efforts culminated in a MoMA exhibit featuring the iconic "solutions," each with its own distinctive approach and signature. The players included Stanley Tigerman, Robert A. M. Stern, Charles Moore, Anthony Lumsden, Michael Graves, and Allen Greenberg. Each BEST solution became an expression of each architect's style, but often on steroids. My own personal favorite is Stanley Tigerman's solution, which is simply a mid-century suburban tract home that has been artfully rescaled to perhaps four times its correct size. In the partially opened front door stands a twenty-two-foot-tall Mary Tyler Moore lookalike welcoming the shoppers. The actual entry to the store was through the slightly opened garage door, positioned as if to allow the family cat to enter—but in super-scale it was high enough for customers to enter the *big* house.

While the entire exercise further called attention to (and, in some cases, criticized) the good-natured architectural folly, in my opinion none of the star architects succeeded at the level SITE had demonstrated in its architectural restraint and its genius in creating a commentary on the state of big-box retail architecture. More significant, however, was the manner in which the approach was providing BEST products a unique identity and a differentiated experience for the consumer. Unfortunately, the genius of the Lewis family in engaging the SITE firm in the creative exercise would not prove to be a significant enough step against the changing tides of retailing. In January 1991, BEST filed for Chapter 11 bankruptcy protection and a second filing took place in 1996. By 1997, the company had liquidated its assets, but was able to pay ninety-six cents on a dollar to unsecured creditors. Today, much of the Lewis art collection can be seen at the Virginia Museum of Fine Arts.

## ADAPTIVE REUSE OPPORTUNITIES CONTINUE

By 1984, the work was steady enough for SteinDesign that I felt comfortable taking the next step—renting space for my growing firm. Sadly, in January of that year, Dad had finally succumbed to the cancer after a long, tough fight. By then, there were three of us working out of my apartment and I felt I needed a separate home to go back to at the end of the workday. It was always odd running into an employee as I was making my way to and from the bathroom in the morning wrapped in a towel.

The Minneapolis warehouse district was undergoing a minor rebirth as old manufacturing buildings were being renovated into Class B office space. This was beginning to attract younger creative firms (mostly Boomer-owned) with similar needs. I signed my first lease for about 1,000 square feet in the newly renovated Kickernick Building on First Avenue North at the edge of downtown and proceeded to design the space that would ultimately burnish our young, but thriving, brand. We would spend the next twenty years, almost to the day, signing five different leases, with three different building owners, in three spaces.

Life was good. My business had taken off, and after being single for ten years, I had found my perfect complement. I met the love of my life, Cheryl Stern, in late 1984 and we were soon making plans. We married in the summer of 1986, she exchanged a consonant for a vowel, and I got a new and fulfilling life beyond work.

Specialty retail design brings with it some unique challenges and opportunities, and I have referred to it in previous chapters as the architectural equivalent of fast food, implying that it happens very quickly, usually in about a dozen weeks from first meeting to grand opening. Further, it has a built-in shelf life generally considered to be in the area of three to five years. This is supported by the fact that many (if not most) mall leases have a negotiated length of three to five years, and there is almost always a remodeling clause that forces a tenant to update. The stores we were designing back in the early to mid-1980s were for small chains like Goodman's and the Record Shops, along with many entrepreneurs who generally had very shallow pockets. As we were learning our craft, we were finding out what probably seems obvious, that the rollouts for our established clients with multiple locations were more profitable than the one-offs for the start-ups. Because many of the one-offs were for new businesses, we often received smaller fees even though we worked twice as hard. We also often found ourselves playing the role of business and branding consultant as well as store designer, but ultimately that became a role that I truly enjoyed and with it came great satisfaction. The good news was that with each of these new start-ups came an opportunity to experiment with some new materials and merchandising concepts without thinking in terms of having to replicate the concept over multiple locations.

Unfortunately for us, we were beginning to get some attention from other competing architects and designers in town. More and more of them wanted to add a retail project to their portfolio so much so that they would often be willing to give the work away, essentially as a loss leader. These same firms often were funded by the income from other more profitable work at their firms—work we didn't have. However, more often than not, we were able to sell our expert retail knowledge that few if any of our competitors could match.

## SITE OF MINNEAPOLIS'S ORIGIN

One of the most significant historic sites in Minneapolis is an area bordering the upper Mississippi River adjacent to St. Anthony Falls, the only natural waterfall on the upper Mississippi. The area was inhabited by businesses at the turn of the twentieth century as river traffic became a vital link to commerce. In the mid-1980s developers saw the viability of converting those commercial buildings into retail and entertainment complexes. We benefited from this because we were hired for many additional store design opportunities, virtually all with young start-ups. One thing we did learn early on was that the astonishingly tight budgets of these projects forced a type of problem solving and simplified brand aesthetic that became a valuable discipline, one that ultimately served us well even when the budgets got bigger later on. In some ways it was like a design "boot camp" where we had to be incredibly resourceful, often using hybrid off-the-shelf items to bring the projects in on budget.

One such project was located at the newly renovated St. An-

We also often found ourselves playing the role of business and branding consultant as well as store designer.

thony on Main retail complex, which became the focus of much of our design activity. Our clients were two young men planning an upscale young men's boutique called Dimitrius. The store was to have a lean, urban, fashion-forward look; and "lean" also described the budget. In fact, the entire project budget including design, build-out, and fixturing was less than the project fees that we would be charging a mere half-dozen years later. (We were paying our dues.) The approach we took was to create a neutral foil for the product by utilizing a minimalist approach. We designed a series of angular, unfinished, concrete block walls that would become both backdrops for assembled outfits and structures for displaying shelved and hanging products. We chose a paint and carpet color that virtually matched the warm gray of the concrete block so that the product would visually dominate. The only contrasting elements were a series of out-of-catalog black industrial wire partitions commonly used in warehouses to create secure but transparent rooms. The completed outfits were presented on the three-by-seven-foot wire partitions, which served to cross-merchandise articles in the store while complementing the block walls. The angular geometry of the store was reinforced through the repetition of extremely simple Italian fluorescent trapeze lights suspended from the deck. The three elements—concrete block, wire partitions, and trapeze lights—created a strong background for the contemporary men's product that was featured. The resulting branded environment (including the logo we designed) was simple, clean, contemporary, and most of all cheap! In 1986 we were awarded a Minnesota Society American Institute of Architecture Interior Design Award for the project, one of five such awards the firm received in a two-year period. It was featured in *Interior Design* magazine the same year.

## RHYTHMS OF LIFE AND BUSINESS

It's fair to say that the 1980s were amazing for me personally and professionally. I started my business, received national recognition, found and married the love of my life, Cheryl, and we had our first child, Ariel Beth. Not bad for a geeky kid from Milwaukee. SteinDesign had outgrown its initial office space and committed to a shiny new space, about three times the size of our first downtown digs, just in time for the recession of the early 1990s. We all learn that there are rhythms in life and cycles in business and it's never fun when what goes up comes down, but it happens. I've also come to appreciate that how one spends one's down time has much to do with sustaining a business over the long haul.

By the late 1980s and early 1990s, midsized regional retailers, many of which had built solid businesses over the course of many decades and even generations, were starting to feel the pinch coming from the substantial growth of the national retailers. The greatest growth was coming from the new big-box players that were emerging in virtually every category, giving them buying power and even influence over manufacturers that the smaller regional retailers could only imagine. Many of the bigger regional retailers had strong single-market penetration, and some had stores in multiple states. Although these locally based businesses often had a devoted following along with regional brand recognition, they lacked the deep pockets that bought the expertise and clout of the major national specialty retailers.

Having had tremendous success with the Record Shops, which by then had thirty-some stores, I began to ponder ways of connecting with similar midsized regional retailers in need of our services. We had recently completed some tenant design criteria work for Melvin Simon and Associates for a series of their older

**SteinDesign had outgrown its initial office space and committed to a shiny new space, about three times the size of our first downtown digs, just in time for the recession of the early 1990s.**

properties, and our focus had broadened from the tenant side to the landlord side. Malls and shopping centers establish certain design parameters that tenants must abide by when they design their stores. Initially, when many of the malls were first leased, there was a high degree of regimentation imposed by landlords. As centers grew more ubiquitous and brands wanted to express their uniqueness, the malls complied by establishing broader and more varied parameters for storefront and interior designs. And we were one of the firms retained by the major landlords to establish the new rules. In the process, we gained some additional insights on the issues that landlords were also facing with their changing tenant mix.

In my feverish attempt to bring in new work during this financial downturn, we were doing all the typical things one does to generate new work—making calls, writing letters, and sending out glossy-covered brochures—but it was going nowhere and I was feeling a bit desperate in our big new digs, populated by only a few associates. Since desperate times call for...well, you know, I figured, why not try something new? I whipped together a brochure aimed not at retailers, but at shopping center and mall owners. I offered a seminar aimed at their independent and regional chain retailers concentrating on inexpensive improvements to help them compete with the big retailers, an issue I knew was top of mind with the malls and centers, as more and more of the once prosperous regional players were losing market share.

The program, named inSTORE[SM], was designed to take place at the individual mall(s) of the developer's choosing. I planned a ninety-minute group presentation along with a Q&A, and then the rest of the day would be spent visiting a dozen or so stores at the mall conducting a "SWAT audit." The focus included layout and lighting, fixtures and display, materials and finishes, and visual merchandising, along with a broad trend update. We planned to follow up the visit with a summary that would be sent out to the individual retailers and the mall. I priced it right, and it worked. Not only did I get in front of the type of retailers (and potential clients) we were looking for, but the fact that we were anointed by the mall owner gave the program cachet. The whole strategy forced me out of my comfort zone. It also drove me to bone up on retail trends, got me in front of great audiences, and introduced me to retailers who ultimately became clients. We ran the program for about two years and it eventually morphed into a series of retail trend seminars that have evolved and continued over the past two decades to the present.

> The whole strategy forced me out of my comfort zone. It got me in front of great audiences, and introduced me to retailers who ultimately became clients.

## RESIDUAL EFFECT

As with many immune system disorders, people with CFS are undermined by stressful conditions. It's fair to say that the combination of the bigger office space, a new baby, the economic downturn, and the launch of the *in*STORE[SM] program made for a pretty stressful cocktail. By March 1991, I found myself in bed with the worst (and still undiagnosed) episode that I had ever experienced. Fever, headache, swollen glands, raging sore throat, joint aches, and extreme lethargy had me on my back for two weeks. Blood work was done, depicting a viral condition (typical to my many previous bouts), but no explanation for the symptoms. After considerable research, Cheryl was able to find a specialist in communicable diseases in town by the name of Dr. Alan Kind. He had been working with a number of patients with similar, frequently occurring, viral-like episodes. And after a slew of additional tests to rule out other more exotic and rare diseases, the diagnosis of chronic fatigue syndrome was established.

These kinds of diagnoses are both good and bad. Good in that they are not terminal, not so good in that there was, and is, no cure. What was so enlightening and reaffirming was the way Dr. Kind treated me (and the condition). He was the first doctor I had encountered who ratified many of the holistic treatments that I had incorporated into daily life to stay as functional and productive as I was. He listened intently about how my discovery of meditation, massage, even herbs and nutritional supplements, seemed to prolong my periods of well-being. He shared his insights about the malady, which had only been recognized by the Centers for Disease Control five years prior. Many of the treatments that he had been prescribing to his CFS patients were as much about lifestyle adjustments as prescription medicines. They included ten to twelve hours of sleep a night, regular moderate exercise, withdrawal or extreme moderation of stimulants including alcohol, sugar, and caffeine, etc. And the big one: learning to pace oneself. This was the hard part. At a time when popular culture tells us to tough it out whatever the malady, learning to unplug is a challenging prescription.

Over the course of the next several years, with a truly kind and thoughtful doctor supporting me, I had new insights and learned some new techniques that put me on a course to a much improved state of well-being. The most unremarkable and yet most effective of the things I learned both from the good doctor and the dozens of books I read on the subject of CFS was to listen to my body. In other words, when the first signs of an episode begin to occur—unplug! Through this nasty, yet empowering, episode I developed new tactics for managing a condition that has been life-altering, but never life-defining.

# CHAPTER SEVEN

# BRANDED ENVIRONMENTS AND EXPERIENTIAL RETAILING

7

In chapter one, I describe the movement from an agricultural-based economy toward one based in industry in the late nineteenth century. This dynamic fueled America's growth for the next fifty years, but by the middle of the twentieth century half of the population were employed as service workers. And thus began the transition from an industrial-based economy to a service-based one. By 2011, only nine percent of the workforce was employed directly in manufacturing, with the majority of the workers in the service sector. In 1999, B. Joseph Pine II and James H. Gilmore introduced us to *The Experience Economy* (updated in 2011) in their defining book of the same name, which explores the next phase of the economy beyond services and the ongoing evolution of consumerism and value-based offerings.

Pine and Gilmore's thesis is that there is a logical progression of economic value starting at the bottom with undifferentiated commodities (e.g., coffee beans), which are bought and sold at established market-controlled prices. The next value level up involves the making and selling of goods (e.g., roasting the coffee beans and selling them in grocery stores) with the price/value proposition influenced by processing, packaging, and other lower-level differentiators. The next higher value proposition is when the product is combined with a service (a cup of brewed coffee at a restaurant). The fourth and highest metric represents the highly differentiated offering that results from a staged experience (the brewed beverage is customized to the individual's liking and delivered in a highly memorable, branded venue (such as Starbucks). Naturally, the higher one moves in the economic value progression the more cost is associated, and correspondingly, the greater degree of intrinsic satisfaction is tied to the purchase. Obviously, the art/science of staging such experiences is not an easy one, but when it is done correctly and consistently it can become a transformational experience for the participant, one that in small or not so small ways may change how the individual forever relates to the product, service, or brand.

It has been my life's work to understand the construct behind these transformational experiences, and to be able to orchestrate their various parts and pieces in a manner that ultimately leads to a positive customer experience (a cool store) and a predictable sales outcome (making lots of money). I have sought to lift the veil from the complex underpinnings of their evolution. My curiosity goes all the way back to Jewelry and Toy Center, watching my Dad interact with customers in a way that hopefully influenced their decision to "drop a couple of bucks" on something that they probably didn't need, but in a small way was going to make their lives more satisfying.

Dad really was somewhat of a magician, or it seemed that way at the time. I remember watching him in action, using to his advantage the fact that the store's "vintage" glass-top showcases were so badly scratched that the customer could barely see the object of his or her curiosity. Being an astute reader of body language, he would intervene, "Hey, let me take that watch out of the case so you can see it better." And with almost dancer-like movement he would open the case, reach in for the watch, and simultaneously with the other hand almost magically produce a rather worn, velvet-covered pad to properly "stage" the watch. For me, this was pretty much Retail Theater 101, light-years before Kenneth Walker coined the term. Dad knew that by reducing the barriers between customer and product, in this case the "distressed" showcase, he would be one step closer to meeting his objective. The customer's eyes would light up and the tactile stuff would start happening.

Within the next half minute or so, sometimes with a bit of assistance, the watch would make its way onto the customer's wrist

**Naturally, the higher one moves in the economic value progression the more cost is associated, and correspondingly, the greater degree of intrinsic satisfaction is tied to the purchase.**

and Dad was within a motion and an emotion of closing the deal. But that didn't necessarily mean the customer was walking home with the goods. In the late 1950s and early 1960s, before deficit spending and credit-card debt had begun to fuel-inject the economy, Jewelry and Toy Center's customers (like millions of other hardworking, middle-class Americans) pretty much subsisted paycheck to paycheck. To meet their customers' needs, the twins were among the many merchants who offered "a convenient layaway plan." This meant the customer could put a couple of hard-earned bucks down to hold the watch, and then continue paying weekly or biweekly until the payment was complete and the product became theirs. But it wasn't until the inception of Pill & Puff that the twins fully grasped the larger macro components of branding and store design, which were necessary to meet the customer's needs consistently while building brand loyalty at the same time.

The more I have learned about my craft, the more I've come to believe that what we do is more about shades and tones than distinct blacks and whites in the choreography of space, product, and consumer interplay. We are learning from neuroscientists that there are indeed certain brain states that influence product-recognition purchase choices and that these factors are deeply emotional and as primal as our urges for power, sex, and sustenance. Consequently, learning to manage the customer experience has become an exercise in handling both emotional and intellectual input. We know that our brains are highly complex and at any moment we are consciously and unconsciously processing tons of sensory input. And to complicate matters further, how we process this stuff is also colored by our life experiences, how we are wired, and thousands of other factors. We all process this information differently.

## WHY DOES IT MATTER?

One might well ask—Why does all this matter? And what, if any-thing, does it have to do with the future of retailing? I'm glad I asked. In subsequent chapters we will begin to deconstruct the biggest and most destabilizing issues that retail has experienced in the last hundred years: e-commerce, Internet retailing, and Mobile Electronic Retailing or MEtail[SM], as I have termed it. The price transparency and commoditization of goods and services brought on by a wired world challenge store-based retailing like nothing else in our time. It is my belief that in order for store-based retail to remain viable now and into the foreseeable future, the nature of the in-store customer experience must evolve into something far more engaging, memorable, and immersive if it is to matter at all. If store based-retailing becomes a "race-to-the-bottom," price-driven game, the Internet wins hands down. We will be left with hundreds of millions of square feet of ghost malls and shopping-less centers.

## P & G'S 4Es

In *The Experience Economy*, Pine and Gilmore focus on four realms of experience and how they work together to influence the quality and memorable nature of a location or an event. They are the 4Es: educational, esthetic, escapist, and entertainment. When these qualities are properly blended together they can serve to move the individual from a passive to an active participant and from absorption to complete immersion in an experience. This transcendence is essential in order to create a transformational experience, which is the gold standard for brand building. We have all had many memorable experiences in our lives (hopefully positive ones) in which the 4Es have been at play conspiring to make memories.

In the summer of 2012, my wife Cheryl and I, along with our

**Consequently, learning to manage the customer experience has become an exercise in handling both emotional and intellectual input.**

daughters Ariel and Brianna, took a major vacation—a three-week getaway to Israel and the Amalfi Coast of Italy. It was the longest trip we have ever taken as a family. It was in celebration of Ari's completion of an eight-month fellowship in rural Ethiopia, and Bri's recent graduation from high school and enrollment at Columbia College in Chicago. During our adventure, the 4Es conspired to make the entire experience truly memorable. Entertainment was everywhere with a wide diversity of people speaking many different languages in colorful, open-air markets next to the near-chaotic blending of small scooters, micro cars and gigantic tour buses in a density and at speeds that seemed to defy the laws of physics. Educational opportunities abounded, including many visits to antiquities and historical sites, not to mention the pursuit of palate refinement with each wine tasting. Escapism defined our holiday (as the Europeans so delightfully refer to vacations) as we slipped away from our everyday lives into an altered reality—at least until the American Express bill arrives back at home. And finally the fourth E: esthetic. From the ancient city of Jerusalem to the postcard images of Positano, every day was an esthetic sensory overload that we never wanted to end.

There is obviously a huge difference between the engagement we had in the natural world and the quality and memorable nature of man-made spaces or venues such as those we refer to as branded environments. Certainly it's worth noting that our European experiences were in large part "staged" by divine and/or natural forces (depending on your beliefs). The significant works and contributions of mankind over the ages in the architecture, art, and culture of these places did contribute toward making our summer experiences so memorable.

## STAGING EXPERIENCES

It is the transformative qualities of the 4Es that have become the ultimate goal for experience-stagers in pursuit of brand nirvana. In recent decades, a number of brands have created venues that have had just such an effect on the brand and the consumer, artfully employing the elements of educational, esthetic, escapist, and entertainment. The result leaves an indelible impression on the individual. When the first NIKETOWN opened in Portland, Oregon, it was seen by many as having these kinds of transformative qualities and as going far beyond the established realm of the space, product, and customer interplay. As I have discussed earlier in the book, NIKE has always successfully employed elements of mythology and storytelling in its endeavor to create strong emotional connections to the brand. These measures were further brought to life within that first trend-setting store. The phenomenal staging and interspersing of product, brand, and heritage served to move the customer from a passive viewer to becoming immersed in the brand's story. It felt as much like a museum as a store and produced the result of turning brand advocates into indoctrinated followers. Much of what was conceived and brilliantly executed at NIKETOWN was not new. In fact, it very much emulated the Disney approach of experiential sequence to manage visitors' expectations. In NIKE's case, Mickey Mouse was replaced by Michael Jordan. Without a doubt, many people who visited that first NIKETOWN store were likely to have an altered sense of the brand thereafter.

The same can be said for what Apple has accomplished in its store based retail by creating a destination that exudes the 4Es on a level not previously seen in the category or perhaps in retailing, period. One need only to visit any Apple store, in any location, at almost any hour to experience a transformational love affair with a brand that is holistically conceived, designed, managed, and executed at the highest level. Entertainment is nuanced and multilayered in the Apple store. The leading-edge nature of the brand constantly entertains us with its multiple levels of innovation and execution. Customers go from observers to participants within moments of their entry. Crossing the threshold becomes for many the gateway to the virtual otherworld with a multitude of iThings as the transporting devices. Education is and has always been a key ingredient of the Apple brand. Besides the fact that the digitally adept Generations X, Y, and Z associate the brand with their earliest learning experiences at home or in school, the Apple brand has done much to educate and enlighten us all. As a defining brand component, the Genius Bar signals to the customer the level to which empowerment and shared insight about the brand and its products reside at Apple's core.

Whether we are conscious of it or not, humans are phototropic—we're attracted to light. Hence, we escape into the Apple store environment like a moth goes to a flame. The light level and ultra-cool color temperature (5400–5600 kelvin, for all you lumen geeks) gives the store a cool, sleek, cleanliness. The highly structured product staging and attention to the smallest detail give the store a sense of order that is very compelling in our all-too-messy and complex world. Our minds are wired to attempt to create order out of chaos, and when the manufacturer/retailer takes the initiative to order their universe, we are predisposed to buy in. (Pun intended.) However, I believe that the overall esthetic is Apple's greatest conquest, and may be their secret sauce. Apple has, perhaps more than any brand of our time, created a unique, signature design language. And because good design has always been a fundamental and unwavering brand value, their attention to detail and design refinement has transcended every aspect of the brand.

This touchpoint cohesion, from the online web embodiment, to product design, to packaging, to store design, to advertising, exceeds at a level few other brands have accomplished.

As I have mentioned several times, achieving and maintaining this level of cohesive execution is very difficult. It requires a type of organic top-down thinking and universal buy-in that is rarely seen in corporate America, or anywhere for that matter; but when it's accomplished the rewards are astronomical. Throughout the Great Recession, Apple never once had to discount its products, or veer from its course, because they created a brand so defining that popular culture has coined the term "Apple-like" to describe its celebrated esthetic. They are also responsible for elevating design sensibility and awareness in a way few other trendsetting brands have. The obvious question arises whether a Job-less Apple can maintain the company's status as the juggernaut it became in the late twentieth century and continues to be at the beginning of the twenty-first; I, for one, hope so.

## THE DICHOTOMY OF THE SERVICE ECONOMY

The unbridled growth of our service economy is still taking place, and it has often come at the expense of, well, service. You probably have to be a Baby Boomer like me (or older) to remember back to a time when a certain level of personal service was a common component of sales in most any category. The annual visit to the neighborhood shoe store (a notion that would horrify my daughters) was accompanied by the friendly shoe salesmen properly measuring your feet to make sure that the style and manufacture of the shoe, which he would produce from the back of the shop, would be a proper fit. He was often the store's owner, who knew the entire family and had a trusted relationship with every pair of the family's feet—and now he's long gone. Another symbol of that service era

**However, I believe that the overall esthetic is Apple's greatest conquest, and may be their secret sauce. Apple has, perhaps more than any brand of our time, created a unique, signature design language.**

was the milkman. Even with the dependable grocery store within a mile, our families depended on a weekly or biweekly delivery of fresh milk and dairy products. These deliveries would arrive in ubiquitous, properly branded, stand-up vans, driven by uniformed drivers, throughout much of the first half of the twentieth century. In many parts of the country, homes were fitted with milk shoots, small square apertures that were built into the sides of the houses, usually near the back door. These little compartments became the intermediate home for the family's dairy products, until they were retrieved and moved into the fridge. These funny little double-door cavities often doubled as convenient means of entry for the smallest in the family, when a back door key was inadvertently forgotten.

## BING...DING

One of the best-known symbols of this bygone era was the neighborhood service station often found on multiple corners of the neighborhood retail area. This was where you brought the family car to have the gas tank filled and the car serviced. The family would motor up to the bubble-top gas pumps with the car's bias-ply tires passing over a small hose on the asphalt pavement, triggering a friendly bell—bing! This signaled the trusted mechanic to drop his wrench, approach the driver's window (always with a smile and a personal acknowledgement) with the familiar opening query: "Fill 'er up?" Moments after the customer's go-ahead nod, fuel began to flow into the tank, signaled by a friendly "ding" from the pump that noted each of the $0.299 gallons of Fire Chief Supreme gasoline being dispensed into the Chevy. The attendant would quickly reappear at the driver's window rattling off a series of gratis service offers that were a ceremonial part of the weekly visit. By then, if the attendant was on his A game the window rag (usually kept in the right rear pocket) was already being employed to clean off the windshield. "May I check under the hood today?" was almost always the next question, and it was as common back then as "Want fries with that?" has become today. The big difference being that the fast food question invites an up-sell, while the under-the-hood query is more about added value and relationship building. Of course, if lifting the hood and checking the straight-six's vitals (employing the rag in the left back pocket) led to the sale of a quart of oil, it would indeed benefit the station owner, but the objective had much more to do with properly maintaining the car and serving the customer than upping the sale.

With the under-the-hood vitals checked, all the windows cleaned, and the tank filled, the final procedure was for the attendant to check the air in the tires, using the requisite gauge that every attendant carried in his chest pocket. When the routine service was complete, the attendant would settle up, which usually required a sprint back into the station to get change from the five-dollar bill for the fill-up. But before leaving the station, the attendant would in all likelihood politely remind the motorist that it was time to bring the car around for an oil change and a tune-up (plugs, points, and condenser). Like the shoe salesmen's obligation to the family's feet, it became the implied responsibility of the neighborhood service station to assist with the care and maintenance of the family's transportation. This commitment was ratified in most of the major brands advertising of the day; remember the familiar jingle for Texaco gas stations, "You can trust your car to the man who wears the star, the big red Texaco star."

These neighborhood service stations of the day also took on another identity for many of us. Whereas, the corner bars were the local watering holes and social exchanges for those twenty-one and over; many of these gas stations became an ad-hoc hangout and for younger, driving-age kids. They also became the source

**"May I check under the hood today?" was almost always the next question, and it was as common back then as "Want fries with that?" has become today. The big difference being that the fast food question invites an up-sell, while the under-the-hood query is more about added value and relationship building.**

of wrenching knowledge, the go-to place when one's first car lost its go. For me and many others, these hallowed halls of grease became the source of a job, often providing the first real paid-employment experience to earn extra spending money. My ultimate goal, like many other kids of the day, was to have my own set of wheels, at least for the summer. My parents' acceptance of my plan was based on the condition that I would get a part-time job to support the car. This seemed quite reasonable and I began my search.

In Milwaukee, the first petroleum company to begin moving away from full-service stations was Clark Oil, which was started by Emory Clark in 1932. By the mid-1950s, Clark had 500 stations throughout the Midwest that focused on selling gas and oil without service bays and mechanics. This made Clark a leader in the move toward a simpler business model that would ultimately take hold several decades later. In the summer of 1964, I secured my first real job at the Clark station on Port Washington Road in Glendale, Wisconsin, the suburb immediately west of Whitefish Bay. Getting the job green-lighted my purchase of a black 1960 Ford Falcon two-door sedan for $600. It was a low-mileage, one-owner car in excellent shape, complete with an economical (and rather lifeless) 170-cubic-inch 6-cylinder engine; but, it did have a three-on-the-tree manual transmission that gave it a bit more pep. Having received my driver's license only about six months prior while driving an automatic, I had not yet mastered the art of three-pedal motoring, but I was hell-bent on learning. After a week of embarrassing stumbles, over-revving, and stop-sign restarts, I finally mastered the rhythmic clutch in, gear in, clutch out, gas in routine that is the secret handshake of the fraternity of true motor heads. I had reached the outer periphery of cool.

## THESE WERE HAPPY DAYS

What I had not yet realized with my newfound job and set of wheels was that over the summer of 1964 I would make my own personal connection with what was to become a legendary Milwaukee pop-culture icon.

Port Washington Road was a commercial strip, lined by bowling alleys, restaurants, muffler shops and a mix of low-level retail. Directly across the street from the Clark station was The Milky Way Drive-In, which was the epicenter of 1960s car culture. In order to get as many hours as I wanted (working for $1.10 an hour, I couldn't be choosy), I often had to work nights and weekends. Naturally, I had imagined driving up and down Port Washington in the Falcon (with my teen heartthrob, Janet Bernstein) on weekends. Instead, I could be seen wearing a baggy, white-and-black pinstripe Clark uniform, which was at least three sizes too big for me, and all the pins, belts, and cuffing didn't much help. I was back to geek city. I have to admit, however, that the first couple of Saturday nights that I worked will forever remain in my aging memory banks as being special and eye-opening.

There were two distinct traffic patterns on the Port Road at night. One was the high-speed movement of cars north and south, punctuated by the rock 'n' roll soundtrack of the 1960s. This was occasionally interrupted by sounds of burning tires on asphalt. The other traffic pattern was slower, with the cars moving back and forth across the street into and out of my station, and back to The Milk, as the drive-in was known. Naturally, no matter how many bodies any given driver was able to load into his/her night ride, the pooled funds had to be split between sustenance and fuel. So, the routine was to drive into the station, buy three or four gallons, run to the restroom, get a pack of smokes, jump back into the car, and

**I finally mastered the rhythmic clutch in, gear in, clutch out, gas in routine that is the secret handshake of the fraternity of true motor heads.**

motor across the street again for fries, a cherry Coke, and more scoping out of who was with whom and who was driving what.

Now, I was a pretty busy guy with eight pumps on the drive (with a capacity for at least ten cars at any given time). I had to keep the window and grease rags straight, manage pockets full of money, and get everything else that came with the job done. Because we were responsible for any losses on our shift, I had to make correct change on the fly without the aid of a calculator or computer. Even when I was not manning the place by myself (which did happen on occasion), there was not much time on a given Saturday night to just hang out.

Then there was the occasional visit by toughs from the other side of town. They arrived complete with slicked-back hair, side-burns, and the requisite T-shirts with a soft pack of Camels rolled up in their sleeves. They also brought a bit of "attitude." The contrast between the visiting toughs and the locals could not have been more profound, which was highlighted by the mostly blond-haired "Bays" (for Whitefish Bay) in their madras short-sleeved shirts and laundered cutoffs. While I was a bit apprehensive and on guard at first, I really found that these visiting characters added an element of almost exotic diversity and intrigue to the mix. Some of them even became regulars at the station. As the summer progressed, I also became pretty friendly with a number of the Milk's carhops and they, too, broadened my horizons. On nights when I didn't get a break, I would phone in my order and one of the girls would meet me in the street with my dinner. "Here you are, honey. I bet you must be starved." (Did she call me honey?) For a pretty sheltered suburban kid, I was seeing, hearing, and learning stuff that wasn't part of the curriculum at Whitefish Bay High, and I loved it.

Ten years later, another Whitefish Bay High student, Tom Miller (who actually graduated from neighboring Nicolet High in 1958) became the executive producer and cocreator of the TV show *Happy Days*, which ran from 1974 to 1984, and it put Milwaukee on the sitcom map. During a *Milwaukee Journal* interview that Miller gave in 1977 he reported that, "Arnold's [the drive-in in the show] is a compilation of everyone's recollections of the drive-ins of the '50s, it's just The Milky Way was closest to me when I grew up....in Whitefish Bay." In a subsequent 1986 *Journal* interview Miller told a reporter, "Richie Cunningham was me, and Richie's mom was definitely my mom, Lavern." Apparently, Henry Winkler's character, Fonzie, was a unique creation for the show, one that is now forever ingrained in American pop culture. "There was no Fonzie among the kids I knew," said Miller, in the same interview. Had Tom Miller been working with me in the summer of 1964, he would have found any number of Fonzies who made their way across town into my Clark station.

**Had Tom Miller been working with me in the summer of 1964, he would have found any number of Fonzies who made their way across town into my Clark station.**

## RETRO FIT

The image of the neighborhood service station is etched into the Boomer memory banks and remains a source of nostalgia now fifty years hence. So much so that the businesses that trade on midcentury automobilia (selling everything from original-condition gas and oil signs and perfectly restored gas pumps to "authentic recreations" of articles bearing classic American brands) have become a huge business. In 1994, we were contacted by Craig Runkel, a young entrepreneur and Mall of America (MOA) retailer, who had been part of one of the mall's early retail-incubator programs. Among the many innovations that the mall's co-developers and managers, Melvin Simon & Associates, did from the onset was seek out entrepreneurs with unique concepts to test and develop for the mall. One such program involved short-term leases for developing only the front portion of unoccupied storefronts, or bump-backs, as they were called. These temporary tenancies served to test new concepts and the chops of enterprising retailers. Neither party made a long-term commitment or invested a large sum of capital—call it the retail equivalent of speed dating. Craig ran one of these start-ups, specializing in nostalgic brands and products from the midcentury, many with a strong auto connection.

Based on his tremendous sales, Craig was able to successfully negotiate a conventional five-year lease for a mall space and approached us to help bring his vision for a little slice of 1950s nostalgia to the MOA. After a number of meetings, I became quite familiar with Craig, the products he wanted to sell, and our shared passion for all things motoring. We began to chat about creating a highly authentic midcentury service station to act as a backdrop and stage for his nostalgic merchandise. Needless to say, the idea hit home with me on many levels and we were off and running.

## CREATE THE HOOK

With over 500 stores and over 40,000,000 visitors annually, each and every retailer at MOA is in a battle for the customers' attention. There is a highly planned visual stimulus going on everywhere and we know that the shopper's decision to enter a store or walk on by takes place in mere seconds. With the trifecta of a limited storefront, a tiny footprint, and a very slim budget, we were challenged to create something that would make a statement among the pack of regional and national retailers on all sides, above, and below. Given the enormous cost of rent at MOA, retailers need to maximize every square foot of floor space and every linear foot of wall space for product, and it would have been logical to bring the glass line or storefront up to the lease line as most others retailers do—but we didn't.

We felt from the onset that in order to engage customers in the nostalgic storyline of the neighborhood service station, we really needed to create retail theater that would properly stage an event so we approached it much more like a theatrical stage set. We sought to make the themed destination as true to the 1950s memories as budget and space would permit. From our initial concept sketches to the detailing, we incorporated, borrowed, and re-created all of the elements associated with the memory. The first twelve feet in was the presale transition space, which included the driveway, fuel pumps, a vintage motorcycle, outdoor billboards, and the accurately detailed service station exterior, complete with service bay entrance and customer area. Positioned behind the overhead garage door, stands (an almost) full-scale hydraulic lift complete with a mid-'50s Nash Metropolitan lifted eight feet off the floor being "serviced." The walls in the service bay were broken up into four-foot display bays and merchandized with nostalgic products, which continued into the customer service area. This area was framed by a huge curved-glass window in the style of many period stations and it was sheathed in turquoise and white porcelain panels, a signature material of the era.

What made the concept work was not that it was unique, since retro gas station imagery and references are commonplace. It was successful because our fixation with theming authenticity and the accuracy of the execution challenged one's perception of what's "real" in the 1,500-square-foot store. As in any book, movie, or play, it is the writer's objective to take you to another place, and tell a story that moves the audience. For those old enough to identify and take a brief trip back to childhood our story had meaning. For a father to engage a son or daughter and share a recollection of what life was like in the 1950s, it meant something even more significant. Customers bonded around our story/store and hopefully

**With over 500 stores and over 40,000,000 visitors annually, each and every retailer at MOA is in a battle for the customers' attention.**

got "lost" in Runkel Bros. American Garage, at least for a moment or two.

## TAKING SERVICE TO A (MUCH) HIGHER LEVEL

Customers visiting mid-twentieth-century service stations bought more than just gasoline; they purchased a myriad of products and services for their cars including oil, filters, fan belts, and tires—lots of tires. The gradual demise of the neighborhood service station, like so many independently owned and run businesses, left many products and services without a location to access them. It created new opportunities for entrepreneurs anxious to fill those voids while creating more clearly defined specialty offerings. This led to the emergence of new product/service segments in the last quarter of the twentieth century. Certainly, the Stein twins demonstrated this in the health-and-beauty segment. But when it came to selling tires and creating a high-level customer experience, no one in the country succeeded at the level of Minnesota's Tom Gegax, founder of Tires Plus.

Tom's professional career began right out of college in 1968 with Shell Oil Company, where he worked until 1976. That was the year he and his business partner, Don Gullett, started Tires Plus from a sketch on a restaurant napkin, and they built it into a ten-state, 150-store, $200-million success story. Tom's success was anything but an out-of-the-chute blast to the top. Tom and Don recognized that the customer experience associated with buying a set of tires was pretty awful. Most of the garages and repair places were dirty, dark, and dreadful places with customer service to match. It was certainly anything but pleasant and uplifting. So, they set out to reinvent the customer experience for the tire-buying public and along the way rewrote the book on team building and personal service. The duo understood that creating a high level of quality, personal service for each and every customer coming into their Tires Plus stores was going to require a new, holistic culture and set of disciplines that hadn't yet been seen in the industry.

Tom had a healthy appreciation for the kind of team building that happens in the sports world under the guidance of a great coach, and Tires Plus became one of the pioneers of using the sports vernacular of coaches, teammates, and huddles to create a strong sense of common purpose and a winning team. This was conceived and implemented from the corporate level on down (or up) to the store level. Head Coach Tom also knew that the best way to create a "culture of caring" was to demonstrate an honest concern for the well-being of his team. Tires Plus was a pioneer in integrating wellness programs at the corporate level by hiring a full-time wellness coach, along with implementing programs in weight and stress management and smoking cessation. Tom even employed shiatsu massage to help his team members deal with the stress that accompanies a fast-growing company on a mission to reinvent a retail service category. Tom's unique approach was quickly being noticed by corporate leaders throughout the Upper Midwest.

Demonstrating a commitment to the team's well-being gave credence to Corporate Commandment #1 at Tires Plus: "Thou shalt be caring." Giving caring, world-class service to Tires Plus's guests was the company's mission. Making the customers feel like guests started by creating the cleanest, most comfortable, well-lit service environments ever seen in the business. Spotless uniforms, cappuccino machines, comfortable chairs, and kid-friendly areas further differentiated the Tires Plus experience.

Head Coach Tom applied a unique approach to both instilling and bringing the message home to the team by coming up with some very practical and effective methods of mentoring. He

**So, they set out to reinvent the customer experience for the tire-buying public and along the way rewrote the book on team building and personal service.**

knew that making best practices stick at the store level requires more than just a demonstration of what those best practices are. He taught his trainers the tell-show-involve method of creating a culture of service. Tell them how to do it; show them how to do it; watch them do it and offer feedback; and finally, watch them do it again, and they will own it. In 2000, Tom sold Tires Plus to Bridgestone/Firestone and serves as chairman emeritus. Today, more than a decade later, one need only call any one of the hundreds of Tires Plus stores across the country (mine's on speed dial) to hear, "It's a great day at Tires Plus." Tom and Don's teachings and guidance are still very much in play.

After creating and nurturing such a phenomenal business success story over the course of a quarter century, it might be well expected for the principals to relax and reflect on a job well done, but that is simply not Coach Tom's style. The highly effective management methods developed and perfected at Tires Plus made Tom a sought-after business and life coach for company owners, corporate executives, and agents of change. Tom's passions for a broad range of environmental, health, and philanthropic causes spurred the development of new companies and foundations, channeling his seemingly limitless energies. Tom has become a highly requested public speaker and successful author. In 2005, with assistance from a cowriter, Phil Bolsta, Tom wrote *By the Seat of Your Pants: The No-Nonsense Business Management Guide*. The book became a best seller, with Sam's Club alone selling 60,000 copies. In 2007, the book was reedited and rereleased by HarperCollins under the new title *The Big Book of Small Business*, and that edition also became a best-selling business book. It was endorsed by the likes of author Ken Blanchard (*The One Minute Manager*), Richard Schulze (founder of Best Buy), and Tom's friend and spiritual guru Dr. Deepak Chopra. I'm proud to say that I was among the FOTs (Friends of Tom) asked to contribute a case study to Tom's amazing book, and I will share the small contribution in a later chapter.

## ANOTHER CHANGE 'AGENT'

We live in a time of accelerating change. Businesses and careers that were thought to be perpetual from one generation to another are ceasing to be so. They're being replaced by new product and service offerings that are meeting our ever-evolving cultural, lifestyle, and technological needs. Only a few people could have imagined just a decade ago that the essential pocket accessory of our time would be a computer more powerful than all of mission control during the moon launch era of fifty years ago. At the same time, it would be equally difficult for most us to imagine the state of "the new, new normal" that our kids or grandkids will be surrounded by even a decade from now. Fast is simply getting faster. Thankfully there are always those dreamers among us who see the new reality long before it exists; these are the visionaries that we refer to as *agents of change*.

In chapter five I discuss the element of emotion at the core of a great brand, and the power of storytelling and mythology to propel a brand into having an otherworldly embodiment. One agent of change, who saw the future before it arrived, was a twenty-four-year-old wunderkind by the name of Robert Stephens, who started a business fixing small computers in Minneapolis in 1994 with $200. What differentiated this brilliant young computer nerd from the throngs of other young techies was his understanding of the power of branding to differentiate what he had to offer. Stephens had a particular fascination with the television series *Dragnet* and its lead character Joe Friday played by actor Jack Webb. *Dragnet* was one of those early TV serials that had an indelible effect on many of us growing up during its initial 1951 to 1959 run in TV's black-and-white days. Friday and his partner Bill Gannon, played superbly by Harry Morgan (of *M\*A\*S\*H* fame), would arrive on the scene of the crime in their black-and-white squad car, dressed in white shirts and narrow black ties, flash their badges at the still-traumatized victim and things would get better (and worse) thereafter. This was as iconic and powerful an image of the era as Superman, but cooler.

So with Roberts's initial two hundred bucks, white shirt, black clip-on tie, and "Chief Inspector" badge, he became a one-man fighter against broken hard drives, jammed floppy disks, and hero to the terrified neophytes of the new digital era. And he called himself the Geek Squad. The first years were lean (ramen-noodles lean) but eventually he got enough money together to bring on some additional, similarly equipped, "Special Agents" along with a pretty beat-up little Renault Dauphine painted to look like Friday and Gannon's "black-and-white" with a mostly black body, white doors, and the prominent Geek Squad logo on both front doors where you would expect to see the police department badge. Even the logo had tongue and cheek built into it because rather than placing the "q" in Squad in the typographically correct position (with the tail of the q properly descending), Robert took liberties and misplaced the descending tail of the q as if to say, "I'm making new rules." The brand's simplicity, cheekiness, and self-deprecating humor combined with Robert's ability to triumph over every imaginable challenge of the young and rapidly growing digital age got him noticed by small and midsize businesses throughout the Twin Cities metro area. His reputation for digital "crime-solving" spread to the entertainment world and he became the on call go-to guy for rock musicians playing in town. He would take Mick Jagger's calls at all hours from any location. (Wouldn't you?) The power of the Geek

Squad brand grew, fueled by Robert's marketing and tech genius. Before long the beat-up foreign cars that spent as much time in shops as on the road were replaced with shiny, new specially ordered black VW Beetles with white doors. At the time, they were the only custom paint orders VW did.

I had the good fortune to sit down with Robert in our offices in the Minneapolis warehouse district as things were really building for him and his company. He possessed all the characteristics of an overachiever. He had a sense of absolute confidence about his mission—and was fueled by a level of passion and clarity that was common to other change agents I had met in the past. He talked about his brand as if it were a living organism that was part of his DNA. He also shared with me that he had a standing offer from Disney Studios to tell his story, but that he was in no hurry to take them up on the offer—he was much too busy. In 2002, a mere eight years after its founding, Robert sold the Geek Squad brand to Best Buy for, as they say, an undisclosed amount. The acquisition became a crucial turning point in the tech retailer's ongoing attempt to differentiate its brand in the marketplace and address the perception that the lack of service in their stores was contributing to the commoditizing of their brand. Thanks to Robert's impact on their Richfield, Minnesota, headquarters, the trustworthiness of the Geek Squad brand did, in fact, produce the desired halo effect Best Buy had been aiming for. It also created a new, high-margin service offering for the company to build upon. And build they did. As I write this there are reported to be more than 20,000 Geek Squad agents worldwide, still dressed in their iconic white shirt and black clip on tie initiated by Chief Inspector Stephens two decades earlier. In 2012, at age 42, Robert left Best Buy and moved to California to start something new. I can hardly wait to see what the Chief Inspector comes up with next.

**The trustworthiness of the Geek Squad brand did, in fact, produce the desired halo effect Best Buy had been aiming for.**

## SPEAKING IN ONE VOICE

Ken Walker always emphasized brand connectivity with all aspects of the brand needing to "speak in one voice." I've always liked that analogy. It brings to mind the difference between the relative chaos and discord of orchestral musicians warming up, in stark contrast to the harmonic sounds that follow the maestro's tapping of his baton. We talk about the high brand value that will result when all of the brand touchpoints are in sync. These often include the presale (advertising, marketing, brand management); the in-store experience (store design, graphics and signage, fixtures, displays); the execution (sales training, customer service, cross-platform connectivity); and the postsale (delivery, installation, customer satisfaction assessment).

As I mention in chapter five, after Ken sold his company he could do high-level consulting, but he couldn't do design projects due to a noncompete clause. That circumstance led to a series of highly rewarding collaborations between Ken and our firm. Ken was contacted by an investment group that had taken over a small, but unique, mattress manufacturer based in Minneapolis called Select Comfort. The company started by Robert and JoAnn Walker (no relation to Ken) in 1987 was in dire need of a complete brand makeover. At the time of the private investor acquisition, Select Comfort had a handful of stores, nominal sales through direct marketing, and almost no brand recognition. What the product had going for it against the Big Three Ss (Sealy, Serta, and Simmons) was a completely new system of support that eliminated the inner springs by substituting them with air chambers. Not only did this minimize pressure points and provide better support, but it made it possible for each individual to adjust his or her side of the bed to the desired firmness. In 1994, we received a call from Ken explaining the opportunity and requesting that we prepare for a meeting at Select Comfort's headquarters in one of the Twin Cities' suburbs.

Ken has never been a man of many words. Like many New Yorkers he speaks succinctly and in abbreviations. He briefed me in the car on the way from the airport to Select Comfort's headquarters that he was going to assume the position of project director, but that we were going to do the heavy lifting design-wise. Once there, we were introduced to all the key players, including the young but seasoned president of retail, Brent Hutton. Brent had climbed the retail ladder fast, starting on the floor of Radio Shack, working his way up at the Tandy Corporation, and eventually leading three different businesses.

Ken spoke eloquently to the corporate heads in the room about how we intended to make Select Comfort into a bona fide brand and make the market understand the benefits of their unique technology and care about it. I remember thinking at the time, "holy crap, when he says *we*, he really means *me*." I could feel my throat drying and hair graying as I smiled and attempted to look calm and confident. I remember him saying something about bringing them the A Team, which just happened to be locally based and that we think very much alike. Now, my parched throat and graying head were swelling as well. It was all a bit surreal.

Rarely in life does one find oneself in the eye of the kind of perfect storm we just had. The combination of a major brand reinvention, being anointed by the likes of Ken Walker, having an investment group with really deep pockets, and a revolutionary product concept only happens every so often—and it had just arrived on my doorstep. Things started happening very fast: proposals were written, data was dumped, and a "walking-around sense" (Hutton-speak for getting a feel for existing

**Ken Walker always emphasized brand connectivity with all aspects of the brand needing to "speak in one voice."**

stores) was achieved. Because of the importance of achieving a national brand status, as Ken had proposed, we felt we needed to bring in graphic design co-conspirators, and I contacted our friends Bruce Rubin and Jim Cordaro of Rubin Cordaro Designs in Minneapolis. Bruce and Jim were like-minded in their design approach and we all shared a healthy respect for one another's work.

Hutton was taking a very bold direction with his plans for store size and locations given the conventional wisdom of how mattresses were sold, which was usually in department stores in areas laid out like a congested parking lot. Brent's strategy was to put the new stores in major malls, in small 1,000 to 1,200 square foot stores, featuring no more than about three beds. This counterintuitive approach was designed to move the category away from a purely destination-type purchase to building brand awareness and sales in a more impulse-driven matter. None of which was arbitrary or capricious. The research that the company had done showed that many people slept on mattresses that were long past their useful life; they rarely thought about replacing them; and their quality of sleep and general health were often affected. But, the real jewel in the data dump (probably driving the design of the new store more than any other factor) was that the product was so good and so unique that even in the few poorly designed existing stores, once they got a customer to actually lie down, the sales conversion rate was through the roof. This gave us real insight as to design direction and our course of action. The other oddity of the product category as it existed was that the store's walls did not need to be covered in product, which invited us to think very differently about the presentation.

Our design mantra became "Get them in and lay them down"— the customer, that is. We knew that the new mall locations would generate a huge customer traffic count that was highly uncommon for the category, as was the unique "air bed" technology. Our job was to create a hook that would be hard to ignore, in order to drive customers into the store even if the last thing they were thinking about was a new mattress. The walls of the store became ten-foot-high by fifty-foot-long billboards, featuring iconic figures lying down on Select Comfort mattresses against a backdrop of billowy clouds. We had a broad variety of huge and recognizable iconic images, from the Eiffel Tower and Big Ben to John Wayne. And they were all assuming a horizontal position on a Select Comfort mattress. Smack dab in the middle of the billboard was a graphic that simply dealt with the beds' top-line features and benefits; thus combining both emotional and intellectual components of the unique brand.

The concept proved to be a hit, and in the course of two and a half years we designed and oversaw the build-out of 145 stores across the country. During the height of the expansion, we were doing two stores a week and had a staff of five devoted to the effort. From our introduction to the brand in 1994 through 1997, we saw the company's valuation jump from $20 million to $200 million. Over the past twenty years the Sleep Number brand has gone through many phases of growth and contraction, but to this day it remains among the top-ten retail brands in terms of dollar-per-square-foot generation. We were proud to be a small part of this interesting brand repositioning story.

**Our job was to create a hook that would be hard to ignore, in order to drive customers into the store even if the last thing they were thinking about was a new mattress.**

# CHAPTER EIGHT

# FORMATS IN FLUX/ CHANGING CHANNELS

Traveling outside the U.S. is a wonderfully enriching experience that offers opportunities to learn about other cultures as we gain a new perspective on our own. Whenever I am fortunate enough to go abroad for either work or recreation, I am always struck by the amount of time people in other countries devote to casual relaxation and socialization; and this occurs almost anywhere beyond borders of the U.S. In towns and cities large and small, it seems that people take gathering and just hanging out far more seriously than Americans do. While the focus of many American lifestyles has long been informed by the NIKE slogan "Just Do It," our global neighbors have figured out how to "Just Be."

## IN SEARCH OF THE NEW 'THIRD PLACE'

In the late 1980s, American urban sociologist and writer Ray Oldenburg coined the term "the third place" in his books *Celebrating the Third Place*, and *The Great Good Place*. He suggests that casual gathering places such as pubs, cafés, coffeehouses, and even post offices are at the heart of a community. He argues that they're important to a civil society and civic engagement. Oldenburg's third place is separate from the two other social environments he defines: home, the first place; and work, the second place. And it could be argued that for many late-twentieth-century and early-twenty-first-century Americans, devotion to both the first and second places has often left too little time for the third. While it seems that in many great centers of civilization, a strong sense of place was at the core of centuries-old planning to meet cultural, civil, and community needs, in the U.S. these same needs are often met by good old capitalism and corporate ingenuity. Leave it to Starbucks to institutionalize the third place.

The first Starbucks coffee shop opened in Seattle, Washington, in 1971, but it wasn't until one of its former employees,

Howard Schultz, purchased the small chain of six stores in 1987 from the original owners that the company's growth began and its impact was felt outside of Seattle. By 1989, there were forty-six stores across the Northwest and Midwest. When the company went public in 1992, it had grown to 140 outlets and that number mushroomed to over 1,000 by 1996. In 2000, as the store count topped 3,000 units, Schultz stepped down from the CEO position to focus on global industry issues. Schultz had led the way in sustainable business practices from early on, and his efforts helped to establish licensing agreements to sell Fair Trade Certified™ coffee in the U.S. and Canada. In 2001, working with Conservation International, Starbucks introduced ethical coffee-sourcing guidelines. Unbridled expansion from 2000 to the onset of the 2008 recession added over 13,000 units and matters were getting very much out of hand. As a result, Schultz came back to the CEO position in 2008.

## TREND CONVERGENCE

**Schultz was not only a premier brand builder and marketing genius, but he was also tuned in to the fundamental underpinnings of trending.**

Schultz was not only a premier brand builder and marketing genius, but he was also tuned in to the fundamental underpinnings of trending. In retrospect, more than a modicum of trend convergence and synchronicity fostered the environment and helped set the stage for the growth of the Starbucks brand. When we speak about cultural trends we are acknowledging a marked and lasting change in behavior brought on by circumstances and events. Unlike transitory fads, which come and go, these trends generally have an effect over long periods of time, often a decade or more. When multiple trends converge, their impact and influence become greater than the sum of their parts. For Starbucks, the intersection of a number of micro trends combined with a force like the building of a monstrous wave that lifts a surfer and moves him or her a great distance at tremendous speed.

Schultz brilliantly tapped into a number of these trends during the growth years at Starbucks. They included a strong tolerance for higher prices (fueled by the growing economy); changing tastes and an affinity for a personalized offering; desire for a more caffeinated beverage (which may have gone hand in hand with our sleep-deprived culture); the desire to "belong" to a strong and recognizable brand; and perhaps most important, the fulfillment of the third place need. While acknowledging the universality of Oldenburg's theory, we should also note that there were some unique micro trends that played into Starbucks presentation of itself as a carefully staged third place.

Spawned by the growth of the Internet in the 1980s, the growing popularity of PCs and fax machines, and the economic downturn in the 1990s, there was a new workplace phenomenon taking place in the U.S. This was manifested by two parallel dynamics. First, was the SOHO (small office/home office) movement with a significant number of business start-ups created in several service areas. Whether this was a result of corporate downsizing (which I would argue began more than a decade before 9/11) or the "flattening effect" brought on by the Internet, a "digital democracy" was created that was allowing individuals to do things that used to be the exclusive providence of corporate America. Complementary to the SOHO micro trend was that of big businesses deploying telecommuting and outsourcing as a means of stripping away the excesses of the bloated behemoth companies that were built before the global economy began to impose a new cost-cutting diet. This became known as "homesourcing" (a combination of outsourcing and telecommuting) and it began gaining acceptance during that same period.

## BOWLING TEAMS AND OFFICE FOURSOMES BE GONE

The upshot was that many workers were no longer participating in the daily socialization and human interaction that was an essential component of the old workplace. They were working from home. Gone were the bowling teams and office foursomes of yesteryear; they were replaced by de facto solitary confinement. And what better way to become a part of the socialized fabric than to make Starbucks the SOHO satellite office. Recognizing the opportunity to fulfill this third-place need, Schultz and his design team staged an experience that drew upon all of the iconic emotional triggers that made the daily indulgence justifiable at almost any price. The stores' environment embodied aspects of anyone's glorified home, from the fireplace to the overstuffed chairs. It was devoid of any fluorescent lighting that one would associate with an institution, and its earthy colors seemed to come directly from the Ralph Lauren saddle, horse, and hay-bale palette. There was even the element of familiarity and recognition that one seeks in a third place where your favorite barista knows you by name (Norm!) and the formula for your favorite caffeinated concoction. How could any homesourced person or SOHO start-up resist such a temptation? Schultz knew they couldn't.

As I write this, Starbucks is in sixty-one countries worldwide with over 17,000 stores. While the unmatched growth and burnishing of the iconic brand has not been a straight shot (make mine vanilla) it has become a legendary branding and marketing success story that owes at least some of its success to the fulfillment of the collective need for the third place.

**Schultz and his design team staged an experience that drew upon all of the iconic emotional triggers that made the daily indulgence justifiable at almost any price.**

## AMAZON—LIKE THE RIVER

The dot.com boom of the 1990s had similarities to the Gold Rush of the mid-nineteenth century. Both were based in northern California, and both promised immense wealth. The latter was linked to the seventy-ninth element on the periodic table (AU, gold) and its pursuit was focused on California's El Dorado County. This certainly explains why Cadillac chose that name for its most expensive model back in the 1950s. The former was based on the fourteenth element of the periodic table (SI, silicon), and while the name Silicon Valley was coined by California entrepreneur Ralph Vaerst in the early 1970s, the center is actually in Santa Clara Valley, California, which became home to most of the high-tech businesses involved with silicon-chip production. When the emphasis moved from semiconductors to innovations in software and Internet services, there was plenty of venture capital around to realize the visions and ambitions of thousands of newly minted twentysomething millionaires. And it would seem that sometime in the mid-1990s many had the same dream to monetize the rapidly growing Internet.

In the early 1990s, Princeton University graduate Jeff Bezos (born Jeffrey Preston Jorgensen) left a high-paying job at a New York hedge fund to set up just such an Internet retail business. His decision coincided with U.S. Supreme Court ruling *Quill Corp. v. North Dakota*, which decided that the lack of physical presence in a state exempted a corporation from having to charge and pay sales and use tax to the state. Bezos saw this as an obvious advantage to begin selling products on the Internet. He thought that locating his new company in a lesser-populated state would give the greatest advantage to the largest numbers of his soon-to-be customer base, so that drew him to Washington State. The company was first incorporated in 1994 as Cadabra, but was soon renamed Amazon. Bezos felt that the scale of the Amazon River, one of the world's largest, along with its tie to Greek mythology made the name more appealing and appropriate to his sizable mission. In July 1995, Amazon sold its first book over the Internet, and thus began what has become one of the most disruptive chapters in retail's ever-changing history.

## THE INTERNET PURE PLAY

Ironically, it wasn't Bezos and Amazon that garnered the greatest attention early on from the conventional store-based retailing community. This was due in part to the fact that unlike the more highly publicized (and even greater leveraged) start-ups promising an overnight game change, Bezos was in it for the long haul. He didn't even plan to turn a profit for four or five years. It also appeared that he was focused on competing exclusively with the nation's booksellers, who were becoming quite hot and bothered by his early impact—enough to garner lawsuits from both Barnes & Noble and Walmart. The biggest splashes during e-commerce's infancy came from a whole plethora of Internet "pure plays," as they were known. These were the higher profile web storefronts that had no brick-and-mortar stores (like Amazon), and they were spending heavily not to build infrastructure, but to get attention (unlike Amazon). Largely funded by dot.com boom money, most were setting up shop right and left, and with deep pockets behind them, they were spending enormous advertising budgets to build their recently created brands. Almost overnight, previously unknown names like Buyitnow.com, overstock.com, FreeShop.com, boxLot.com, and Mall.com were popping up on primetime TV urging us to "shop naked," if we were so moved. Meanwhile, conventional store-based retailers were either in denial over the whole

**Bezos felt that the scale of the Amazon River, one of the world's largest, along with its tie to Greek mythology made the name more appealing and appropriate to his sizable mission.**

thing, assuming that it would run its course, or a few began dabbling in this new, highly unfamiliar territory. While a few store-based brands began to embrace the new fad, there was little doubt that these noisy newbies were creating more than a modicum of consternation among the major retail chains.

## QUICK EDUCATION

I've attempted to wear two hats over much of my career: one as a retail planner/designer, and another as a trend forecaster, or at the very least, an avid observer and interpreter of all things retail. I know that from time to time one hat fits better than the other, and it's often difficult to wear both without looking like a Dr. Seuss character. But I have found that keeping my head in both games has been enlightening and has benefited my clients and audiences. With the success and publicity surrounding our *in*STORE[SM] seminar program, I was invited to speak at the 1999 National Retail Federation (NRF) Convention held in New York's Javits Center. Naturally, I was reading everything that was published about the new e-tail phenomenon in preparation for my address, and I attempted to give the audience some perspective about the likely trajectory of this new beast they were all seeking to decode. I boldly suggested that many of the new Internet pure play storefronts may be, in fact, a flash in the pan. I likened it to the dozens of obscure automobile brands that first arrived on the scene at the beginning of the twentieth century— the ones that came and went faster than they ran. That information brought smiles. What was not received as well was the idea (that I had the audacity to share with a room full of retail executives), that e-commerce was not going away and that it would ultimately become just one more touchpoint in their brands' embodiment, and they needed to embrace it. Things got really quiet.

To my surprise and delight, my address was received well

enough that I was invited to speak at NRF's Expo 2000. I felt doubly compelled to "bring the goods" when I returned in the new millennium. In the fall of 1999, I attended one of the first national conferences on Internet retailing, called *e-retailing '99*. It was sponsored by Shop.Org, which was affiliated with the NRF, and what an education it was. This was my first exposure to a completely new mentality, one that defied most everything I had experienced in the retail industry, along with basic precepts of "the process." At the conference I heard one twentysomething speaker after another talking rather casually about launching Internet concepts, just to "get traction" (a term often repeated)—and then quickly pulling them down, rebranding, and relaunching the websites. It seemed as if they were making things up as they went (which they were) and that money was no object (which was the case).

The speakers at the conference were a mix, mostly dominated by pure-play start-ups, but there were a few traditional "bricks and clicks" players (those with business conducted on physical premises as well as on the Internet) present too. There was a striking difference in the approaches of the two groups. The pure plays were largely the young guns whose objectives were to get "up and out," to launch and sell. The bricks-and-clicks participants were there just trying to understand the new language at least enough to take it back to corporate and attempt to sell it. I was also hearing stories from the seasoned retail veterans that exemplified the estrangement and conflict that this new universe was presenting throughout their corporate ranks. "Our media ad people don't know how to communicate to our Internet ad people." Naturally, this was only the tip of the virtual iceberg, with much more distressing confusion to come before the old guard would learn to embrace the new kid on the block.

**What I didn't realize at the time was that I was not only experiencing a pivotal point in retail and consumer trending, but I was also observing a cultural clash of epic proportions.**

## GENERATION FLUX

What I didn't realize at the time was that I was not only experiencing a pivotal point in retail and consumer trending, but I was also observing a cultural clash of epic proportions. The newbies measured their progress and evolution in nanoseconds and IPOs, while traditional retailers evaluated over seasons, quarters, and generations—completely different mind-sets and goals. The business model that had built and propelled retail over the course of the last hundred years was based on sourcing, distribution, and marketing according to established protocols, and even with ongoing changes in procedures, rarely were those adjustments radical. This is in stark contrast to e-commerce, which was largely driven by techies who were never schooled in the command-and-control idiom that drove much of twentieth-century retail. They had no rules to follow in this uncharted territory. And because the entire tech business has been about disruption and constant warp-speed reinvention, these new "titans of e-ness" were functioning by their own rules, or lack thereof.

It could be argued that e-commerce, along with much of the tech world, was being developed by what *Fast Company* editor Robert Safian would identify as "Generation Flux" a dozen years later. Generation Flux is not defined as a demographic like Boomers, Generation X, or Generation Y (aka the Millennials), it describes a psychographic or mind-set that tolerates and even embraces the unknown, and its players come from each of the aforementioned demographics. This change in mind-set foretells as radical a cultural change as the one that took place over one hundred years ago when America was moving from an agrarian, farm-based economy to one that centered on manufacturing. This new information- and technology-based economy was bringing with it chaotic disruption, not as a transitory condition but as a constant state of affairs. In the face of this new normal, the comfortable norms of business—from established business models, the forty-year career, and the rise up and down the corporate ladder—are all breaking down. And nowhere is the impact of this seismic change more profound and destabilizing than in retail. However, even in this time of extreme chaos one constant remains, and this truth would have been as comfortable and intuitive to Al and Lou Stein as it became for Steve Jobs and Jeff Bezos, and that is: Know your business mission! As I mentioned in a previous chapter, Dad always said, pounding away on the kitchen table, "If the retailer thinks they're one thing on Tuesday and something else on Friday, how is the customer supposed to know what they are?"

## TOYS R LATE!

Returning to the NRF Convention at the Javits Center in January 2000 was another heady experience. I had received invitations to speak abroad as a result of my 1999 NRF speech, which had given me additional confidence, and by then the dot.com boom had quickened its pace. The audience's anxiety over the high-flying phenomenon that had pumped e.com stock prices and PE (price/ earnings) ratios into the stratosphere was palpable. The industry had just come out of Christmas 1999, which was one of the first holiday seasons in which a significant number of store-based retailers had delved into the new Internet sandbox to compete with upstarts like Amazon and other pure plays that were starting to build traction. While an increasing number of Americans were ready to give the web a try in the months leading up to Christmas '99, the impulse came before many of the store-based retailers had mastered the back-end fulfillment, which was the one thing that Amazon had concentrated on from day one. Suffice it to say

**In the face of this new normal, the comfortable norms of business—from established business models, the forty-year career, and the rise up and down the corporate ladder—are all breaking down.**

that for some retailers the experience was not pretty. For example, Toys R Us sold much more online than they could find the means to deliver on time, and "Toys R Late" became their moniker for the '99 holiday season.

Amazon, meanwhile, was holding its own on the all-important, back-end fulfillment component, but it was starting to get some bad press on the conditions their workers were enduring to keep the wheels on the bus. The message I shared with the NRF audience (after my revelation at the 1999 e-commerce conference) was to continue to embrace the new brand touchpoint, because it was becoming clear even in its infancy that it was not going away. We also had learned that some of the more savvy retailers were already partnering with experienced back-end fulfillment operators (like Amazon) rather than attempting to do it on their own. While no one in the audience, myself included, could have anticipated the dot.com implosion and financial meltdown that would occur less than sixty days after my appearance, we were already seeing many of the pure plays succumbing to the rise-and-fall syndrome that only foreshadowed the big bust that was two calendar pages away (back when we still had paper calendars). Although Internet sales circa 1999 had yet to top one billion dollars, it was already growing in double-digit increments with each consecutive year. This pattern would continue over the next dozen years before surpassing a quarter trillion dollars by 2012. The final point I shared with the audience in my wrap-up was the notion that many in the room would see the day when people will have forgotten that Amazon started as an online book seller.

## NEW RULES

Much has been written and said about the Internet becoming a great equalizer and a source of empowerment to many. The Internet has enabled individuals and small groups to perform tasks that could only have been accomplished by large institutions only a decade ago. It has also given a voice to people around the world who previously were unseen and unheard. It has changed our culture and society like nothing in human history and made the world a much smaller place. It has also become the go-to place to research everything from medical maladies to large and small purchasing decisions. Initially, the shopping research was aimed at larger items with long purchase cycles, things that consumers buy infrequently like cars and appliances, but it wasn't long before there was information (both credible and otherwise) available about virtually every possible product and service offering imaginable. Today, if we need to learn anything about anything we simply Google it!

As far as retailing is concerned, the Internet has contributed to what authors Robin Lewis and Michael Dart dub "Wave III" in their book *The New Rules of Retail*. *New Rules* makes a compelling argument for three distinct eras in U.S. retailing; and I touch on those eras in previous chapters. Wave I describes the era of producer power in the early half of the twentieth century. This was the period when the demand was greater than the supply and, consequently, consumers were pretty much forced to accept whatever was available and had virtually no influence over pricing. Wave II was the post-WWII era, which became a marketing- and distribution-driven economy (as depicted in the TV show *Mad Men*). During this time we witnessed a massive expansion of product variety and brands along with virtually every major retail format that we have come to know. It included the development of department stores, specialty retail, big box, and category killers. Wave III supports Pine and Gilmore's treatise as the greatest transformation yet, with the birth of the experience economy in which genuine experiences and

**The message I shared with the NRF audience (after my revelation at the 1999 e-commerce conference) was to continue to embrace the new brand touchpoint, because it was becoming clear even in its infancy that it was not going away.**

customized products trump mass-market dynamics, and real value is championed over bling. Although Lewis and Dart place e-commerce in Wave II, I would argue it fits more comfortably in Wave III as the game changer behind the disruption that has led to the customer being in control instead of the producer, distributor, or retailer. Today's customer wants what they want, when they want it, and at the price they are willing to pay.

## WOW, NOW, AND HOW OF RETAIL RELEVANCE

Wave III has brought with it three operating principles that are essential to the success of any entity currently operating in the retail space. According to Lewis and Dart they are: neurological connectivity, preemptive distribution, and value chain control. I call it the *wow*, *now*, and *how* of retail relevance. Without executing these three principles, it has become difficult, if not impossible, to achieve success in the new era of the experience economy. While we have already briefly discussed the power of neurological connectivity to influence consumer behavior and brand value, as we begin to dig into the world of e-commerce, e-tail and MEtail[SM] (mobile electronic retailing) it justifies being revisited. Neurological connectivity (the wow) refers to the way that our brains work when all our senses are engaged—sight, sound, smell, taste, touch, and the sixth sense, that of the mind. I like to refer to this phenomenon as sensory sync. Truly experiential retail (think the Apple Store again) engages all of our senses and does it in a holistic manner that tells us the brand and all its touchpoints are fully integrated. This level of getting it together is necessary for any brand that is in search of the gold standard in brand positioning and becoming the defining brand in a product or service category.

The next strategic operating principle in the trifecta is preemptive distribution (the now), getting the product or service to market ahead of the competition—in other words being "fleet first." Sometimes this means taking the store to the consumer, at least figuratively speaking. A more literal translation was the experience my wife and I had when we were celebrating our twenty-fifth anniversary in Cabo St. Lucas, Mexico. For any bona fide shopaholic, the combination of sitting on the sun-baked, white sand beaches while local venders parade past with endless collections of silver jewelry certainly defines bringing the product to the customer, and doing so when all of the senses are fully engaged. Time to market has undergone severe compression and it will continue as more retailer/manufacture relationships demand it, and evolving technologies enable the customer to have highly customized offerings made available to them in minutes and hours as opposed to days or weeks.

**Truly experiential retail (think the Apple Store again) engages all of our senses and does it in a holistic manner that tells us the brand and all its touchpoints are fully integrated.**

## GETTING VERTICAL

The third principle is value chain control (the how), what I think of as conception to consumption. We have already discussed how much of a game changer this became for retailers like The Limited to redefine a specialty retail segment by taking control of all aspects of design, production, and distribution. Controlling the entire value chain has certainly been a factor in Apple's success. Vertical integration is becoming the last hurdle for many brands on the retailing and manufacturing side of the equation. Retailers like Target have been largely responsible for the monumental change in the perceived value of generic, or store brands. The public's perception of quality and value for this category has moved from a strong negative only a decade or so ago, to an overwhelming positive. Target brands including up & up, Merona, and Mossimo have been so widely accepted (even preferred) that they have helped change the ratio of national brand names to that of private label house brands, in favor of the latter. And this shift has strongly influenced margins as well as brand loyalty.

From a manufacturer's standpoint, there are few major brands out there that haven't at least experimented with controlling their brand's value and messaging at point of sale by becoming their own retailer, as Apple did. Lest we forget, Gap started out as the go-to place for Levi's until their brand name became at least as strong, if not stronger, than the Levi's they were selling. The other means by which manufacturers control their brand is through store-in-store or branded shops, as demonstrated by our Brunswick Pavilion. To list the major brands that have taken one or both of these directions would fill a chapter in this book. A few notable examples include Calvin Klein and Ralph Lauren (fashion); Nike and Under Armour (sports); Weber Grills and John Deere (outdoor); and Andersen Windows and Pella (home improvement). These tactics will continue as popular brands continue the tug of war with fewer, larger, and more powerful retailers. Their success depends on their ability to control their brand message and avoid the commoditization associated with decreasing real estate and presence in multibrand, big-box or department store formats. To make matters worse, Target, Costco, Walmart, Dick's Sporting Goods, and most of the other mass-market retailers are all experimenting with house brands—from golf clubs to garden shears—to compete with and steal market share from the major national brands.

The last bodies to fall in this fight for value-chain control are the independent distributors, who were the essential link between manufacturers and retailers over the course of the last century. These entities were responsible for getting products from manufacturers to legions of retailers, large and small, from big cities to small towns across America. Over the course of the last half century, we've witnessed the number of unique retailers diminish while the nature of the relationships between manufacturers and the larger, dominant retailers have radically changed. Manufacturers used to go to market with products, models, and features aimed at the American consumer (whoever that was). Today, in the interest of differentiated product offerings and the retailer's increased marketing prowess and buying power, the major retailers often influence, if not dictate, what will appear in their aisles. These stronger retailer/manufacturer relationships are another factor influencing the roles and perceived value of many middlemen. And with continued pressure on margins and increased pricing transparency brought on by the Internet, many of these independent distributors' roles are no longer cost justified. Middlemen have already become part of sales history in some sectors, and in the areas where they still function, their days are numbered. Simply put, multilevel distribution models are the analog equivalent in a digital world of sourcing.

**Simply put, multilevel distribution models are the analog equivalent in a digital world of sourcing.**

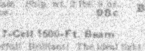

# MARKET
# OF ONE

9

The world of business is in a constant state of flux with an ongoing dynamic of development, deconstruction, and reinvention. For retailers, this has been most pronounced in the way they've had to adapt to the changing purchasing patterns of their consumers, which has been driven, at least in part, by the influence that the Internet has played in creating pricing transparency, along with new and seemingly unlimited supply options. I've watched Internet online sales in the U.S. go from a few hundred million to a quarter of a trillion dollars in a decade and a half, climbing a minimum of 10 percent year on year. Store-based retail appears to be in steady decline, and in my opinion, e-tail is still in its infancy. In order to analyze and understand the nature of these changes and try to predict what's next, we have to get our heads around one of the most destabilizing dynamics of our time: social media. Perhaps no single social experiment in modern human history has had the far-reaching and profound effects that social media has had on billions of individuals of all ages around the globe.

## GETTING VERY SOCIAL

As of the third quarter of 2012, Facebook surpassed one billion active users including at least 7.5 million under thirteen years old (the legal age of registration). When we are not posting and uploading the latest images devoted to capturing and sharing "a moment in the life" we are busily sending and receiving text messages of 140 characters or less on Twitter. And collectively we are doing so at the rate of half a billion tweets a day. Be assured that by the time you read this chapter those statistics are likely to be woefully inaccurate. This passion, preoccupation, or obsession (depending on one's degree of participation) has had, and will continue to have, a profound influence on the marketing and selling of goods and services worldwide. Meanwhile, we are all leaving tracks of information about who we are, and what we like and don't like, and these responses are providing vast amounts of "big data" to keep supercomputers churning, all in the name of brand loyalty and selling stuff.

To understand the likely trajectory of this digital madness and the implications for the retail industry, it is instructive to briefly re-examine the demographics of the six generations who currently occupy our great country. We are doing so to better understand what has become known as the digital divide, drawing a comparison between the digitally adept versus the novice adapters. We should acknowledge that it is due to the increased attention to health and diet along with advances in medicine that we are living longer than at any time in history—making it possible to talk about six generations of living Americans.

In my years of research into the whole notion of demographic demarcation I have come to the conclusion that there are no universally accepted break points between one generation and another. Also, behavioral scientists recognize that there are overlaps from generation to generation and that the overlaps appear to be getting larger generation to generation. In addition, echoing the signs of the zodiac, being on the cusp of the next generation also influences behavior. While I've already discussed the dangers of broad generalities associated with generational demographics (in contrast to more objective psychographic analysis in chapter four), I'm going to share what might be called a hybrid or composite demographic overview in order to gain some insight on the digital divide and how retailers and marketers are likely to deal with it.

**The GI Generation (1901–26)-** These were the children of World War I and the participants of World War II. They experienced the economic boom of the Roaring Twenties followed by the Great De-

**Perhaps no single social experiment in modern human history has had the far-reaching and profound effects that social media has had on billions of individuals of all ages around the globe.**

pression. They benefited from an increase in public schooling and the first child labor laws. They were all about community, pulling together, and being team players with strong moral compasses and even stronger senses of right and wrong. Uniformity and formality were highly valued. They married for life and, with few exceptions, never planned for retirement. They bought and paid for only what they could afford and often made do with the basic necessities.

**The Matures, or the Silent Generation (1927–45)-** Tom Brokaw refers to these folks as the "greatest generation," and rightly so. They were the brains and brawn behind the greatest expansion of business and commerce in the country's history. In the process, they became better off financially than their parents. They were WWII and Korean War vets. Many started their careers in the same company that they would ultimately retire from. Family was very important and their children were being indulged in ways they never were. They were able to plan for retirement and spend freely from their hard-earned savings, pensions, and social security. They witnessed the swing era, big bands, the blues, and the dawn of popular music.

**Baby Boomers (1946–64)-** At seventy-seven million strong, they have had an outsized influence (good and bad) throughout their lives. Regrettably known as the "me generation," Boomers have been regarded as being a bit self-righteous and self-centered. They would assume the nicknames of "hippie" and "yuppie" and were raised with rock 'n' roll, counterculture, peace, love, television, and the dawn of mass marketing. They lived through the Vietnam War, the assassination of two Kennedys and Dr. King, along with the civil rights and Vietnam peace movements. The birth control pill and the acceptance of divorce gave rise to new attitudes toward sexuality. Now retiring at the rate of 10,000 per day, this group will reinvent retirement on many levels. The rocking chair will be replaced by rock climbing. Some will start new businesses and others will become global expats at a rate not previously seen. Many will live to recreate as long as they worked to create.

**Generation X (1962–82)-** Baby Boomer divorce rates and two working parents gave them the nickname "latchkey kids," making them independent and self-reliant at an early age. Vastly reduced birthrates for this group have decreased their generational clout. They rebelled against and mistrusted institutions, government, and the Boomer generation before them. They grew up dealing with drugs in school and the AIDS epidemic, and were a part of the disco and hip-hop cultures. They postponed marriage, but accepted cohabitation. Reacting against their parents' obsessions over job and career, they choose to work to live rather than the other way around, resulting in shorter work stints and more career changes than was common in the past. They were the first generation to see computers begin to influence education and they were the earliest adapters to the new language.

**Generation Y (1980–2000)-** Known as the "Millennial Generation," or "Millennials," and as "Echo Boomers," they reflect the Boomer generation in many ways. With eighty-seven million births (approximately one third of the U.S. population) their sheer numbers will have a significant economic impact for years to come. Also like their Boomer predecessors, they are more respectful of authority and more optimistic than Gen X before them. These folks are definitively on the digitally adept side of the digital divide because the computer has always been a part of their lives. They embrace text messaging as a means of shorthand communication, they are brand loyal and smart consumers, and their spending helped pull the country out of the Great Recession. Living in a 24/7 world, they've been under a lot of pressure to excel, and they have managed to develop the ability to process much information while redefining their community via the Internet. They are global citizens and consequently they feel responsible for a shrinking world's growing problems. They do share one trait with Gen X, which is that they also choose to organize their work lives around their broader interests and expect the workplace to change accordingly.

**Generation Z (1995–2010)-** Also known as "digital natives," they are facing some of the most significant challenges of the modern day, including terrorism and the effects of climate change. In addition, their vastly reduced numbers compared to the Millennials before them mirrors the relationship that Gen X has to the Boomers. Gen Z will exist in the shadow of Gen Y and will probably rebel against them. They have grown up with the Internet, cell phones, laptops, and all things digital. They are comfortable with and dependent on technology, and they place a high value on being socially networked and engaged. Their lives often blur the lines between virtual and actual reality. They have become highly adept at multitasking and seeking interactive and stimulating formats over passive entertainment like TV with particularly simple, well-designed formats. As globally connected individuals, they are flexible and more tolerant of diverse cultures different from their own. They are also in touch with the environmental impact of products and brands and respect good corporate stewardship. Looking forward, many of them will work at jobs that don't even exist yet. Their small numbers will, however, make them highly marketable at a time when minorities become the majority as traditional ethnic and racial barriers melt away.

## DIGITAL DIVIDE AND CONQUER

Reflecting on the evolving digital adaptation of America's consumer we have to take into account (as marketers do) the sheer numbers of Generations X, Y, and Z. Together these consumers account for more than half of America's consuming population, and they represent even greater spending power now, and for the next three decades. While the Baby Boomers are by no means allergic to digital devices, and in fact represent a huge online market, it's the attitudes, habits, and inclinations of the Gen X, Y, and Z combination (who I will nickname Gens3) that will create warp speed change and format destabilization like nothing in the last century of retail.

Witness the fact that some of the smartest (and wealthiest) entrepreneurs and change agents are investing unimaginable amounts of capital in finding new ways to monetize the social media phenomenon. There isn't a week that goes by that another new start-up or alliance isn't formed to leverage the legions of the digitally connected, while utilizing the collected personal information (big data) to market in new, effective, and even more personal ways. Facebook, Twitter, Amazon, eBay, Apple, and Yahoo, as well as untold numbers of little-known (but well-funded) start-ups are in hot pursuit of the secret ingredient that will produce a successful net recipe that will send legions of followers looking for the *love button* resulting in a Wall Street jackpot of mega proportions.

The undeniable truth is that for all three of our key demographics, their most-prized possessions are their smartphones or other web-enabled devices. These objects represent the freedom, social connectivity, and power that previous generations associated with a driver's license, car, telephone, favorite hangout, or "pad," or all

The undeniable truth is that for all three of our key demographics, their most-prized possessions are their smartphones or other web-enabled devices. These objects represent the freedom, social connectivity, and power that previous generations associated with a driver's license, car, telephone, favorite hangout or "pad," or all of the above.

of the above. It provides everything necessary to connect, relate, learn, escape, invent, or reinvent one's persona—and shop. The frightening truth for retailers today and tomorrow is that with the point of sale now tucked away in a backpack, back pocket, or purse, how will the retailer, brand bearer, or mall owner engage this new, highly mobile consumer? Simply put, the concept of the store has changed forever. The issue of where and how the customer actually engages with the brand has taken on new meaning and importance to manufacturers, retailers, and anyone remotely interested in selling goods or services.

## FROM MULTICHANNEL TO CROSS-CHANNEL TO OMNICHANNEL

Multichannel retailing is hardly new. Mail-order retailers Montgomery Ward and Sears & Roebuck, after establishing hugely successful catalog businesses in 1872 and 1893 respectively, began opening stores. Sears was first in 1925 and Ward's followed in 1926. Within two years Ward's had expanded to over 240 outlets. The mail-order catalogs were focused initially on rural America, in order to provide the farmers with comparable, dependable goods that the "city folk" had access to. The first Ward's and Sears urban-based retail outlets still could not inventory all of the tens of thousands of products that the four-pound catalogs contained. By 1904, Montgomery Ward's had reached a printing of three million units when the total population of the country was less than seventy-seven million. If you consider the average family size back then, that would suggest that there was at least one catalog (from both Sears and Ward's) for every five or six homes in the U.S—talk about market penetration.

Today's multichannel selling universe is infinitely more complex and fractured and is in a constant state of flux when compared to the mail-order days of old. We've also seen the leading brands adapt from a multichannel to cross-channel mind-set, realizing that the consumer thinks first about the brand, *not* the distribution channel. In addition, the leading or defining brands always keep in mind the who, when, and how any particular consumer will choose to engage with a specific brand touchpoint—and it's an ever-evolving and totally dynamic phenomenon. Methods of brand engagement are no longer predictable and are becoming as fluid and varied as the target consumers. More important, customers don't differentiate one brand touchpoint from another when it comes to the emotional quotient and neurological connectivity that leads to brand value. In other words, a brand message can be well executed in advertising and marketing, but if the in-store experience falls flat, the entire brand suffers. As online retailing continues to grow, fed by smartphones and the attitudes of the Gens3 driving them, the goal of marketing must be finding a way to embrace omnichannel thinking. This means a completely holistic and integrated brand embodiment across all channels. It recognizes the important fact that the consumers may engage any and all of the brand's touchpoints at different times, and that they expect an engaging, fluid transition that meets their personal needs. The next wave of brand retailing will offer a host of new tools to strengthen this connection between the brand touchpoints. But as I suggest in previous chapters, the only way to create the kind of brand unity that will be required is to blow up the silos. Silo thinking is contrary to and undermines the omnichannel objective. Because today's retail universe relies on a unified shopping experience, the corporate structure that conceives, designs, and builds this connection to the customer must be equally holistic and connected in its strategy and execution.

**Methods of brand engagement are no longer predictable and are becoming as fluid and varied as the target consumers.**

## METAIL<sup>SM</sup>—CAUSE OR ANTIDOTE TO SHOWROOMING?

The three converging trends of the smartphone's capability and acceptance, the desire of Gens3 for constant mobile access, and the rapid growth of online retail are coalescing and becoming a major game changer. As I mention in chapter seven, I created the term MEtail<sup>SM</sup> (mobile electronic retailing) as a logical handle for this phenomenon. The moniker also recognizes the degree to which these devices support the personal styles and preferences of the populace to search, research, share, edit, and purchase goods and services any time and anywhere. This change wave is forcing retailers to address the fact that retail websites designed for PCs, Macs, and laptops don't work well on a 3.5" diagonal screen. In addition, the search depth that was customary on a full site is no longer essential for many of the mobile searches being conducted. Hence, reformatting was necessary to make MEtail<sup>SM</sup> work as efficiently as it needed to. The leading and defining brands in most categories have been quick to address this.

For today's retailers, enabling customers to take the Internet with them has proven to have unintended consequences, and it can be another destabilizing factor, particularly at the big-box, commodity end of the spectrum. These retailers were already fighting a slowly recovering, post-recession economy with tighter margins brought on by the price transparency on the Internet as well as competing with the behemoth Amazon. Retailers are now dealing with customers coming to price shop their stores using them as their own private (and very expensive) personal showrooms and then making the purchase online. (This is also known as "showrooming.") To add insult to injury, many shoppers have the audacity to hit the competitor's buy button even before walking out of the store. Nielsen Research tells us that two-thirds of the smartphone-equipped users will in fact use their smartphones in the store to research products and prices online. So how is a retailer supposed to recognize and account for this behavior as part of the new normal?

There are broad-based movements currently underway to tax online sales in an effort to level the playing field, and it appears that this is inevitable. That aside, I believe there are fundamental efforts that the retail industry can (and must) make to address showrooming, but they must do so proactively. The implementation of these available tools, which I will explore next, are also essential to maintaining store-based retail as a viable and integral brand touchpoint as web-based retail continues to grow. Remember, if store-based retailing attempts to compete with the Internet on price alone, it almost certainly will lose.

## EXPERIENTIAL RATHER THAN PRICE DRIVEN

The nature and quality of the in-store experience must be compelling enough that price alone will not be the deciding purchasing factor. The experience must be relevant to the consumer's needs, which means engaging the emotional and intellectual components of decision-making in a manner that resonates with the shopper on a meaningful level. We recognize the importance of assisted discovery, which helps the customer "decode" the store and move him or her from observer to engaged participant. This can be achieved through an intuitive layout, logical adjacencies, and unmistakable way finding. Tapping into the Internet within the store environment holds endless possibilities and is essential to creating an omnichannel experience. But, it also puts pressure on the retailer to approach all touchpoints in a holistic manner so they "talk" to

> The nature and quality of the in-store experience must be compelling enough that price alone will not be the deciding purchasing factor.

one another. Well-designed and placed graphics and signage in the store will assist with category and departmental organization as well as provide the customer with appropriate topline information, which is essential in decision making. At the brand and product level, quick response (QR) codes can enable access to deeper levels of information that aids in editing and choice making, as well as understanding features and benefits. Using iPads and other digital readers can provide Intranet or network web capture to expedite both assisted and unassisted selling. If executed correctly, the store works harder and salespeople become closers and order takers to a greater degree.

## SOLUTION-BASED VS COMPONENT-BASED RETAILING

Most every product or service purchased by today's consumer is part of a larger lifestyle/personal style framework and should be thought of in that way. When we buy a big-screen TV it relates to home entertainment. When we buy a bike it relates to recreation, exercise, family bonding, or all three. In order for the store-based retailer to make the store visit less about price and more about higher value aspirational goals, the customer experience must tap into the broader lifestyle and personal triggers that lie at the heart of the purchase. This broader solution, or lifestyle-based approach, should plant seeds for future visits while generating cross-category sales. Staging the store to readily promote these softer, more individually informed values generally results in longer customer visits, larger purchases, and greater brand loyalty. One only need visit a Cabela's store to understand how effective this type of solution/lifestyle-based retail approach can be. When the store brand addresses these higher level and personal lifestyle issues, the perceived value of the brand rises as well as the margins.

## INDIVIDUALIZING THE EXPERIENCE—
## BEING THE EXPERT

Whether the product or service being purchased has a long or short purchase cycle, the customer's need-to-know becomes key to the editing phase of the purchasing process. For the in-store experience to have a high perceived value, it must (both passively and actively) assist that customer with choice making. This emphasizes the importance of presenting recognized brands and properly edited offerings. In the study of Costco in chapter five, we learned choice can be double-edged; too much choice can be worse than too little. Our time-strapped customers want to believe the retailer has pre-edited the offerings to save them valuable time and expedite making a choice. With a smartphone in hand and the employment of QR codes and other emerging technologies, the retailer opens up the "endless aisle" option that expands choice beyond the standard or in-store offerings. Meanwhile, we can expect that the expansion of loyalty programs will bring dynamic pricing into play, further recognizing the customers' devotion to a retailer or brand and rewarding them accordingly. This all goes further toward the market-of-one promise. This is the result when the retailer's message has been so well defined and targeted that the customer feels as if he or she is a preferred recipient of a unique and high-value product or service offering. Access to highly trained sales personnel when interpersonal engagement is warranted further cements the brand's expertise and intelligence because it builds trust.

## LIVING IN A MOBILE WORLD

We live in an amazing time; one in which ever-changing technology is making life easier and more complicated all at the same

**Most every product or service purchased by today's consumer is part of a larger lifestyle/personal style framework and should be thought of in that way.**

time. Many of us have become slaves to our digital devices; they have become central to work and play—perhaps in not altogether healthy ways. Our hyperconnectivity has become both an asset and a real burden. Work doesn't seem to end with the completion of the workday. And it has become a full-time job keeping up with our legions of friends and family, not to mention knowing what Ashton Kutcher ate for breakfast. (I just dated this book again.) And socialization seems to be taking a real hit in the process. It has become accepted etiquette for people to be together socially, while any numbers of these individuals are "virtually" engaged in something else. But enough ranting!

It has become very clear that we are only beginning to feel the impact technology will have on retailing in the near future. The implications will affect every aspect of the purchasing experience, the nature of what a store will become, and how it will function. Technology will affect the size, configuration, location, and number of outlets a retailer will have. It will also have a profound effect on shopping centers and malls throughout America, a topic I explore further in chapter eleven.

## WHOLE NEW VOCABULARY

The half-life of many of today's new technologies is getting shorter and shorter, and I know that in presenting and defining some of these, one runs the risk of making a book appear dated almost before it gets published. But, I would like to touch on some of the most obvious developments that with individual or collective use are likely to have a profound effect on the retail world. These include nonlinear quick response (QR) codes, radio frequency identification (RFID), near field communications (NFC), and geo-tracking applications. Interfacing these technologies with today's smartphones will continue to influence all aspects of the customer experience for the foreseeable future.

**Quick Response (QR) bar codes-** Universal product codes (UPCs), labels otherwise known as linear bar codes, were introduced in 1974. GS1 MobileCom, based in Brussels, Belgium, established the design and implementation standards globally of these one-dimensional labeling systems. Since their introduction, UPCs have reshaped the nature of product identification and tracking worldwide. Its simplicity of use has brought the UPC system great acceptance, despite the shortcoming that data was limited to between twelve and twenty characters. In 1994, the QR code system was invented by the Toyota subsidiary Denso Wave for use in the auto industry. These two-dimensional codes vastly improve on UPC codes in that they enable the encoding of 7,000 characters, including text, URLs, or other data.

Because this platform is easily downloadable to virtually any smartphone, retailers and manufacturers have been experimenting with its application in numerous ways. In-store scanning can link the consumer to the brand's website for general promotion and brand building. At point of engagement, the QR codes can be effectively used to enable the customer or sales assistant to access in-depth information on a product line or particular model—a practice that's also referred to as extended packaging. The QR code can also be used as a method of geolocating where a code has been scanned. This can be done either through embedded location information or cell phone tower triangulation. QR code scanning has been linked to increased sales conversion rates.

**RFID (Radio Frequency Identification)-** These mini chips (only slightly larger than a grain of rice) have been used for tracking everything from cargo and cattle to house cats. They've even been approved by the U.S. Food and Drug Administration for use on people. (Parents, do you know where your children are?) In retail, RFID is used for data transfer and back-of-house operations, including pallet identification and a host of inventory-control issues. The convergence of this technology with that of smartphones is bringing RFID technology out front and promises to be a key ingredient in delivering an omnichannel experience for the customer.

*In Sync-* RFID-embedded floor fixtures and sales kiosks can improve the shopping experience by telling the customer what sizes and colors are available beyond what is displayed on the floor. It can make suggestions about coordinated product offerings and even enable the customer to access sales help or simply have the product sent to her home. Cross-selling doesn't have to stop with what's physically in-store. The technology can suggest infinite online sales options (endless aisle) that are likely to strike a chord, based on that particular customer's likes and dislikes. Suddenly MEtail[SM] becomes everyone's personal shopper.

*E-fficient-* Waiting in lines (and even checkouts) could become a thing of the past. With RFID-enabled fixtures communicating with the user's smartphone, the purchase may be consummated via mobile banking. Security is assured since the customer uses a personal digital code (fingerprint or retina scan) to verify account access. RFID helps retailers learn shoppers' preferences and shopping patterns to facilitate loyalty programs as well as shout-outs when new, "preferred" products are available. The dynamics of the data sharing enables the retailer to create highly personal offers for key customers (market of one) that drives traffic when excess inventory or slow sales periods warrants it.

*Social Synergy*- An RFID "smart mirror" takes the customer experience to a whole other level and converts the changing room into an experiential destination. Approaching this customer focal point, the smartphone tells the customer what price she will pay for the item she is trying on, and the level of discount associated with her loyalty status and/or combining the purchase with the wide variety of matching pieces or accessories being viewed. She is also just one touch away from linking to selected social-media friends for a thumbs up or down on the purchase. Once a decision is made, the sale is consummated by tapping the phone and she's on to the next purchase.

**NFC (Near Field Communications)-** As promising as RFID will become in retail, NFC may have an even greater influence on how we live, shop, and interact with others. NFC is an offshoot of RFID, but is designed for close-proximity exchange. The NFC tag sends a small current, which creates a magnetic field that is recognized by the customer's smartphone and turned back into electrical impulses and ultimately data, instantaneously. There are essentially two forms of the technology: passive and active. A passive NFC tag is one in which the device sends out information that can be read, but does not itself read information back. For example, an NFC-equipped sign on the front of a store might send out a special offer when contacted by a passing customer's cell phone to entice them into the store. Active devices (sometimes referred to as peer-to-peer) can both read and send information and are likely to become the ultimate retail game-changers. The "cashless society" that futurists have talked about is likely to become a reality by employing active NFC technology. Many of the Android phones that are currently in circulation have NFC capabilities. Google Wallet and MasterCard PayPass are two examples of NFC technologies

> The "cashless society" that futurists have talked about is likely to become a reality by employing active NFC technology.

that allow for instant, cashless transactions. They turn a smartphone into a virtual wallet. Secure channels and encryption would be used to protect against theft, and code authorization would ensure that lost or stolen devices are not compromised.

With the smartphone's ability to hold rewards points and loyalty program information, as well as a plethora of customer lifestyle information and personal preferences, a shopping trip can be a highly individualized experience. The level of product intelligence and advice that can be shared between the consumer and the retailer is infinite, whether a live salesperson becomes involved or not. A highly personalized shopping experience can be pre-planned by the customer around an event, preferred brands, or product sequencing (geolocating). Selections are made throughout the trip and the phone is waved at the card reader on the way out of the store. Social media will likely begin to leverage "tapping" or "bumping," a phenomenon that will allow two similarly NFC-equipped smartphones to share information or engage in a special "friending offer" or interactive game. It has been predicted that by 2015 nearly a third of all smartphones sold will be NFC equipped.

**Geotracking and Geolocating-** It does not take a lot of imagination to envision the myriad ways that retailers will soon be engaging customers through the three aforementioned emerging technologies. The opportunities compound themselves when you add aspects of geotracking and geolocating to the mix. Imagine the added dimension of a shopping trip when the customer's smartphone guides the trip based on the personalized selection criteria that have been preprogrammed. Apple began a patent application in 2010 for utilizing geolocated software for two specific realms of shopping, which they defined as "casual shopping" and "targeted shopping." Casual shopping constitutes browsing and would include current location, personalized maps, special offers, style search, new arrivals, and access to special services. Targeted shopping on the other hand involves finding specific products or stores and includes store locator, special events, product search, reserve and pickup, and available inventory. While general geolocating technology has long existed, one can only imagine how the addition of NFC will enhance both shopping types; perhaps it will be known as iFindit!

While Apple has yet to announce the introduction of NFC to its iPhone as I write this, rumors abound. The focus of the buzz is Apple's likely introduction of what has come to be known as iWallet, their NFC-based mobile payment solution. It is suggested that along with mobile payment will come a host of complementary financial management tools, such as credit card management, the necessary parental controls, as well as a fingerprint reader that is so smart it can initiate different functions based on which finger is being used.

## BRICK AND MOBILE

In addition to the aforementioned technologies, retailers are experimenting with a host of other shiny new tools, including augmented reality (AR), holograms, and motion-detecting video walls that interact with the customer, all of which are intended to engage and entertain the shopper. These new devices in and of themselves will not save or transform store-based retail, nor will they overcome showrooming. And, in my opinion, showrooming is not really the central issue, it's merely a symptom of the changing times. Our focus should be on reimagining the store environment in a way that makes the actual experience truly transformational and in sync with omnichannel thinking. It will be up to leading brands and in-

> **Apple began a patent application in 2010 for utilizing geolocated software for two specific realms of shopping, which they defined as "casual shopping" and "targeted shopping."**

novative retail planners and designers to master all of these new implements to reimagine and revamp the in-store experience. The goal is to blend the best aspects of the virtual and digital technologies with actual product and human engagement in experiential ways the Internet cannot achieve. The ultimate objective will be a unique and personal experience that delivers on the market-of-one promise.

I've always believed that consumers want and need both the social interaction and tactile experience of purchasing products—it's the dynamic that has made the town market a gathering place throughout history. The timely convergence of these new technologies that complement social media, e-commerce, and MEtail[SM] should lead to a new way of interacting with products in a manner that is highly personal and individualized as well as fast and efficient. This "brick and mobile" interface will complete the omnichannel experience and help to bridge the virtual/actual reality modes.

I do believe, however, that there is a new case to be made for the pure showroom concept along the lines of a BEST Products store that we discussed in chapter six—only on steroids. As merchandising dispersion continues to get amped up—through the kind of regional distribution centers Amazon is currently investing in, for example—we will see an even faster product-to-consumer timeline. This may mirror the effect that FedEx brought to the shipping world. If you take onsite product stocking out of the retail store equation, one could imagine state-of-the-art, interactive showrooms that are just that. These venues would intertwine product, brand, information, entertainment, and social media in an entirely new manner more like a tradeshow than a store, but one that is consumer-centric. Once the product selections are made and products purchased, it will be up to the customer when they want them delivered to their homes (uncreated, installed, networked, and demonstrated) in minutes, hours, or days. This is totally consistent with the type of cost-benefit that would further strip unnecessary expense out of the channel, while investing heavily in the front-end customer experience that pays big dividends. One can predict that Amazon could become a key player here. A truly experiential brick-and-mobile concept employing the best MEtail<sup>SM</sup> technology has the capability of delivering a personal, highly customized, and truly omnichannel type of engagement that customers would want to experience, and brands would "pay" to participate in. I will talk more about this, along with the concept of RaveRetail® in chapter eleven.

## RESHAPING THE FOUR P'S OF RETAILING

The brick-and-mobile world will ultimately reshape and reconfigure retail's four Ps: product, packaging, pricing, and promotion. The product itself will become more interactive with extended packaging that will communicate directly with smart devices. Mobile phones will replace loyalty cards while providing a host of personal services. In-store navigation will be smartphone-assisted, guiding every aspect of the shopping experience. Advertising and promotions will be sent directly to the phone in sync with location and brand preference. And self-scanning and self-checkout will be facilitated by mobile payment.

Executing all of this new technology will not happen without bumps in the road. And trust between the retailer or brand and the consumer can be a delicate thing for even the most brand loyal among us. There is great value in personalizing products and services and contextualizing the relationships between the retailer and the customer. But much can be lost if customers believe their personal privacy was compromised along the way. It will become even more important that retailers remain vigilant in the implementation of the new technologies so consumer relationships and trust

> **The timely convergence of these new technologies that complement social media, e-commerce, and MEtail<sup>SM</sup> should lead to a new way of interacting with products in a manner that is highly personal and individualized as well as fast and efficient.**

built over time are not affected.

## ASSISTED DISCOVERY

If not handled properly, all of these wonderful cyber tools may also yield a very expensive flash in the pan (remember Sony's Metreon?) if the basic fundamentals of customer engagement are not heeded. Through the years we have learned a lot about moving customers from passive observers to engaged participants in this wonderful world of retail design. Along the way we have distilled some fundamentals under the heading of assisted discovery. We have also worked to create some tools to facilitate implementation of these fundamentals. Assisted discovery acknowledges the fact that consumers approach products and purchase decisions from different points of view. They may have vast differences in their brand and product knowledge. They may be at very different places in the purchasing cycle. They may have different comfort levels with digital technology. Another factor at play is that different customers have varying desires for salesperson engagement, which is also likely to change when they are empowered to readily decode the store and begin the editing process. Add to this that in-store sales personnel have varying knowledge levels and communications skills, and generally move around a lot in the company (departments, roles, etc.). In addition, during the all-important peak times in most stores, the ratio of salespersons to customers diminishes greatly (except, it would seem, at Apple).

With all these factors in mind, along with the designer's overriding purpose of creating a predictable outcome for the retailer, there needs to be a map of sorts that guides the customer through both the emotional and intellectual aspects of the sale. The term "map" should be thought of not in literal terms but in more subliminal terms—a map that helps decipher the layout, design, product adjacencies, and wayfinding, which are all part of designing a user- and brand-friendly space. This assisted-discovery path involves the intuitive layout and wayfinding, editing brands, and product offerings. It facilitates making a choice and expedites the sale, and the result is an experiential sequence dynamic from beginning to end. Whether these fundamentals employ display and selling systems that utilize old-school analog or new-school digital technologies (or both) their application needs to meet the specific objectives of assisted discovery. Factoring into assisted discovery is the element of consumer empowerment, which is a very important part of today's retail equation. We have already discussed how the convergence of such trends as the downsizing of America, distrust in once-trusted institutions, and the Internet have all conspired to make the consumer a more self-reliant decision maker around purchases both big and small. When we sit down to dinner and are interrupted by three sales calls on the landline no one answers anyway, we no longer wish to be "sold" anything. Instead we now wish to be empowered to purchase. With this idea in mind, today's retail environments work to be responsive through the application of assisted discovery, which plays out in four parts.

**When we sit down to dinner and are interrupted by three sales calls on the landline no one answers anyway, we no longer wish to be "sold" anything.**

## LEPSync

There is a combination of emotional and intellectual components in decision making and the assisted-discovery method takes both into consideration. It is also important to point out that for the formula to work there are many other elements in the store's design that must be dealt with before these tools are employed. It is essential that the layout be intuitive, enabling the customer to quickly decode the store. This requires clear pathways and departmental locations, as well as logical product adjacencies. Humans innately associate order with comfort, and chaos with discomfort.

The more quickly we can scan and understand an environment the more readily we are likely to move from being passive to becoming engaged. The blueprint that we use to assist the customer through the assisted discovery "funnel" includes four key aspects of way-finding and choicemaking which are: lifestyle and brand imagery, empowerment content, product information, and shelf-facing labels (LEPSync). This information quartet uses multiple types of content ranging from large-scale graphics down to the most granular of product/pricing information. It may also blend analog and digital media depending on budgets, product categories, and core customer.

**Lifestyle/Brand-** This is the graphic hook that is usually large in scale and implies distance readership. Think of this as the widest part of the funnel. Depending on the nature of the retailer, whether in a single brand or multibrand environment, for this category of graphics to be effective it must be highly readable and recognizable. This graphic content will set the stage from a lifestyle point of view, help in the brand positioning, or both.

**Empowerment-** This is where product category and choice making begins to come into play as the funnel begins to narrow. Different types of graphics, usually verbal and visual, will assist the customer with the first level of product editing. In a single-brand store (e.g., Apple) this is very straightforward, in the more common multibrand environment, the process becomes more complex. One of the brand-management issues in either big-box or department store formats is how to handle the duality of the primary brand (Macy's, Penney's, or Best Buy) against the plethora of suppliers' cobrands (Calvin Klein, Ralph Lauren, Sony, etc.) that are all vying for attention within the multibrand space. Too often this becomes a visual fight that ends up undermining both the primary and cobrands. The entire department store industry has lost many of its legendary store brands due in part to the lack of differentiated offerings. Many of them succumbed to the growing strength of the national name brands and cookie-cutter arrangements of their ubiquitous branded shops. This ultimately contributed to losing their own unique identities, many of which were generations in the making. Some of the more successful department store operators have had success with organizing their stores more around customer lifestyle, which is more in tune with what the customer is thinking. Target is one of the few general merchandising retailers that has done a good job incorporating national brands with their popular proprietary brands while keeping the Target brand clearly dominant. Their way-finding hierarchy facilitates both category identification and the process of making a choice without letting cobrands become too dominant.

**Product Information-** Moving down the funnel to the more granular information is where the customer begins the more in-depth process of editing offerings. At this level the features and benefits of a particular brand or product come into play. One of the retailers' objectives is to offer topline information that assists the customer in eliminating the products and brands that appeal least, and begin comparing and contrasting the range of items that meet their particular needs related to function, price point, and other essential criteria. This is where some of the emerging digital technologies begin to shine. While the topline product information may appear in conventional analog format, there are infinite opportunities for the retailer and the manufacturer to incorporate QR codes, RFID, NFC, and other technologies to enable the customer to drill down to more in-depth information. This may employ the customer's

> The blueprint that we use to assist the customer through the assisted discovery "funnel" includes four key aspects of wayfinding and choicemaking.

smartphones, as well as integrated iPads, kiosks, and other digital enablers to help the customer through the editing process. This also becomes an important in-store omnichannel link.

The other key factor driving the appropriate use of these technologies is that they complement both unassisted and assisted selling. In today's fluctuating marketplace, sales personnel cannot possibly keep up with every manufacturer, every product line, and the ever-changing product offerings in the store. Add to this the fact that the work life-span of any given salesperson can be measured in hours and days, as opposed to months and years. Also, the speed with which product technologies change in almost any industry make it easy to see why the stores must work harder at the tasks traditional sales personnel used to be expected to do. With the proper implementation of both old signage formats and new tech toys, the salespeople can interface with a more informed customer, who is likely to have formed questions specific to their needs. The result is that salespeople spend more productive time with customers while conversion rates increase. Sales associates become order takers and sales closers, while the store systems assist the customer through making a choice, which is what today's shoppers are looking for anyway.

**Shelf-Facing Labels-** The bottom of the funnel or the spout is the shelf-facing label. As these items start getting smarter, they too may provide the customer with a myriad of helpful and useful information to create increased value for the in-store experience, as well as saving the customer valuable time and money. Besides the obvious list price of the products, we are likely to see new aspects of dynamic pricing take place that begin to reflect the entire value chain converging to benefit the consumer and the retailer/manufacturer. Factoring in the customer's smartphone-stored coupons and loyalty status, the dynamic price seen on the smart label or the customer's smartphone display may also reflect supply-chain dynamics. Too much of a particular product in the channel may momentarily drive the cost down, whereas weather-related interruptions or other scarcities will raise the price and this may occur without human intervention. You can be assured that these kinds of tactics will become a part of the in-store retailer's arsenal as they battle the continuing showrooming phenomenon.

**The other key factor driving the appropriate use of these technologies is that they complement both unassisted and assisted selling.**

# CHAPTER
# TEN

# FADS, TRENDS,
# AND PRETENDERS

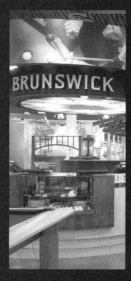

Frequently, what may begin initially as a transitory fad can eventually work itself deeper into the psyche of the masses to become a bona fide trend. On rare occasions that trend can grow deep enough roots to transcend from trend to lifestyle. Such has been the case, in my opinion, of the wellness movement over the past forty years. The term "wellness" can first be credited to Dr. Halbert L. Dunn. Born in New Paris, Ohio, in 1896, he attended medical school at the University of Minnesota and did his fellowship at the Mayo Clinic in Rochester, Minnesota. In 1929, Dr. Dunn became the first biostatistician hired by the Mayo Clinic, and he spent the next thirty years working in the area of vital and health statistics. It wasn't until the late 1950s that Dr. Dunn began lecturing on the concept of wellness, which became the basis of his book *High Level Wellness*, published in 1961. By the mid-1970s the ideas stemming from Dr. Dunn's book were beginning to bloom with the emergence of the holistic health movement. In 1975, Dr. John Travis opened what is believed to be the first wellness center in the U.S. in Mill Valley, California.

While the term *wellness* does not appear to have a universally accepted definition from a strictly medical point of view, it implies freedom from disease. Wellness has also become associated with a balance of mind, body, and spirit that produces an overall sense of well-being. Its tenets often involve a reintroduction or integration of alternative therapies many thousands of years old. Until recently these therapies were discredited by the modern practice of Western medicine, which tends to focus more on curative rather than preventative medicine. Many of today's medical schools and practitioners have opened the door to a more blended approach that includes treatments and therapies long associated with Eastern medicine, including meditation, acupuncture, massage, and even herbal therapies. This has stimulated an evolution in thinking within popular culture regarding the medical profession. Attitudes have moved away from the strict notion that many of our parents had of the doctor's sole responsibility being to heal disease. This has morphed into a more interactive, doctor-patient dynamic around preventative medicine, and maintaining a state of wellness through a better diet, more exercise, and achieving a healthy overall balance in one's life. There have also been many faith-based programs that have offered a spiritual approach to family, life, and relationships felt to be essential in achieving balance and fulfillment. This is in contrast to the popular secular promoters of wellness such as Drs. Andrew Weil, Deepak Chopra, and Mehmet Oz, whose work has had a profound impact on a society in search of a higher level of spirituality and meaning, not to mention selling many books.

## MORE OR LESS

It's certainly been recognized that many of the health challenges and maladies that twentieth-century, middle-class Americans suffer from are a result of our abundance, and the relentless pursuit thereof. Our bodies, which were designed for movement and foraging for food, forage no more and eat too much. And the aftereffects of our hyperconsumption and squandering of the earth's resources have left us with an environment where too often the air, water, and land are too toxic to breathe, drink, or grow our food. As a society, we are also coming to terms with the unintended consequences that many of the chemicals, additives, and preservatives we have so liberally injected into our livestock, infused into our soils, and packaged into our foods are making us sick. Growing up in suburban Milwaukee in the midcentury we rarely encountered kids with food sensitivities or allergies. Nowadays, school kids have become very aware of which of their friends can't eat nuts, dairy, wheat, berries, gluten, soy, or fish for fear of a reaction.

It's certainly been recognized that many of the health challenges and maladies that twentieth-century, middle-class Americans suffer from are a result of our abundance, and the relentless pursuit thereof.

One can only imagine that our bodies are reacting to the chemical assault on our environment and the alteration of our foods over the past millennium, a multipronged assault our immune systems have not been able to handle.

As one of the unfortunate canaries in the coal mine with multiple chemical sensitivities, I've learned (the hard way) which "everyday products" and "ordinary inhalants" will send me gasping for air or start me down the rapid spiral toward a chronic fatigue episode. These include cigarette smoke, perfumes, paints, pesticides, molds, dust, and even common household cleaners. I've learned which aisles in the grocery store to avoid (cleaning supplies), which segment of the department store to bypass (perfume), and which section of the garden store to circumnavigate (pesticides) for fear of even momentary exposure to the bags, boxes, or bottles of the offending products. I even found myself in the luxurious yet unfortunate situation of having to return a brand-new European performance sedan with less than 1,000 miles due to the off-gassing of VOCs (volatile organic compounds) being so overwhelming that driving the gorgeous thing was making me very sick. So much for the wonderful "new car smell."

## WHOLE NEW APPROACH

As the public's awareness of the effects of synthetic pesticides, chemical fertilizers, and additives have increased, the movement toward organics and the demand for safer, healthier foods has also been growing. While organic farming dates back to the 1940s, in response to the industrialization of agriculture, it did not begin to affect consumer buying habits until the late 1970s or early 1980s. Even then it was only a small emerging movement, but what had been previously dismissed as a cult-like fad by many was taking root in America. And surprisingly, the most significant player in this burgeoning trend came not from progressives in California, or from East Coast intellectuals, but from deep in the heart of Texas.

Two college dropouts, John Mackey and his girlfriend Renee Lawson, met while living in a vegetarian housing co-op in Austin Texas. In 1978, after raising $45,000, the two started a health food store called Safer Way (a spoof on Safeway Foods). Two years later, after merging with Clarksville Natural Grocery, the business was re-named Whole Foods. They grew the concept through acquisitions and by savvy merchandising and marketing. As the concept of nat-ural and organic gained broader acceptance, they honed their skill at creating retail stores that exuded visual appeal through im-peccable merchandising and product display. Fresh produce was being merchandised more like jewelry at Tiffany's than the fruits and vegetables stocked at chain grocers or typical health food co-ops. They recognized that customers were willing to pay a premium to get products that were locally sourced, certified organ-ic, and free of many of the additives and preservatives that were contained in far too many of the products at most of the nation's major grocery chains.

In 1997, the company introduced its 365 Everyday Value pri-vate label brand, one that has been lauded as one of the most successful, high-value private label offerings in the business. That line has become the benchmark and template for similar lines and private label offerings by many of the premium grocery retailers nationwide. In 1999, the company opened its hundredth store and that same year the company launched WholeFoods.com, which was ultimately replaced by WholePeople.com. In 2009, with the increasing controversy over genetically engineered foods—more often referred to as products containing genetically modified or-ganisms (GMOs)—Whole Foods took an industry lead by putting its 365 Everyday Value brand through non-GMO verification. In ad-

Two college drop-outs, John Mackey and his girlfriend Renee Lawson, met while living in a vegetarian hous-ing co-op in Austin Texas. In 1978, after raising $45,000, the two started a health food store called Safer Way.

dition, they have set a 2018 deadline whereby all of the products in their North American stores must be labeled to indicate whether they contain any GMOs, a move that effectively forces their entire supply chain to comply. With this action Whole Foods will become the first national grocery chain to establish full GMO disclosure and product transparency.

By 2013, the chain had grown to 350 stores, with revenues closing in on twelve billion dollars. While their growth and history have not been without controversy, they have received their fair share of recognitions, including a variety of Environmental Protection Agency's Green Power Awards in 2004, 2005, 2006, 2007, 2010, and 2012. In addition, the company has made a significant attempt to source products from local growers that can meet their rigid standards. Some of their markets employ what the company calls a forager, whose job it is to source local products for specific stores. This not only supports small organic farmers in an area but also meets specific customer demands and regional taste preferences. In the U.S., no single retailer has had either the impact or success that Whole Foods has had in bringing a small niche consumer movement to a nationwide trend, which has changed the face of grocery stores throughout most of the country.

What can't be readily measured is the degree to which their best-in-category brand has changed the entire food retailing landscape while increasing the public's awareness and desire for healthier foods. One such demonstration of the rising health food tide lifting all boats is with Target's recent decision to enter the crowded waters. In 2013, Target introduced its Simply Balanced brand, which includes about 250 SKUs of products that are free of artificial colors, flavors, and preservatives and about 40 percent of that line is USDA-certified organic. The bigger impact can be seen across the entire grocery spectrum from large-scale commodity players to the upscale specialties. Categories featuring organics and healthier offerings have been among the key growth areas across the board, in response to the public's increasing awareness due in part to the Whole Foods effect.

## KARMIC COINCIDENCES

In 1986, SteinDesign was busy balancing some new regional and national clients with local independent start-ups. While both the design fees and the construction budgets for these smaller local projects were rather tight, they often allowed us design freedom that some of the larger projects did not. I also enjoyed the mentoring role that came with the younger retail entrepreneurs. One such start-up was a small fitness/wellness concept in the St. Anthony on Main redevelopment where we had already completed several projects. While fitness equipment stores were not uncommon, one that devoted a portion of the store to personal fitness training and lifestyle coaching definitely was. Our client Cari Johnson was a former dancer whose career was cut short by a spinal injury. Rather than submitting to surgery with only a 50 percent chance of improvement, Cari became devoted to finding an alternative path out of her constant pain. That path led her to a Japanese doctor trained in chiropractic, acupuncture, and shiatsu massage. With treatments and visualizations Cari was soon pain-free and was now motivated to share what she learned and experienced with others. She received a degree in exercise and dance physiology, as well as training at the Shiatsu Massage School of California, which became transformational for her. She moved from California to Minneapolis in 1985 and felt her pathway to helping others might be through a wellness concept that mixed retail and service.

We designed a dynamite store for Cari called 4Fitness, which was as lean in concept as the sculptured bodies being promised.

To meet the tight budget we borrowed a techie design aesthetic from the fitness equipment itself, to keep the overall branded environment theme-appropriate. The concept featured a destination coaching and consultation area in the back of the store. Privacy to the individual consulting stations was accomplished through the closure of giant, bright blue, eight-foot-tall by three-foot-wide panels that were interconnected, allowing them to open and close in tandem. We were very proud to have the project become the recipient of a 1986 Minnesota Institute of Architects Interior Design Award (juried by Ray Eames). Most important, 4Fitness had gotten Cari started on her path to strengthening and healing others, but this was only the beginning of what was yet to come in her career.

## READING THE SIGNS

In 1989, I was boarding a westbound plane on my way to a project in California, and I found Cari coincidently assigned to the seat next to mine. She was on her way to Asia, where she had arranged an apprenticeship with a master/doctor of shiatsu, acupuncture, and herbal medicine. On the flight to the West Coast we got caught up. She talked about her excitement in taking her career to the next level, and I talked to her about my challenges in managing my CFS, she suggested that I give Shiatsu a try. After a year of intense study in Japan, Cari had received her teacher's blessing to teach Shiatsu in the U.S. Traditional Japanese bodywork or Shiatsu is thought to be over 5,000 years old, though there is speculation that the treatment's origins stem from India and may actually be considerably older. The technique combines two forms of Asian bodywork and is based on principles of traditional Chinese medicine. It uses the thumbs, fingers, and palms to stimulate key pressure points on the surface of the skin to promote the body's natural, self-healing abilities, and it strengthens the flow and balance of *qi* (pronounced *chi*), meaning vital energy. In contrast to the more popular forms of Swedish massage, which is performed when the client is au naturel, Shiatsu is performed on fully clothed clients.

Cari's return to the States coincided ironically with my prolonged and very deep CFS episode in 1991. At the time, she was practicing and teaching from her home and I made an appointment for some bodywork. While I had been receiving occasional massages for years to manage stress, I wanted her insights about how Shiatsu might bring me back to my wellness baseline and help me manage my episodes. My first visit started in what seemed to be a rather odd, but soon familiar routine. As is the case with many forms of Eastern medicine, Shiatsu practitioners learn to "read" pulses, but not in a way that a Western doctor would. Because Eastern medicine focuses on strengthening the body's own ability to heal, part of the training has to do with assessing imbalance in energy (qi) and determining the origins of the imbalance. Students are trained to read and understand the complex nature of the body's pulse—the deeper and more subtle rhythms that relate to energy levels and various organ imbalances that are thought to be the origin of "dis-ease." This becomes the road map that guides the practitioner and gives him or her insight as to where to concentrate treatments to regain balance. To our Western "take two of these, and call me in the morning" sensibilities this sounds pretty strange, but it works. My initial visits were focused on getting me back to some semblance of normal, but in time I learned that with regular treatments I was able to prolong my periods of well-being and have shallower and shorter CFS episodes when they did occur.

In 1992, Cari formally founded the Minnesota Center for Shiatsu Study (MCSS), which opened with twelve students. In 2001, MCSS merged with Northern Lights School of Massage Therapy,

**I learned that with regular treatments I was able to prolong my periods of well-being and have shallower and shorter CFS episodes when they did occur.**

offering instruction in both Asian and Western massage therapy, and changed its name to CenterPoint Message & Shiatsu Therapy School & Clinic. Under Cari's and partner Jackson Petersburg's direction, CenterPoint has become one of the leading schools in the Upper Midwest and has trained thousands of students to become practitioners of massage, Shiatsu, and the healing arts. Besides CenterPoint's devotion to education and training, they have become the go-to source for corporations and educational institutions in the Upper Midwest who understand the health benefits of Shiatsu massage and the value of healthy and productive employees. One such corporation that has availed themselves of CenterPoint's services was none other than Tires Plus stores.

## THE LARGER PLAN

My own personal pursuits of wellness have been a long and winding road, to paraphrase a Beatles' song. I have learned that managing a chronic condition is a continuum of doing many small things with consistency to remain relatively symptom free with a reasonably high energy level. It affects virtually everything I do— what and when I eat, how much I sleep, how much exercise I get, my daily meditation, and Shiatsu massage twice a month. I've learned the importance of a meaningful and fulfilling career, a positive attitude, and the support of a loving family. I've also learned that maintaining an openness to "the infinite possibilities of the universe," as Dr. Chopra writes, and learning to "read the signs" (like finding Cari Johnson in the airplane seat next to mine) are also valuable strategies. This mindfulness and paying attention can be potent and beneficial as we deal with the myriad of challenges that life has in store for all of us.

Through another series of cosmic coincidences, Cheryl and I found ourselves invited to the home of Tires Plus founder Tom

Gegax in the late summer of 1998. Tom was on the board of the Chopra Center for Wellbeing in La Jolla, California, and had become a close friend of Deepak Chopra. Dr. Chopra was in Minneapolis to deliver an address and Tom was hosting a reception for friends and acquaintances in honor of the occasion. By then, I had probably read a half dozen of Dr. Chopra's books devoted to holistic health and alternative medicine. As the author of over seventy books, including twenty-one *New York Times* best sellers, Dr. Chopra is one of the most prolific authors of our time, selling over twenty million books translated into some thirty-five different languages worldwide. The opportunity to meet him was more than a little exciting. While standing in a reception line holding onto a glass of wine, I was contemplating what great insights might come out of this karmic event. As I was getting closer to him, my mind was spinning, and my fingers holding the wine stem were getting a bit moist. I introduced myself, and told him I was a fan (like he had never heard that before). And out of nowhere, I asked whether he thought it was strange that the recent passing of two significant female role models (Mother Teresa and Princess Diana) should happen mere hours apart. (Talk about obtuse.) He looked straight at me and in his soft and gentle voice uttered, "There are no accidents." Point taken.

**He looked straight at me and in his soft and gentle voice uttered, "There are no accidents." Point taken.**

## CHANGE OF STATE

By the early 1990s, the Baby Boomers were beginning to confront middle age, while their parents were entering the golden years and feeling the physical effects of the natural aging process. Along with the public's evolving attitudes toward wellness, there were changing attitudes around aging brought about by longer life-spans, improved health care, and a belief that the last phase in one's life could be about new beginnings rather than endings. In 1993, my firm received a visit from a woman named Margaret Everist who had a history of working in banking and finance, and who said she wanted to "get into retail." She had been negotiating for a small space at Southdale Center, and it was on the strength of her concept that Southdale was even talking to a retailing neophyte.

Because Margaret had no previous retail experience, the leasing department required that she present a fully developed concept before they would commit to a lease. They recommended that she visit us to get packaged, as we often referred to it. This included concept development, layout, and sketch rendering. On her initial visit, she brought a box of products that reflected her concept; she placed it carefully on our glass conference table and began to tell her story. Her presentation of each of the oddly shaped, plastic, metal, and wooden items gave no clue as to the nature or intent of her new retailing endeavor. When all the items had been placed neatly in front of us she described them as "aids for daily living." This was a term that was completely new to me and the others in the room. She went on to explain that the products were all designed to address the common conditions and physical limitations that are often associated with aging. They included tap turners, special bottle openers, illuminated magnifying glasses, specialty utensils, clocks, playing cards with oversized numbers, and much more.

While some of these products were available at pharmacies, they were generally found on metal gondolas (next to the metal crutches), were poorly merchandised, and were often seen as institutional, with an overwhelmingly negative overtone. To our client's knowledge there had not been a specialty store anywhere in the country that had given proper attention to the branding and positioning of this evolving product niche. She was intent on launching the first concept of its kind to deal with these unique items in a manner that was positive and life-affirming. I liked the premise. I had recently read a number of articles on the evolving attitudes toward aging, and I knew that this was an important part of the wellness movement.

The ergonomic, user-friendly designs of the products invited us to reinvent the category around positive imagery, warmth, and empowerment. Ms. Everist felt that all of these values were as important as the products that she planned on selling. In addition, because many customers might not be able to identify many of the objects, let alone understand how they work, we knew that we were going to have a unique merchandising challenge ahead of us. Another challenge, besides the relatively unfamiliar product category, was our client's lack of retail experience. By this time in the firm's dozen-or-so-year history we had developed a reputation for added value based on our expertise in brand building and our results-driven approach to design. So it wasn't unusual for leasing agents or mall tenant coordinators to recommend us based on our mentoring ability and our design skills, and I was very proud of that. But with that endorsement came the additional time and labor involved with issues outside of project norms. Again with this project, we had to confront the seemingly omnipresent characteristic of start-ups—a tight budget that factored into every design decision.

As the project got underway and we dug into the product category, it became apparent to us that the store needed to function as much as an interpretive display museum as a store. This would be essential to provide the customer with the topline information that helps to explain the features and benefits of the varied products. It was simply not an option to depend on the manufacturer's packaging to tell the story. This project highlighted the customary interaction between the retail space and the product being displayed, and it was made even more challenging by the miniscule

**To our client's knowledge there had not been a specialty store anywhere in the country that had given proper attention to the branding and positioning of this evolving product niche.**

750-square-foot space. This macro/micro interplay of designing the space and the display systems simultaneously is essential in order to end up with a functional and integrated aesthetic. This is somewhat similar to the exterior/interior balancing act that brings proper form to architecture. Given the role that environmental graphic design would play in assisted discovery, we reached out to our friends at Rubin-Cordaro Designs at the onset of the project so we could conceptualize the graphic and signage system early on. The elements they created would act almost like didactics (explanatory signage) in a museum and aid in empowering the customer. We also brought in a consultant who specialized in geriatric environments to guide us along the way. We referred to her as the "geriatric police."

## WHAT'S IN A NAME?

The store's category "aids for daily living" presented a unique challenge in coming up with a name and graphic identity because HIV/AIDS was very much in the news and on the minds of many Americans. The Academy Award–winning movie *Philadelphia*, starring Tom Hanks and Denzel Washington, and featuring Bruce Springsteen's haunting and memorable title song had come out in 1993. The movie was the first major drama to deal with HIV/AIDS and we were very cognizant about the subject and the shared term (aids/AIDS) during the naming process. To keep the concept life-affirming and positive our team came up with Life Enhancements as the brand name and Bruce Rubin and Jim Cordaro created a very simple, friendly, and inviting brand identity to complement the name. The store had a great launch and created tremendous buzz, but it may have been a bit ahead of its time. Today, two decades later, I rarely get through a capabilities presentation that includes this project where I'm not stopped and questioned by clients who are as intrigued as we were by the thoughtfulness of this concept.

## TAPPING A TREND

The process involved in converting a trend such as wellness into a viable retail concept is a very tricky one. It requires proper timing, clarity of concept, brand building, appropriate product mix, deep pockets, tactical execution, and lots of luck. Even when the best and most successful retailers attempt to leverage what looks to be an untapped market opportunity, it does not always lead to success. Such was the case when Best Buy decided to craft a wellness concept twelve years later in 2005. They understood that there was indeed a void in the marketplace, and that women were the lead decision makers related to purchasing products in the wellness category. They also realized that their Best Buy stores did not appeal to women, and they needed to address this head on when designing a female-friendly retail environment.

After several years of research and untold expenditure, Best Buy, in conjunction with health-care providers Park Nicollet Health Services and Prairiestone Pharmacy, launched EQ Life, a destination health and wellness concept aimed at an upscale female consumer. The concept was clear, the name—not so much. The notion, playing off the idea of adding equilibrium to the lives of many stressed-out, multitasking, female consumers, became too much to explain when the name didn't express it all. Add to that the possible confusion over the concept of emotional intelligence (EQ) or the equestrian magazine of the same name. In February 2005, the 18,000-square foot store prototype opened in Southdale Square in Edina, Minnesota, just a stone's throw from the venerable Southdale. It offered a wide variety of services, including a complete spa and salon, wellness programs, yoga, and Pilates. Also available were nurses and dieticians, a complete pharmacy,

**The process involved in converting a trend such as wellness into a viable retail concept is a very tricky one.**

a Caribou Coffee shop, and even the tech services of the Geek Squad. The 10,000-SKU product mix was even more diversified than the service offerings. They included many health-oriented consumer electronics, exercise equipment, air purifiers, and heart- and blood-pressure-monitoring devices. On top of that they offered makeup consultations, aroma therapy, and other herbal health and wellness consumables. They even threw in portable DVDs, MP3 players, laptops, and cell phones for good measure.

Naturally, I couldn't wait to visit and get a walking-around sense of the concept. It was a bright, attractive, pleasant and female-friendly environment, which spared no expense in its execution. There were lots of able-bodied Qs, as they referred to their sales associates, who according to the promotional information were there to "guide you to sound answers and options to meet your individual needs." After about an hour in the store, I left feeling overwhelmed and a bit confused as to what they were trying to be. It seemed to me as if a viable 5,000-square-foot wellness concept was hidden inside an 18,000-square-foot store, and it was trying to find its way out. I could only imagine that the process must have been overwhelmed by "and let's try this, too" thinking. By April 2006, a little more than a year after opening, Best Buy closed the Southdale Square EQ Life store and sold its majority interest in the brand and two other locations to Mike Marolt, the former Best Buy SVP who had led the effort. The two remaining stores were closed within the year.

## THE DICHOTOMY OF CHOICE

In chapter five, I discuss Costco's use of edited offerings to its tremendous advantage. It's clear that the consumption pendulum has swung from "more is better" to "less is more." Many factors have caused this swing, including time-pressed consumers, decreasing attention spans, plain economics, and the fact that too many choices impedes rather than assists in decision making. One of the industries that learned this during the last twenty years was the paint and decorating industry, in which we had been very much involved beginning in the late 1990s and into the new millennium.

In 1996 we were approached by representatives from Colwell Industries on behalf of Color Guild International, which comprises more than fifty-five independent paint manufacturers and retailers from fourteen different countries. The independent paint and decorating industry was being challenged by the unbridled growth of big-box retail stores like Lowe's and Home Depot. As an industry leader with strong ties to both the independents as well as the big-box players, Colwell asked if we could help their retailers and manufacturers understand how to position their companies in the face of the rapidly changing DIY market space. We were happy to oblige and, as always, we dove in deep and got dirty attempting to learn as much as possible about the industry—from the commodity big-box players to the smaller independent paint and decorating centers who were feeling the most pain from the industry's ongoing transition. Our association and involvement in this category predated the explosion of DIY cable programming, such as HGTV, which has brought the subject of home decorating and home improvement to an even broader consumer audience and made the category more approachable.

A little background is in order. Our client, Colwell Industries, was a privately owned, Minnesota-based supplier and manufacturer of paint chips and other sampling materials to the paint industry in the U.S. and abroad. When you visit any paint and decorating store, many of the little swatches along with the entire color systems were probably supplied by Colwell. In addition, their in-house color consultants help create and update the paint lines for paint

**It's clear that the consumption pendulum has swung from "more is better" to "less is more."**

manufacturers, large and small. The other unique thing about Colwell is that while a significant amount of their products end up in big-box stores, they have been devoted to the success of the many smaller independent paint lines through their leadership and association with Color Guild International. Colwell was preparing us for an opportunity to address the Color Guild Association at an annual meeting in Washington, D.C., in 1996 to discuss general consumer trending and, more specifically, how to deal with the changing retail landscape within their painting and decorating category.

Our research demonstrated a replay of what had been happening over and over in the evolution of retail in the U.S. with the dominance of big-box concepts and their destabilizing effect on the generations-old independent retail channel. The response in the past to this "invasion" was for the independent to try to compete on price rather than to distinguish themselves on service and other higher upmarket values, and the result has usually been a bad outcome. As with most other segments where this story has played out, the strongest of the established players gets better and survives and the weakest perishes, which was exactly what was happening in this sector. Simultaneous to my new assignment was the small but highly significant emergence of a brand- and lifestyle-driven phenomenon that would begin to revolutionize the paint industry, and bring with it the seeds for renewal and re-invention. This emerging trend also suggested a pathway for the independent paint and decorating retailer to differentiate their offerings. And, as is so often the case, these transformational events are either disregarded or misunderstood except by those who know how to read the signs of change.

## RALPH AND MARTHA

It was conventional wisdom within the paint industry that a paint line needed to have something in the area of 1,400 to 1,500 colors to be viable, and that was the case for most of the paint lines currently on the market. In 1995 (a year prior to my being retained by Colwell), Ralph Lauren introduced a lifestyle-oriented line of paint that had about one third the number of colors of the average paint line, and it was priced two to three times higher than the (perceived) comparable paints on the market. Many of the paint-industry insiders thought the idea of a fashion icon selling paint was heresy and that the market would reject the notion out of hand. Plus, as I was told by many members at the Color Guild conference (who seemed to fixate over the chemistry of paint) it certainly wasn't worth the price. My message to the audience was that Ralph Lauren (RL) wasn't selling paint (which is a commodity), he was selling color (which is emotional), and it correspondingly had greater perceived value—hence the price. You could hear a pin drop in the room. I went on to explain how RL was taking a completely different approach to selling paint—one based on the customer's desire to "belong" to the high-value RL brand and lifestyle, which has been carefully and expertly crafted and managed over the years.

This concept was in stark contrast to the industry's preoccupation with chemistry, coverage, and cleanability—all of which are important traits, but not very emotional. I reinforced the notion that the consumer was "programmed" to respond in a positive way to the brilliantly designed and conceived palette along with corresponding lifestyle imagery, which was designed to evoke the aspirational and romantic emotions associated with the RL brand. The palettes were divided into collections that helped the customer focus on choice making with names like Urban Loft, Vintage Masters, Thoroughbred, White Wash, and Island Brights. And in proper RL brand vocabulary, the swatches were presented with the properly coordinated lifestyle imagery that corresponded to

> The response in the past to this "invasion" was for the independent to try to compete on price rather than to distinguish themselves on service and other higher upmarket values, and the result has usually been a bad outcome.

the theme of the palette. The presentation of the line's 532 colors made it infinitely more shoppable than a conventional paint line three times that size. The fact that my audience found all of this brand imagery language so foreign was quite understandable, since even Ralph Lauren had to pitch several paint manufacturers on the concept before one would bite.

The entire Ralph Lauren discussion helped me tee up the idea that the independent or small-chain paint retailer should choose to move upmarket a bit to separate themselves from the commodity big-box players that were here to stay. We talked about focusing on things that engage the customer in the more emotional aspects of style and design in the home, and to use their stores to set the stage for redecoration. I also informed them (much to their surprise) that paint cans don't sell paint, but the proper use of color and decorating ideas do. I referenced the fact that Restoration Hardware was selling tons of the single shade of gray paint that they used in their stores because the customer gets a great feeling for how the color would look in their homes. Another indicator of the power of lifestyle branding in the DIY home-improvement category came when Martha Stewart completed a deal with Sherwin-Williams in 2001 for her new paint line with color offerings that turned out to be even fewer than Ralph Lauren's at a total of 416. In 2010, after a long-running stint in Kmart, a new Martha Stewart Living line of 280 colors replaced the Ralph Lauren paint line at Home Depot. That introduction came along with the brilliant idea of offering (high-margin) eight-ounce paint samples that enabled customers to test the color at home before committing to the purchase.

A final thought on the dichotomy of choice hit home when talking about the rapidly contracting wallpaper industry of which many of the retailers were infinitely aware. I shared my observations of watching customers on a Saturday afternoon (in some of their stores) fighting through book after book of wall covering samples to the point of overwhelming exhaustion. The unbridled depth of choice and complete lack of shoppability had already contributed to the near-demise of this once-vital home décor component.

## COBALT & SCARLET<sup>SM</sup>

Well, despite that fact that I had apparently shaken things up at my first Color Guild speaking gig, I was soon invited back for the following year, but this time I had a larger story to tell. In planning for the 1997 meeting with my friends at Colwell, I devised a strategy that I felt could really prove helpful in attempting to take the independent retailers to the next level. Because many of the upmarket concepts I was suggesting were abstract at best, I proposed having Colwell retain us to design an upscale paint and decoration prototype that would help the smaller players visualize the direction that they might take to remain viable against the big-box stores. After a number of meeting and discussions, we were off and running.

I knew from the start of the venture that the implementation of any concept that we developed was a long shot at best. But I also knew that bringing this segment of the industry closer to the light would continue to position Colwell Industries as a leader—as a visionary company—which I knew was important to them. As our design team began the exercise, I made a number of programming decisions that would guide the design effort. They included the idea that color is at the core of interior design decision making and that paint purchasing is often part of a larger redecorating effort, or it could be. I felt that, by and large, the industry had done a pretty poor job when it came to cross-category selling that was solution-based versus product-based. We felt the opportunity ex-

I referenced the fact that Restoration Hardware was selling tons of the single shade of gray paint that they used in their stores because the customer gets a great feeling for how the color would look in their homes.

isted for a retailer to help the customer make the transition from one product category or "surface" in the home to another within the three or four key product areas that common remodeling projects incorporate. We believed if this was done well, the products could be more readily cross-sold and coordinated like accessorizing in fashion. This also plays into the idea of empowering the consumer to feel smarter and more secure in their interior-design and home-decorating decisions. We knew that this was an issue due to the number of high-color swatches that are chosen by customers and the amount of beige paint that ends up being applied. I felt the industry was primed for an overhaul and that the independents that had the common insight and financial wherewithal could lead the charge. (I am forever an optimist.)

My thinking at the time was influenced by my visits to Home Depot's Expo stores that were launched in 1991 and had grown to around eighteen units by 1997. I knew that consumers were responding to the more upmarket home-decorating environment represented in the Expo concept, and I was also aware that Home Depot had originally planned to open 200 units. I also felt strongly that the stores were too big and overwhelming for many consumers. And while we were focusing on a far more limited offering in the new decorating concept, I felt that our footprint was likely to be less than one-tenth the size of the Expo behemoth. We focused on just four key decorating segments: paint, wall covering, floor, and window treatments. A prominent pathway or "drive aisle" would lead to a large circular color selection area positioned in the center of the store like the hub of a wheel, where the customer could begin their design efforts. We were even planning to offer leading design publications "air rights" to have their monthly magazine covers enlarged to billboard size and displayed above the central color selection area. Customers in the color area would be provided a swatch kit to organize the various color and material samples displayed in each product category.

The rest of the retail area was divided into four large quadrants radiating out from the wheel's hub, corresponding to each of the main product areas. After selecting color samples, the customer begins selecting finish samples in each of the decorating segments to add to the personalized decorating kit. This was seed-planting for future sales or immediate cross-selling, and it gave the customer a sense of a holistic process and ownership in decision making. Naturally, trained personnel would be available to help interpret the customer's needs. We had identified a few selected cobrands in each category to keep choice making manageable and were planning on developing a house brand that would have coordinated offerings in each of the key product categories.

When it came to developing an identity we wanted something that was color-centric and evocative. After a thorough naming process, we chose the name Cobalt & Scarlet[SM], feeling it was memorable, emotional, and covered the color spectrum nicely. We felt that if the concept were executed well across all of the brand touchpoints, then the branded Cobalt & Scarlet[SM] products would have a high perceived value and the corresponding high margins of any well-conceived and properly managed house brand. We developed extensive layouts and digital renderings that were quite crude by today's standards. We packaged the plan's rationale and commentary in beautifully bound books for distribution at presentations. And with the assistance of our friend and past Select Comfort client, Brent Hutton, we even went so far as to write a complete business plan around the concept. We did this to determine the financial viability of the concept and build credence around the brand.

The initial unveiling of Cobalt & Scarlet[SM] was at the Color Guild

**We knew that this was an issue due to the number of high-color swatches that are chosen by customers and the amount of beige paint that ends up being applied.**

International fall meeting in Cancun, Mexico, in 1997. We positioned the concept not as something that we expected members to actually realize, but rather the direction that we believed the industry ought to take in response to the changing retail landscape. We talked about how pieces of the concept could be implemented to help reposition some of the retailers—so their showrooms would become more style driven and customer friendly and less of a commodity-focused environment. Word spread throughout the industry, primed by Colwell's strong connections, and within the year we were invited to share the concept with upper-level executives at Benjamin Moore, Sherwin-Williams, Behr Paint, and Mohawk Carpet. We were also invited to speak at the Painting and Decorating Retailers convention. I had hoped that we would be able to find a partner or partners to launch the concept, and when Chicago-based independent paint and decorating retailer J.C. Licht (a leading member of Color Guild) asked us to present the concept in Chicago, we had renewed hope of its realization. This seemed even more of a possibility when we were taken to a site they had in mind for Cobalt & Scarlet$^{SM}$, but ultimately, it was not to be.

The entire experience over the course of nearly three years was challenging and very rewarding. While all of our efforts and time spent far exceeded the fees Colwell paid us, we got in front of many industry leaders and prospective clients, which in time did pay off in the form of other project opportunities.

## COMING BACK HOME

As I outline in chapter four, by early 2001 Brunswick Billiards was starting to have great success with the Brunswick Pavilion concept that we had helped launch. The early adopters were seeing impressive year-over-year increases and new dealers were buying into the program. By then I had met enough of the dealers and been in enough of their stores to know that even with a decent-looking, store-in-store concept there were many other factors that were negatively impacting sales and undermining the overall brand and customer experience. Because the margins in the billiard business were traditionally so good, many of the dealers were making decent money selling tables out of stores that were, shall we say, subpar. Generally speaking, little was being spent on tenant improvement, product display was largely an afterthought, and many of the locations could only be described as "destination" at best. As I've mentioned before, my dad described locations like this as a "second story above a vacant lot." One of the big issues that further cut into sales was the fact that many of the dealers, as previously mentioned, believed they needed to have three, four, or more different billiard brands to meet a customer's needs. This left Brunswick sharing space with lesser-known brands, or worse than that, the iconic brand became the calling card only to have the retailer end up selling the customer a cheaper product.

Around this time John Stransky, the president of Brunswick Billiards, and I were on one of our numerous visits to potential Pavilion candidates when during a lunch break I broached the subject of creating a standalone Brunswick branded store. First, it could be used both as a test concept to prove the viability of a single-brand store as well as a more highly evolved home entertainment concept incorporating a best-in-class product mix and merchandising techniques. Second, it would present a unique opportunity to leverage the rich Brunswick heritage while controlling the entire customer experience. I was confident that by creating an entire brand-centric destination we could dispel the belief that a dealership needed to show competing brands to give the customer the necessary selection and price points. After my well-prepared pitch, John smiled and admitted that it was something that he and his people had talked about before, but he didn't feel that it would be an easy sell to the corporate higher-ups at Brunswick Corporation. Brunswick had been stung some years prior when they ended up owning a retail chain after one of their dealers got severely upside down, and they did not want to repeat that experience. Since I am not one to readily take no for an answer, I asked if he minded my spending some of my own time contemplating the opportunity, and he was fine with that. So, contemplate I did.

Actually, that contemplation soon morphed into a full-blown business plan, which pretty much consumed the next six months. I was confident that with the proper strategic planning and tactical implementation we would be able to create the defining brand in the industry. This included writing a comprehensive business plan for a Brunswick home entertainment center along with a financial pro forma, assisted once again by Brent Hutton. The planning document covered demographics, an industry overview, strategic opportunity, plan implementation, executive team, and the numbers. We took on the prospective product mix, ideal store size, strategic locations for initial and subsequent stores, as well as a financial overview including operational expenses and expected revenues. We even went so far as to do preliminary naming and graphic identity. My intention was to clearly define the opportunity and illustrate the process of its realization. I was a man on a mission.

There was nothing particularly radical about the concept, except that it was intended to be very Brunswick brand-centric and empowering for the consumer with equal appeal to both men and women. While billiards was clearly the focus, we intended to engineer the cross-selling of many of the furnishings and accessories that complement an entertainment room, family room, or den. One of my criticisms in visiting many of the channel retailers was that they displayed too many product SKUs in a category and never very well. This inhibited rather than enhanced the process of making a choice. In addition, few of the competitors in the industry displayed furnishings and accessories in ways that were compelling or stylish.

We knew that even if Brunswick corporate liked the concept and rationale, as manufacturers they didn't have the retail operational expertise to launch and operate such a concept. By this time I had Hutton intrigued enough by the concept that I suggested that with his decades of experience in opening and running hundreds of retail stores for Tandy Corporation and Select Comfort that he had the operational skills and credibility John Stransky would need to sell corporate on the concept. In July 2001, I met with Stransky and presented the completed package along with Brent Hutton's credentials. John seemed impressed by the entire effort and naturally needed to digest the package before presenting it to his corporate peers. In late August we were given a go-ahead to move to the next level of discussions and planning.

## A MOST MEMORABLE MEETING

The next step was to get Brent and John together for a face-to-face meeting, which was planned for the afternoon of September 11, 2001, at the Brunswick Billiards headquarters in Bristol, Wisconsin. Brent and I planned on flying into Chicago's Midway Airport and driving to Bristol for a midafternoon meeting. My flight was scheduled to land a little before 8:00 a.m. Chicago time. As soon as my phone went live I had a message from Brent, already on the ground, that one of New York's World Trade Center towers had been hit by an airplane. By the time I deplaned at the arrival gate people were huddled around monitors trying to understand what had transpired in Lower Manhattan. I got as close as I could to a

One of my criticisms in visiting many of the channel retailers was that they displayed too many product SKUs in a category and never very well.

monitor and picked up on the chatter among other horrified travelers when we were all shocked to see a second aircraft disappear behind the second tower and a horrific explosion. By the time I met up with Brent, the news was spreading that the airport was going to shut down. Huge lines were beginning to form, in and around the car rental areas, and attempts to get through to any of the rental agencies by cell phone were futile. Brent had the presence of mind to use one of the many vacant pay phones to secure probably the last available rental car to get us on the road for our hour drive to Bristol. We listened to the car radio on the road as the magnitude of the tragic and mind-boggling events in New York City and Washington, D.C. were unfolding.

Our meeting in John's office was nothing like I had envisioned or planned over that past six months since the lunch when I first bounced the idea off of him. Naturally, the mood was somber because we were all concerned for everything and everybody near the World Trade Center and the Pentagon. The last thing any of us could get our heads around was a new business venture at what appeared to be one of the darkest moments in modern American history. And yet, even though we were all transfixed on what we all knew was likely to be a watershed moment, I couldn't help but feel that one of the likely outcomes of the horror would be the drawing together of families and the reassessment of the things that truly mattered in life. I shared those thoughts with my two friends and business associates, and they agreed with my observations.

Two years and twelve days after that horrific event, the Brunswick Home & Billiard prototype store opened in Wilmette, Illinois, an upscale, North Shore suburb of Chicago. The effort represented the most intense and rewarding planning, design, product research, location assessment, and prototype build-out of my career. Our small design team included Curt Lund, Angela Ford, and Jeremiah Albrecht. They assisted Brent and his staff (headed by Steve de Alcala) in developing the national retail prototype. There was a lot at stake. We were more emotionally invested and had assumed a broader sense of project involvement and oversight than at any time in my professional past. Besides being responsible for the concept and the retail design, our team oversaw naming, graphic identity, product categories, product research and purchasing, location assessment, as well as construction supervision and visual merchandising. We attended furniture markets in both High Point, North Carolina, and Chicago, and we established the style vocabulary for the range of the products that would complement the various billiard table styles. We even went so far as to have our friends at Chicago paint retailer J.C. Licht print and co-brand color swatches of the paint colors that we used on the walls of the store's product vignettes. This small but valuable style gesture enabled the customer to take the color swatch back to any of the J.C. Licht stores in the greater Chicago area and have the paint mixed for them.

The store was a success from opening, and within a matter of six months it had become the highest-volume Brunswick Billiards retailer in the country. The store was used to share best practices with the legions of Brunswick retailers throughout the country and it appeared in the February 2004 issue of *Visual Merchandising and Store Display* (VM&SD). In 2005, Tom Gegax's best-selling *Big Book of Small Business* featured an account of my (initially unfunded) efforts to help a friend and business associate, John Stransky, make a case for a concept whose time had come and my going beyond the realm of the expected to move an iconic American brand to the next level.

The store was used to share best practices with the legions of Brunswick retailers throughout the country and it appeared in the February 2004 issue of *Visual Merchandising and Store Display* (VM&SD).

## WHERE AMERICA USED TO SHOP

We've watched popular brands ebb and flow in the marketplace, affected by changing consumer trends, market innovation, and corporate leadership. Once the Stein twins sold the successful Pill & Puff chain to a New York–based investment group back in the late 1970s, things moved in a very different direction from the vision of its founders. The brand became a low priority and finding ways of generating higher store sales were the investment group's core objectives. It appeared that these short-term objectives were at the expense of the concept's purity. In less than half of the short twelve years that it took to build the chain it was neutered and destroyed. I'm sure it was a hard thing for the twins to watch. A like-minded buyer could well have taken the chain from its tiny Milwaukee roots to regional or national prominence, but that was not to be.

There is a similar but far more meaningful and historic story playing out in America today as one of the most venerable and enduring retail brands of the twentieth century is succumbing to a painful deconstruction at the hands of a profiteer. Richard Warren Sears and Alvah Curtis Roebuck might well have dreamed that their retailing phenomenon that started back in 1893 as a mail-order catalog would grow to become the country's biggest retailer by the early 1980s, and this was indeed the case. What would have been less imaginable for these two pioneers would be to have their company's brilliant achievements, brand notoriety, and financial assets devolve rather precipitously, as has been the case in recent years. And worse yet, is to have the company appear to so many retail industry onlookers as having morphed from a retail behemoth to a kind of hedge fund for a wealthy investor. I'm certainly not smart enough to understand all the ins and outs and ups and downs that have taken Sears from where it was three decades ago at its zenith to where it is today. I'm sure that the growth and success of many of the general merchandising competitors like Target, Walmart, Kohl's, and J.C. Penney's have had had an impact. Combine that with the overall contraction of the department store category and the drop in traffic at the malls where most of their stores are located, and the result is that it has been hard sledding in recent years for Sears. But there has also been a lot of denial and half-baked attempts to prop up the old girl. What has also been widely recognized by the retail gurus and market observers goes back to the fundamentals that we touched on earlier in the book and the point my dad made over and over at the kitchen table: Retailer, know thyself!

Like many retailers in this country, in its phenomenal history Sears has excelled in some pursuits, such as selling hard goods, and fallen short in others, such as the "softer side." In fact, where they have succeeded they have done so at a very high level. The Kenmore, Craftsman, and DieHard brands attained the kind of brand-value equity and customer loyalty that few brands have reached and sustained. I would also argue that the positive attributes of those individual brands probably exceed the Sears brand in the minds of the general public, which does not happen very often. For some years there has been a belief that Sears still could reposition the brand around its strengths and become viable (and profitable) once again. It would, however, require some very strategic thinking and painstaking tactical execution. Hundreds of stores would need to be closed and/or downsized, plus hundreds of millions of dollars would have to be spent on repositioning. This could result in a smaller and more highly focused company, one that could once again become an industry leader that provides goods and services people want and need. And a department store no more.

> There is a similar but far more meaningful and historic story playing out in America today as one of the most venerable and enduring retail brands of the twentieth century is succumbing to a painful deconstruction at the hands of a profiteer.

The good news is that, in my opinion, trending is on their side. As global warming continues to affect the severity and frequency of storms, which are having an impact on virtually all of the country, there will be greater interest across a broader spectrum of people to manage this new reality and invest in protecting their homes and property—we might call it *survivalist lite.* There are a whole host of products and services that Sears could promote by leveraging its Craftsman brand in this arena. These include both preventative and reparation products and services. Sears could be taking a leading role in energy conservation and renewable energy technology including monitoring and alternative energy retrofit (wind, solar). There is a strong nationalistic leaning toward U.S. brands and homeland innovation that Sears could take advantage of through its Kenmore, DieHard, and Craftsman brands in the repositioning process.

Sears's ability to "own" the home appliance business should have made Best Buy's recent move into this sector more difficult than it has been. Sears's depth, breadth, and brand equity in Kenmore should make them the undisputed, go-to retailer when it comes to home appliances. This also opens the door to the fertile ground around the home services sector that currently exists. We can also anticipate new service offerings to the aging population in response to the strong desire that people have to remain in their homes beyond their ability to perform some of the necessary upkeep and maintenance. Sears would be a trusted name associated with economical and professional repair services that would allow the aging population to maintain independence as well as retrofit for handicapped accessibility and other minor in-home modifications that will aid in quality of life.

On the automotive side, Sears could be playing a much bigger role in the lucrative, multibillion-dollar automotive aftermarket the sales and installation of both utility, cosmetic, and electronic components and services for cars and trucks. The Craftsman and DieHard brands, with their association to auto sports licensing, could be better leveraged to involve the entire family in sponsorships and events in and around the stores. Sears could become an advocate for hybrid automobiles by providing high-output charging stations in malls and centers that they occupy, along with satellite charging areas in selected markets (even by charging for the charge). There are limitless opportunities to save the Sears brand if only the inclination for brand preservation and repositioning were there. I look at this timing and opportunity to be similar to when Steve Jobs returned to Apple as it was verging on bankruptcy. Except in this case the stakes are higher, as is the opportunity for an innovative reboot. But it will take a visionary like Jobs to make it happen, and I for one am not highly optimistic. I think the powers that be are only pretending to be retailers, and a legacy and important piece of the American retail fabric hangs in the balance.

# CHAPTER ELEVEN

# THE FUTURE OF RETAILING

We continue to watch as a slow economic recovery takes place after the Great Recession that marked the first decade of the new millennium. While the cause of the downturn can be attributed to many factors, there were already several trend convergences at work that suggest we were sitting on the precipice of fundamental cultural and economic change. Whether you believe we are in a U-shaped recovery or a V-shaped one, the general consensus is that the economy is improving, people are being rehired, retailers are ordering goods, and consumers are spending. Even housing values appear to be rising nationally. However, the consumer trending does not bode well for reabsorption of the retail real estate that sits vacant in the nation's malls and shopping centers.

## AMERICA THE OVER RETAILED

The country is simply over retailed. There are too many storefronts chasing too few customers who have different needs and priorities than they did in the 1970s, 1980s, and 1990s, when most of the centers were built. Boomers who fed the growth are dealing with their underfunded retirement programs while they're cutting up their plastic. Millennial students are entering tough job markets with unprecedented, mortgage-sized college debt without any property to speak of other than their iWare. And Generation Z is spending less and getting more at Target, while text messaging and social-media updates have become a more pressing priority than hanging at the mall. Meanwhile, we are all embracing e-commerce and MEtail$^{SM}$ (its mobile electronic counterpart), which has only just begun to alter the complexion of store-based retail and still has many surprises and more disruption in store. (Pun intended.) And to quote retail anthropologist Paco Underhill, "Many of us are trying to get beyond our lifestyles to something we feel better about."

Most of the biggest specialty retail concepts that have populated the regional malls have reached maturity, and they are contracting rather than growing in the U.S.—plus, there are few new concepts emerging. And we all know what happened to many of the department stores that anchored the county's regional malls—anchors away! Simply put, the regional mall is no longer the darling it once was. Today, malls represent a decreasing asset to developers, real estate investment trusts (REITs), and insurance company portfolios.

What is to become of these meccas of economic indulgence that were driven by the shop-till-you-drop dynamic we thought would last forever? For some, it will be yet another facelift and a remixing of attractions designed to draw us into newly sofa-filled courts. Regrettably, for many it will become a permanent darkening as they wait to become repurposed or reinvented to meet our rapidly changing societal needs. Even with the current economic resurgence, the chance of regaining their 1980s "lust"er is improbable.

Earlier in the book, I discuss the nature of multitrend convergence that ultimately challenges or alters conventional norms. We are currently in a period of just such a change wave driven by a dramatic demographic shift, corporate downsizing, economic stagnation, and rising costs. Combine these factors with an increasing awareness of the perils of the planet, the finite nature of our resources, and a growing sense of responsibility to take action, and we have the makings of macro change. Here, in the final chapter, I attempt to finish painting the picture of what retailing in America will look like in the foreseeable future. Besides building on many of the themes that have already been examined, I explore six trend drivers—big to small, generalized to specialized, national to local, synthetic to authentic, static to kinetic, and discard to repur-

**And we all know what happened to many of the department stores that anchored the county's regional malls—anchors away!**

pose—that I believe are predictors of things to come.

## BIG TO SMALL

I believe small is the new big. Downsizing has become one of the most prevailing trends of our times, and it is likely to continue. Our homes, cars, and corporations are diminishing in scale. Our personal digital assistants, food portions, and even our pets appear to be shrinking. Obviously, there are different forces at work with each of these factors, but overall there is a new sense of practicing economy in areas where "bigger is better" used to rule. In some ways, the stark contrast between compact European scale and American bigness that I observed back in the 1960s has taken root in the States. This has occurred in response to some of the same forces that have shaped European transportation, consumer products, and living conditions in the past. However, most of our downsizing is a result of the effects of mindless consumption and waste.

Virtually every major retailer in the U.S. that has become dominant through big-box or large-format retail has developed newer, smaller-scale formats. Walmart has introduced its midsize Walmart Market, which is about the size of a grocery store, while their Walmart Express comes closer to the size of a convenience store. The latter may be a response to the effect that the dollar stores have had on their business. The creation of City Target is that company's response to the population's movement to the denser urban environments—because for the first time in twenty years our cities are growing faster than the suburbs and exurbs. For Target, these new urban stores represent about a one-third reduction in size from its typical suburban store. Besides responding to a shift in population, the smaller store formats can maximize profitability and allow for stores to be placed in closer proximity to one another. I would also expect to see at some point a micro version of Target which could be inserted into significantly smaller urban storefronts in the future.

In the case of Best Buy, their trend toward a smaller format is in response to the astounding rate of their online sales growth and the effects of "Amazonation," combined with a decreasing demand for consumer electronics, which was their core growth area in the past. This has led to many store closings as well as a focus on downsizing. New branches being tested are 20 percent smaller than their traditional formats. A new cost-control and brand-positioning strategy (with chain-wide implementation) involves subletting floor space to key complementary brands. Called a store-in-store approach, Best Buy has cut deals with both Microsoft and Samsung to run unique departments featuring their products within Best Buy stores. This is similar to the way department stores have been selling cosmetics for decades; traditionally these areas have been sublet and run by the individual cosmetic brands.

This approach contrasts with the more conventional Pavilion store-in-store program we developed to boost sales for Brunswick Billiards a decade ago, a tactic Ron Johnson was planning during his stint as CEO of J.C. Penney. In Best Buy's case, the benefits of subletting space are obvious. It reduces operational overhead while ensuring that the customer will be talking to bona fide brand experts on their product lines. The drawbacks are equally obvious. From a recommendation point of view, many Best Buy customers (me included) often depend on the sales personnel to make recommendations about well, *best buys,* which are based on their expertise on all brands in the store. This initiative could clearly undermine that. The other more subtle, but no less important, effect is whether this new "brand-stand" thinking might begin to under-

**I explore six trend drivers—big to small, generalized to specialized, national to local, synthetic to authentic, static to kinetic, and discard to repurpose—that I believe are predictors of things to come.**

mine the larger Best Buy brand. It's a fine line to walk.

Best Buy is depending on its small-format Best Buy Mobile for much of its sales growth; it reportedly plans on having 600 to 800 units open by 2016. Another proactive move has been the unveiling and testing of Best Buy's Connected Store concept. Best Buy has learned what Apple has known all along, that the chief defense against showrooming is having accessible, well-trained associates who can build a bond with customers. The new idea includes a replication of the Apple Genius Bar called Geek Squad Solution Central. It remains to be seen whether these 'Renew Blue' adjustments in format will be enough to keep the company out of the red and firmly into the black.

*IKEA Thinking*

It may seem like a disconnect to talk about the world's largest furniture retailer under the category of big to small, but no brand of our time has had as much influence on the downsizing mind-set of the American consumer as IKEA has. The efficient use of space and materials expressed through a clean, modern Scandinavian design sensibility are at the core of the IKEA brand. Founded in Sweden in 1943 by the then seventeen-year-old Ingvar Kamprad, the company has grown to over 300 stores worldwide, grossing in excess of thirty-four billion dollars a year with over 500 million annual customer visits. Thinking on a micro level in terms of cost control, simplification, space-saving "flat-pack" storage, and its eco-friendly approach to contemporary design have made IKEA's small thinking very big business. This is also responsible for making Mr. Kamprad one of the richest men on the planet, while at the same time appointing him an ambassador of contemporary Swedish design sensibility around the world. The very inception of the company revolved around designing furnishings for small, efficient living environments found in his native Sweden and that thesis has remained at the heart of the brand ever since. It's also fair to say that IKEA has changed the way Americans think about design and home furnishings perhaps more than any retailer.

## GENERALIZED TO SPECIALIZED

While the biggest retail entities have become ever more dominant and ubiquitous, there is a growing move to smaller and more re-fined retail/service segments. These niche players are filling a void and fulfilling consumers' demands for more specialized products and services in a myriad of categories. In many cases, these con-cepts preexisted as part of a larger retail format but have emerged as free-standing and more highly evolved specialized entities. Star-bucks was a prime example of this some thirty years ago. Many other product/service concepts are emerging to meet changing consumer needs where existing services have not.

### Augmenting Health Care

The convenience of dropping by the Target Clinic with a feverish child in tow while on a weekly Target run has been a godsend for many a time-pressed mom or dad. There are now estimated to be 1,400 similar convenient-care clinics throughout the U.S. The big-gest of these is the CVS-owned MinuteClinic that has opened 650 units in thirteen years. Studies have found that visits to these retail clinics can run anywhere from 30 to 80 percent less than a visit to one's family physician, an urgent care clinic, or an emergency room. The clinics are run by nurse practitioners and physician assistants, and CVS claims that for the thirteen million patients served they are receiving a 95 percent customer satisfaction rate. Another indica-tor of rapid change in the health care industry is the emergence of

> **No brand of our time has had as much influence on the downsizing mind-set of the American consumer as IKEA has.**

retail outlets for insurance providers. With the growth in individual buyers associated with the Affordable Care Act, Blue Cross Blue Shield and United Healthcare are opening retail outlets to assist customers signing up for coverage and to handle claims questions.

The rapid increase in health-care costs, decreasing employer participation, and our increased penchant for taking control of our own well-being has spawned another niche concept in health care with ANY LAB TEST NOW. This remarkable upstart offers thousands of clinical lab tests at affordable, transparent prices to proactively take control of your health. This first-ever direct lab-testing concept provides a broad range of à la carte testing services including allergy, paternity, teen drug, hepatitis, STD, and DNA testing, and biometric screening, among others. There are over 145 stores currently open; some also offer physician-patient phone conferences through AmeriDoc telemedicine services. This is certainly not your father's or mother's idea of medicine, but it clearly points to the rapid changes in what customers are demanding to aid in both preventative and curative health options while seeking cost transparency.

The Boulder, Colorado-based Pharmaca is taking yet another approach to wellness in their integrative pharmacy approach. What Whole Foods has done for grocery shopping, Pharmaca is attempting to do by reimagining the drugstore with a natural approach to health care. Combining both traditional Western pharmacology with complementary and alternative products and therapies, the brand has grown to 24 stores in five states doing $100 million in annual revenue. The brand's developers believe that the concept could readily grow to between 400 and 500 stores nationally, which I don't find surprising. I predict that just like Whole Foods, in a short amount of time, it will no longer be thought of as a niche concept.

Recognizing the fact that 40 percent of the nation's adult population has used some kind of complementary or alternative medicine (CAM) or treatments, Pharmaca is at the forefront of what they refer to as a practitioner service model. Their stores are staffed by traditional pharmacists, as well as Ayurvedic practitioners, naturopathic doctors, estheticians, nutritionists, and herbalists. These alternative practitioners are on the floor and available for consultation. Pharmaca believes their recommendations should not be a substitute for, but can augment, those provided by one's primary care physician.

*Spicing Things Up*

When we travel the world today, whether by air, sea, or cable TV, we are exposed to new foods and flavors that used to be considered rare and exotic. This together with the ever-increasing multicultural influences has resulted in an appreciation and demand for the foods and flavors of our friends and neighbors across the ever-shrinking globe. The result has been a significant growth in America's consumption of spices, and consequently, an increased demand for greater varieties and higher quality of offerings than one might find in the spice sections of our chain grocery stores. While the spice giants McCormick & Co. and Specialty Brands (Spice Islands and Durkee lines) control over half of the approximately $1.4 billion U.S. spice market, one Midwestern entrepreneur has done a miraculous job of creating a niche brand based on many of the success fundamentals addressed throughout the book.

Much like I did, William Penzey Jr. grew up working in his parents' (coffee and spice) business in Milwaukee, Wisconsin. Bill Jr. went on to the University of Wisconsin, where he studied food science and history, being particularly interested in ancient spice trading routes and spice usage in Roman times. After a brief experience with retailing on the East Coast, he returned to Milwaukee,

**What Whole Foods has done for grocery shopping, Pharmaca is attempting to do by reimagining the drugstore with a natural approach to health care.**

and at twenty-two years old he started a spice mail-order business. His venture originated in 1986 with a hand-typed, ten-page catalog that he mailed out to 1,800 customers. Thus began what has become a brilliantly developed and carefully executed niche brand, which is following a unique and clearly charted path to success.

Today, Penzeys Spices mails out hundreds of thousands of its seasonal catalogs—and to even call it a catalog is a misrepresentation of this meaningful and exemplary brand touchpoint. The publication represents the best attributes of a company that has built its brand around a relentless pursuit of the highest-quality spices available anywhere in the world. While the catalog does a wonderful job of providing copious amounts of information on some 300 or so seasonings, that's only the beginning. The heart of the colorful and expertly written sixty-four page (in summer 2013) production is part cookbook and part seasoning anthology that takes a unique look at the history, origins, and the propagation of spices. Its soul is in its devotion to storytelling (verbal and visual) about how good food and love are so often inexplicably intertwined and how the preparation, serving, and enjoyment of sharing food can become transformational whether these everyday rituals are a rarity or a common celebration.

As is the case with many highly successful entrepreneurs, Penzey is fastidious about both the quality and depth of his product offerings, which requires him to fly thousands of miles and expend significant amounts of shoe leather (or rubber). When he is not in Madagascar searching for the best vanilla beans, or Malaysia in pursuit of peppercorns (the catalog lists fifteen different types), he may be returning to India to look for cardamom, coriander, cumin, or curry. The catalog is only a small part of the distinctive Penzeys story. In 1994, Penzey and his team opened their first retail store to complement the initial brand touchpoint, while giving their customers a re-creation of an old-world marketplace with all of the color and fragrance of some of the world's finest spices. The stores succeed at creating an authentic feeling through the use of unrefined wooden boxes, which are casually nested with product informally and almost randomly displayed. The store's layout and visual merchandising is neither slick nor overly staged, allowing fragrances and spice colors to dominate. As of this writing there are sixty-nine Penzeys stores in twenty-nine states.

Whether serving their customers online, through the catalog, or in their stores, they have succeeded in building a niche brand around authenticity, quality, product depth, and customer service, which includes handwritten notes with each catalog order placed. That kind of commitment and genuine relationship building is what makes Penzeys customers feel like family and the brand becomes much more than a label on a bottle. Ironically, they remain one touchpoint short of being a truly omnichannel retailer. The company has yet to jump on the social media bandwagon. Perhaps they feel their customer bond is so strong and authentic that it would be perceived as inauthentic to do so. But some of their avid customers have taken the initiative to create their own Facebook fan page providing a social forum for like-minded brand advocates.

Bill Penzey's love of Milwaukee is manifested in spice mixes named after streets and neighborhoods in and around the city and its suburbs: Mitchell Street Steak Seasoning, Galena Street Rib Rub, and Fox Point Seasoning are a few examples. But the company's dedication to the stewardship and sustainability of their beloved city has recently taken on epic proportions. One of the largest mixed-use developments ever built in Milwaukee was the two-square-mile Northridge Lakes Development on Milwaukee's northwest side. Completed in August of 1972, it was a joint venture between Detroit-based Taubman Centers and Herb Kohl, the former U.S. Senator and owner of the NBA's Milwaukee Bucks. At the core of this development lies the once state-of-the-art, two-level Northridge Mall regional shopping center that was anchored by J.C. Penney, Sears, Boston Store, and Gimbels. The trajectory of Northridge Mall, like too many of this country's shopping centers, is a very sad one, going from boom to doom in a mere three decades. The vacant 800,000-square-foot mall was closed in 2003 and left to be slowly reclaimed by nature, resulting in a huge blight on the vast neighborhood it occupies.

Penzey recognized the importance that the mall once represented to the community and, against some very tough odds, he has been engaged in a highly complex and expensive process to gain ownership of the foreclosed property. Penzey's plans for the enormous site include warehousing, distribution, a retail store, and a visitor center for Penzeys. His efforts have been backed by an incredibly grateful city of Milwaukee that was confronting a very expensive demolition bill. All parties involved believe that if Penzey's plans are realized, the development will go a long way in re-energizing that vast business corridor. The other significant component at play is the role of the private developer in investing huge personal assets without major governmental investment. This is the type of large-scale repurposing and corporate citizenship that will be necessary on many similar sites throughout the country as we go through an economic, social, and cultural recalibration of sorts.

## NATIONAL TO LOCAL

The next significant movement afoot is one that is a reaction to the ubiquity of the "national brand" syndrome that has played out in three acts across the country. The first act began with the suburban flight that brought with it the sanitized shopping center and regional mall architectural idiom. The second act was a reaction to the first by largely supplanting the often generations-old local and regional retailers in favor of the fast-growing national specialty and department store chains. As the tax base and the population left the cities in a dash to the suburbs, urban blight set in at the cores of many cities.

The third act appears to be a slow but recognizable resurgence of the independent and locally based retailer as well as the recognition by many of the big nationals that it is in their best interest to focus on regionalism and celebrate local culture. Back when big was good there was an expectation that for a brand to be viable, dependable, and highly valued it needed to have a strong national look. That image enabled the concept to be readily rolled out from Portland, Oregon, to Portland, Maine, while giving the customer the same studied and tested impression. This McEverywhere formula delivered exactly what it promised—a coast-to-coast processed, perfected, and properly promoted ubiquity. Unfortunately, in the process we lost much of what made our cities and towns unique as the local fabric of each was being rewoven and recut into a not-so-elite, private school–like uniform. And I'm not proud to say I was one of the many tailors who was marking and cutting the cloth. We wanted cheaper goods in greater variety, as quickly as possible. In the process, we managed to lose much of the American manufacturing infrastructure (with the resulting off-shoring of goods), which created and financed the prosperity that resulted in a strong midcentury middle-class consumer and a vital economic engine.

*"So Soon Old, So Late Schmart"*

I'm reminded of a story that is indelibly burnished into my childhood memory. The setting was Stetsonville, Wisconsin, population 200-and-some, not including cows, pigs, chickens, and other live-

> **Back when big was good there was an expectation that for a brand to be viable, dependable, and highly valued it needed to have a strong national look.**

stock. It was 1955, and I was in the company of my dear grandfather Peter Bootzin, whom I introduce at the book's beginning. Papete and I had just taken a five-mile ride from Medford, Wisconsin, where my grandparents resided. While that trip might ordinarily take a few minutes, traveling with Papete in his 1954 Pontiac Star Chief always meant a leisurely journey. I was positioned in the center of the expansive bench seat smack in front of the car's circular, chromed-plated radio speaker, which looked very much like a junior-size steering wheel. Papete insisted that I stay close to him and help "guide" the big midcentury cruiser down the two-lane country road. My small hands were clutched to the faux steering wheel being careful to mimic all of his moves.

Our destination was the small Stetsonville shoe store owned and run by one of Papete's close friends, J. B. Miller, who was also an immigrant from Eastern Europe and one of the few other Jews in all of Taylor County, Wisconsin. The store was situated across the highway from one of my grandfather's few remaining businesses (an IGA grocery and feed store), which by then was being run by my Uncle Ivan. We arrived at Miller's shoe store, which had all of the earmarks of a small rural retail setting at the time. It was spartan, well-worn, and unadorned, with tall whitewashed walls that supported the high, cracked, whitish-beige ceilings. A few round milk glass lights hung from cords and provided a modicum of illumination when sunlight was not piercing through the cracked and dirty store windows. J. B. was sitting in one of the half dozen or so ladder-back wooden chairs, rocking back a bit as he inhaled the smoke of his charred pipe. "Pete!" he shouted, as we entered the store, each creaky wood floorboard tracing our movements back through the narrow space.

We sat down amid the scattered chairs. Randomly stacked shoe boxes were placed around the store's perimeter in no apparent order. Every so often a single shoe sat atop a box, in a halfhearted attempt to display the product; J. B. was not about display. The store had an aroma that was a peculiar mix of dust, mustiness, shoe leather, and tobacco smoke. J. B. smelled a lot like the store when he shook my hand. Even at (just shy of) eight years old, I could sense that J. B. had had a difficult life, and that the ingenuity and drive that allowed Peter Bootzin to prosper in small-town America was not shared by his good friend. We sat across from J. B. and as he rocked back in his wooden perch, he removed the pipe from his mouth, and started in his distinct dialect, "Ya know, Pete. Vee get so soon old, and so late schmart."

Those words of J. B. Miller uttered over a half century ago still ring in my ears when I think about the casual attitude that we Americans have had regarding our great cities. About our race to replace what was a little old and out of style, only to create structures that are far less substantial and aesthetically insignificant. Perhaps today as a culture we have become a bit older and maybe a bit "schmarter." We are also starting to realize that along with losing some of the individuality that made our cities and towns what they were, some of our own identities also got lost in the process.

As the pendulum so often does, it is now swinging back to recognize and celebrate the rich and distinctive local culture and character that differentiates the regions, states, cities, and towns across our great country. Call it new nationalism, big-box backlash, or the fundamental awareness that there is intrinsic value in supporting what is homegrown. This seems to have manifested itself into two distinct movements and trends in retailing: one is top-down and the other is bottom-up. The top-down dynamic represents efforts on the part of national brands to recast themselves as advocates for local culture. Bottom-up is manifested by the rebirth and renewed appreciation for well-conceived and well-run

> **Call it new nationalism, big-box backlash, or the fundamental awareness that there is intrinsic value in supporting what is homegrown.**

local independent retailers that are reemerging across the country.

*Hi, Seattle!*

Every year ten million tourists from all over the world visit Pike Place Market in Seattle, Washington, built in 1903 and opened to the public in 1907. The market, which overlooks the Elliot Bay waterfront, is one of the oldest continually operated public markets in the U.S. In the beginning, its mission was to allow consumers to "meet the producer" of farm products and also to sidestep the middlemen—how about that for déjà vu? In 1970, the market was rightfully added to the U.S. National Register of Historic Places, celebrating both its significance as well as its ability to dodge attempts at gentrification or urban renewal (aka the wrecking ball). Today, the market is home to a wide assortment of locally owned businesses including farmers and fishmongers, restaurants, craftspeople, antique dealers, head shops, musicians, and street performers. There are also 500 year-round tenants who occupy eight different buildings throughout the market's multispace, labyrinthine structure.

In the summer of 2012, Target opened three new City Targets—one in downtown Chicago, one in the Westwood District of Los Angeles, and another a few yards away from Seattle's historic Pike Place Market. Opening these three stores on the same day celebrated Target's latest forays into the urban market. Three months later they would open in San Francisco's Metreon, giving the development new hopes for a glorious retail future that eluded Sony a decade and a half earlier. At about half the size of the typical 140,000-square-foot box, these new and highly visible urban destinations are distinctive not only for their size and location, but for the effort Target went through to locate significant sites and repurpose buildings that had significant if not historic pasts. It's hard to comprehend the degree to which a company like Target must go to first downsize a prototype by 50 percent and at the same time work with the architectural shell of a building that was never conceived around their brand. This challenges the company's engineered customer experience and the refined category adjacencies that are a hallmark of their success. In addition, I suspect a book could be written about the implications of dealing with local preservation groups, as was the case with Target taking on a landmark Louis Sullivan building in downtown Chicago, which I will soon discuss. To Target's credit, the launching of these four stores in significant urban areas gave them an opportunity to move into a new market area and fold its signature brand into a community's fabric in a way that makes it a good and welcome neighbor. While it could be argued that Target may have not gone far enough in expressing the local culture, its red and white ginormous "Hi, Downtown" and "Hi, Seattle" interior billboards made a nice, neighborly gesture.

Another initiative Target undertook in 2012 was to tap into the legions of small specialty shops around the country to offer limited-edition merchandise. While Target has a long tradition of partnering with designers, both new and established, this was another example of Target's "outside the big-box thinking." This was a very brave direction, teaming with small local retailers to create short-term "signature shops" almost like mini pop-up stores within their 1,800 locations and online. The program brought instant and overnight exposure to a handful of independent shop owners around the country and produced some short-term buzz for Target around exclusivity and being big and small at the same time. While Target is to be applauded for the gesture, the concept was short-lived. It must have been very difficult to scale such a program, and one can only imagine the challenges to both the local shop owner and the mothership brand—kind of like an outing

> I suspect a book could be written about the implications of dealing with local preservation groups, as was the case with Target taking on a landmark Louis Sullivan building in downtown Chicago

involving the *Queen Mary* and a kayak. But it is just this audacity of taking on such retail experiments that has brought Target the level of success and brand value that it has enjoyed for more than fifty years.

## *Local Relevance in Chicago*

A far more studied and successful example of bringing local relevance to a national brand venue has been demonstrated with Starbucks's new flagship store located at Oak and Rush streets in downtown Chicago. The in-house design team did an exceptional job of marrying sustainable design with themes that echo Chicago's past, and in the process achieved an aesthetic that is authentic. Since Chicago has long been one of North America's premier rail centers, the design team used reclaimed boxcar wood extensively throughout the space's walls, floors, and ceilings. They also made use of other locally sourced materials including reclaimed brick, cast-iron ornamentation, furniture, and other décor elements. The work of local artisans was incorporated, creating integrated, coffee-related storytelling components, a key part of the Starbucks brand. A giant two-story mosaic mural portrays an oak tree shading a coffee tree as a visual symbol of the company's organic, shade-grown coffee. Square travertine tiles frame the immense focal point using a coffee bean theme that looks like it could have come from architect Louis Sullivan's offices nearly a century ago. This weaving of local history into the branded environments of major retailers is expected to continue as national brands attempt to build a more authentic local relationship with their customers. Not surprisingly, Starbucks has set a very high bar in downtown Chicago.

## You've Got—A Retake

A half century ago the majority of the retailers in cities, towns, and farm communities were locally owned and operated, and they represented a significant part of what made up the economic fabric of our nation. We knew these merchants personally and they knew us. They existed to sell products and services in the communities where they had often grown up, raised families, paid taxes, voted, and worshiped. We inadvertently traded that scenario for bigger stores with cheaper goods in previously unimaginable quantities, styles, sizes, and materials. In the process, we lost jobs and compromised the unique character and identity of our cities and towns. Now that we are left with a kind of stealthy, homogenized twenty-first century retail idiom, many of us long for a little of what we had "back in the day."

Research shows that if consumers are given the choice between purchasing a product or service through either a local or national retailer, at a similar price, they prefer to do business locally. Multiple studies have shown that locally owned independent businesses generate three times more direct economic benefit per dollar spent than a nationally owned business. They contribute to the local character and prosperity of the community and fuel entrepreneurship. In addition, because the majority of indie retailers are in walkable town centers, they are more environmentally sustainable and they add competition and product diversity.

In Nora Ephron's 1998 pop culture classic, *You've Got Mail,* big-box retailer Joe Fox (played by Tom Hanks) of megastore Fox Books (a Barnes & Noble stand-in) does battle with the aptly named The Shop Around the Corner run by Kathleen Kelly (played by Meg Ryan). Fox Books wins handily in the time-appropriate battle of the big box versus the independent. And while love prevails,

**Multiple studies have shown that locally owned independent businesses generate three times more direct economic benefit per dollar spent than a nationally owned business.**

the indie retailer does not. A remake of the movie today, in my opinion, may have a very different ending (retail-wise, at least) for some very fundamental reasons. Local retailers are experiencing a resurgence for the first time in over twenty years. The question is, are we seeing a trend that supports a different outcome for that bookish David-and-Goliath saga? I believe there are multiple, converging trends that bode well for a strong and lasting independent retailer comeback. These include big-box contraction, an end to price wars, a leveling of the playing field, technological parity, and a change in consumer sentiment, which I explore in the next sections.

### Leveling the Playing Field and the End of Price Wars

Every major big-box category killer is in contraction mode. I personally used to believe there was room in the marketplace for two majors in every category; that was before Amazon. We've seen what happened to CompUSA and Circuit City, as well as Borders Books. Best Buy has closed stores and put its real estate on a diet. Barnes & Noble says it will close a third of its stores in the next decade, but don't be surprised if that number increases. I won't begin to list all of the major regional players with double- or triple-digit store counts that succumbed to the one-two punch of the Great Recession and e-commerce. The sheer number of storefronts that steadily grew over the past three decades is diminishing at a faster rate than they grew. Advantage: indie.

Price erosion brought on by the fierce competition between the majors, the independents, and e-commerce players like Amazon has pinned everyone to the same mat. The fact remains that in many product areas the margins have become so thin that the items retailers used make a profit on (like big-screen monitors) are nearly being given away in the hopes of making something on accessories, or other higher-margin products. "The store" is still the optimal place to see and be induced to purchase the add-ons. Once more the independent, with its typically more knowledgeable salespeople, lends credibility to their local brand and can more readily use relationship selling to highly relational Gen X, Y, and Zs.

The other big factor that will contribute to price parity is the proposed Market Fairness Act that is intended to close the gap and level the playing field between the previous tax-free sales on the Internet and the rest of the retail universe. Stores have been charging and collecting 4 to 10 percent tax while e-tail has had a subsidized ride for a decade and a half. Now that even Amazon has stopped fighting the inevitable, it has moved on to its next dominance strategy by building major warehouses in every major city to undermine the one last advantage the big boxes had, which is that of immediate (or almost immediate) gratification. Amazon will be planning on delivering your big screen (and nearly everything else) to your house and install it the same day, even if they are charging you tax on the sale. So as Amazon and the big boxes beat each other silly in the low-cost, low-service, commodity-selling realm, the indie is able to distance itself from the bloodbath. By continuing to position itself as the destination for superior product knowledge, a high level of service, relationship selling, and after-sale follow-up, the indie retailer can charge a bit more for what the buying public longs for, which is to have both a relationship and a great buying experience. The Market Fairness Act will also enable the independent to become a more viable omnichannel retailer. Advantage: indie.

## Technological Parity

The technology gap that used to exist between big national chains and the local merchant has essentially evaporated. Elaborate com-

> So as Amazon and the big boxes beat each other silly in the low-cost, low-service, commodity-selling realm, the indie is able to distance itself from the bloodbath.

puter point of sale (POS) and inventory management systems that were only accessible to national chains not long ago have been scaled to meet the needs of even the single-store retailer. Programs for every aspect of inventory management, reordering, billing, and staff scheduling are user-friendly and inexpensive. Many retailers and service operators are even following Apple's lead in utilizing mobile tablets and smartphones to facilitate transactions on the fly when appropriate. And while every major brand is working hard to get followed and "liked" socially speaking, it is much easier for a local business to manage social networks in a manner that results in real customer loyalty and increased sales. The new POS technology has also made loyalty programs and rebates easier to facilitate and track across channels. This helps the independent create new more customized and targeted programs and offers that match their customer's (market of one) needs and desires. Advantage: indie.

*It Feels Good*

In recent years, our society has watched its once vibrant and rock-solid middle class lose jobs, homes, economic standing, and dignity. Meanwhile, those at the top of the food chain—big corporations, banks, and wealthy individuals—continue to prosper. Suffice it to say, this resurgence of independent retailers will have a lot of goodwill and community support whether they have survived the shakeout or are among the newly minted entrepreneurs behind a niche start-up. Communities hit hard by the downturn and unable to expect much help from state and federal government are looking inward toward local business leaders, educational institutions, and the myriad of independent merchant associations for funding and support. Even the venerable National Retail Federation has launched the indie Retailer.com search engine for over 50,000 independent retailers and those that support them. The fact remains that we all feel better about buying from local merchants who have dealt with pretty strong headwinds in recent years, and it would appear that the winds may finally be at their backs. Karmic advantage: indie.

## SYNTHETIC TO AUTHENTIC

The world of marketing, advertising, and branding has perhaps done too good a job at packaging, positioning, and selling just about everything that we are conscious of during our waking hours. The result seems to be a rejection of the too-slick and too-polished and a new appreciation for all that is genuine. Certainly pop culture's affinity for the unscripted is evidenced by our interest in "reality" entertainment. Although I personally have little tolerance for the bad behavior and self-absorption of many of these productions, I do have a personal favorite that borders on an obsession. Like millions of viewers, I have become transfixed as Mike and Frank unearth buried treasures and genuine characters on the History Channel's *American Pickers*. I believe these shows have struck a chord with the public because of their authenticity and honesty. They show real, imperfect people behaving the way that real, imperfect, yet caring, people behave. *American Pickers* also reminds us that there is inherent beauty in the "rusty stuff," objects from our past that can often tell us stories about people and past lives, American craftsmanship, and what made us who we are today.

### *Getting Real*

Getting real is seen in the style and fashion flip that used to originate on Paris runways to what is now researched and captured

**Suffice it to say, this resurgence of independent retailers will have a lot of goodwill and community support whether they have survived the shakeout or are among the newly minted entrepreneurs behind a niche start-up.**

from the streets of our metropolitan cities. Target employees, like many other fashion trendsetters, are out observing real people's personal expressions as the source of product inspiration, resulting in a bottom-up rather than top-down style migration.

Even "real food" is making a comeback. The neighborhood bakeries that closed down in the 1960s and 1970s as Americans went on white-bread diets have reopened and are flourishing as we begin appreciating the artisan breads that our forbearers baked — no Wonder! Even my car world has caught a case of "genuine-itis" as barn finds that used to go straight into restoration shops are now being paraded around and appreciated (dust, dirt, and all) as time capsules that tell stories about the past. Today, the most highly prized and expensive restored classics and muscle cars are taking a backseat pricewise to unrestored survivors, even ones with the "patina" that comes with age. The mantra is: they can be restored again and again, but they're only original once.

Our new affinity for knowing our heritage and learning about our roots has become popular and highly celebrated. Only a couple of generations ago, American immigrants worked hard to assimilate in order to become a part of the American experience. Many were distancing themselves from the foreign identification and traditions of their birth families. Now that the children and grandchildren of these immigrants have become third-, fourth-, or fifth-generation Americans, they want to learn all they can about their bloodlines. This has become big business for companies like Ancestry.com, the world's largest for-profit genealogy company with 1.7 million subscribers. In the process Ancestry's users have created over twenty-nine million family trees containing over three billion profiles, enabling people from all over the world to uncover or rediscover family histories. This fascination even extends to celebrities, which has led to the creation of TLC's popular *Who*

*Do You Think You Are?*, which is produced in association with Ancestry.com. We've also watched as scrapbookers of all ages have added the digital domain to their scissors and glue obsessions, while a billion or so of the Facebook faithful continue to document and share their lives with their legions of followers.

## Retailers' Recycling History

Retailers that used to devote themselves to the efficient creation of bland, faceless boxes are coming of age and realizing that great, classic architecture isn't a bad place to stage their product. This has led to a renaissance in the repurposing and the rehabilitation of some grand historical buildings that would likely languish and further deteriorate without the long view and deep pockets of these companies. City Target's new Chicago location in the historic Louis Sullivan–designed Carson Pirie Scott building on State Street represents just such an audacious but significant move. Architectural critic Lee Bey noted that "it's a tricky thing bringing the retailer—and its famous red bull's-eye logo signage and color scheme—into one of the world's most celebrated pieces of architecture. But the marriage seems pretty good so far." It sounds to me to be better than pretty good. With today's economy and the phenomenal costs involved in restoring and renovating historical structures like Sullivan's State Street landmark, it's terrific when a company like Target is willing and able to make the kind of expenditure to preserve such a landmark in a manner that millions can enjoy the space while it functions as a place of commerce.

Another architecturally significant structure is the flagship store for the newly repositioned Restoration Hardware (now renamed RH), which has recently undergone a two-year restoration. An affair of the heart had begun two decades earlier between Gary Friedman, then an executive with Williams-Sonoma, and the neo-

> **Retailers that used to devote themselves to the efficient creation of bland, faceless boxes are coming of age and realizing that great, classic architecture isn't a bad place to stage their product.**

classical, red brick and brownstone building in the Back Bay area of Boston. Fast-forward some twenty years finds Gary in the position of chairman emeritus of RH, looking for a flagship store location in Boston. Coincidentally, the 1863 Civil War era structure that had been designed and built as the Museum of Natural History by architect William Gibbons Preston had become available and was in a serious need of renovation.

The 40,000-square-foot building, which would have been far too big for the old Restoration Hardware, is a perfect fit for the brand that has recently evolved from a purveyor of home goods to a full-fledged lifestyle brand. And like the marriage of Target with the grand Sullivan classic in Chicago, RH became the modern-day preservationist for this once grand lady. California-based architects Backen, Gillam & Kroeger were charged with the task of both restoring the building back to its original grace while respectfully retrofitting the old girl with new innards to meet the needs of its new occupant. This began by studying old photos and architectural plans in order to remove mezzanines and other embellishments not part of the original building. A major atrium was reopened to allow for unobstructed views from the main floor all the way up to the gilded and coffered ceiling. The massive former museum spaces lent themselves to the placement of product vignettes featuring the retailer's furnishings and accessories. Experiential destinations consistent with the RH lifestyle brand are interwoven throughout the store. These include a wine bar run by Ma(i)sonry Napa Valley Winery, a cinema devoted to classic movies, and a billiard lounge complete with a rehabbed classic Brunswick pool table.

*Keeping It in the Family*

Heritage brands that have survived decades or even centuries like Brooks Brothers (1818), Lord & Taylor (1826), Brunswick (1845), and Levi Strauss (1850) all have the advantage of legacy and the wealth of brand imagery that many of us have stored in our brand-image memory banks. Maintaining the appropriate balance between heritage and innovation can be a challenge, particularly when the half-lives of technology get shorter and shorter and the quality gap between products and brands shrinks. One American heritage brand that we had the good fortune to work with was Red Wing Shoes. In 1998, Red Wing was planning on opening a flagship store at the Mall of America to display their American-made product and tell their brand story. Ironically, this occurred at about the same time a whole new generation of young consumers, who had little interest in either farming or construction, were becoming enamored by this heritage brand, but for different reasons.

Our indoctrination into the brand and culture was most memorable and became very influential in the conception of the store. The brand values associated with the company, founded in 1905, were about handcrafting and durability, and when we toured the factory it was easy to see why these had become core values. Even today, in this age of robotics and automation, a Red Wing boot is largely handmade on machines that in some cases are as old as the company. Often a single boot may be handled by as many as a hundred hands, sometime belonging to second-, third-, or fourth-generation employees. People I met during my factory visit spoke of how the heritage of their families and that of the heralded brand were intertwined like the stitching through the boot soles. An interesting result of the bond formed between Red Wing Shoes and the people who buy them is the fact that customers will often send shoes back to the factory to be resoled or repaired after years of dependable use, rather than retiring them for new ones.

We worked to incorporate these stories into the retail experience starting with museum-like interpretive displays demonstrating

> **Even today, in this age of robotics and automation, a Red Wing boot is largely handmade on machines that in some cases are as old as the company.**

the process of crafting each boot. We designed "exploded" production models describing each stage of the boot's construction that were assembled in floating acrylic cases. These were complemented by production-line photographs that told the stories of artisans, craftspeople, and the multiple generations of employees whose lives were very much a part of the Red Wing brand. The interpretive museum components were housed in a period-correct interpretation of J. B. Miller's Stetsonville, Wisconsin, storefront. This seemed appropriate as J. B. was one of many independent merchants who had sold Red Wing shoes, and my grandfather had given away Red Wing pottery to his customers for the holidays from the same historic Minnesota town. Throughout the rest of the store we attempted to stage the product for each of the Red Wing family of brands as authentically as possible, creating bona fide vignettes representing construction sites or recreation environments to serve as the backdrops of each display.

## STATIC TO KINETIC

I've talked at length about the phenomenon of omnichannel retail. This new world of brand retailing forces brand bearers to fire on all cylinders to ensure that each and every brand touchpoint is in sync, so that wherever the customer chooses to engage with the brand there is a holistic synergy across the touchpoints. I am and will always be a proponent of store-based retail, and I believe now more than ever we need this traditional "marketplace" for social interaction. Naturally, this assumes that we can *put down the device* long enough to socially interact. The twentieth-century mantra of "build it and they will come" has been dismantled. There will continue to be more store closings than openings, more contraction than expansion of square footage, and more growth in e-tail and MEtail[SM] than store-based retail. That said, store-based concerns are exploring how to engage consumers in highly experiential ways, which is how brand retail will need to reposition and revitalize in order for it to remain viable. The survival of the retailer, the malls, and shopping centers depend upon it.

## Zara and Zumiez

We have undeniably become a culture with an ever-decreasing attention span. I don't know whether we should blame the advertising industry over quick-cut imagery, the popularity of video games, or too much sugar in our diets. Today's consumers (Millennials in particular) have become so accustomed to multitasking that it seems that things that don't move, don't move them. Hence the heading: static to kinetic. Stores that turn product four to six times a year are "so last century." Take Zara's, for example. Customers (like my daughter Brianna) who may visit one of the 1,600-plus Zara stores in any one of the eighty-two countries worldwide on any given week are likely to find a new selection of merchandise to choose from, even if they had visited a week earlier. For this reason, Zara's customers will shop their stores seventeen times a year as opposed to four for the traditional retailer. And because these savvy customers know that what they see won't be there the next time they come, they are motivated to buy with each visit. The fast fashion retailer's near total vertical integration allows its 1,000 designers and product developers to create a constant, low-batch flood of new fashions into the stores. Creating 11,000 distinct items a year is about four or five times what comparable retailers would be undertaking, and because the volume of each style is relatively low, very little ends up on markdown, and the markdowns are never as aggressive as those of their competitors. They keep very close watch on what moves fast or faster and because they can go from design to display in as little as ten days (yes, ten days) they never have to commit to large advance product runs. This amazing controlled value chain has made its founder Amancio Ortega Gaona the third richest man in the world, according to *Forbes*, with a net worth of fifty-seven billion dollars.

Another "Zetailer" that is rethinking retail around the kinetically inclined is Zumiez. Its products are focused on a young consumer, offering clothing and gear for skateboarders, skaters, and surfers. Their 500 stores in North America have an intentionally chaotic feel, stocked with video games and couches to create a comfortable place for customers to interact with each other and store personnel. But it is not the stores or the products that make the brand notable, it's how they choose to market them. For the past thirteen years, the company has sponsored The Zumiez Couch Tour, which brings its young brand advocates together en masse to celebrate their edgy brand, often in retail store parking lots. These highly organized and well-publicized events include live music, pro skateboard demos, celebrity meet and greets, skateboard contests, and giveaways from their major sponsors. For those that can't make it to the nine or so venues each year, the whole thing is available on live webcasts.

The Zumiez Couch Tour and its complementary Best Foot Forward Tour for amateur skateboarders is focused on a young, niche-enthusiast audience, and to dismiss this planned mayhem as just kid stuff would be short-sighted. I believe Zumiez's genius event marketing is the kind of experiential secret sauce that can save store-based retailing if done properly. These events celebrate the lifestyle of their customers and the core attributes of each of their cobrands in a way that checks every box of emotional engagement and "livin' the brand." The buzz built by these events, both online and in stores, generates enormous passion for the Zumiez brand while bringing enthusiasts together to bond around their passion for skateboarding. I believe these types of fan gatherings and brand-centric events are what will make store-based retail relevant and viable in the future. They also close the loop of omnichannel retailing.

## Pop-Ups Live

Another way that brand retailers are getting customers' attention and spurring them to action is through the pop-up store. Pop-ups, like other temporary tenancies, are not new. Al and Lou Stein were opening seasonal Christmas toy stores in vacant storefronts fifty years ago to generate additional cash during the peak buying season. Today's retailers see them as a way to create momentary excitement around a product launch, or to give hot young designers a push. About a decade ago, Target took the idea to a new level opening up Bullseye Bazaars and Bullseye Bodegas that featured exclusive design lines in random, intentionally toned-down retail spaces. Though the Bullseye was prevalent (read overused) the Target name was notably absent. Reebok has tested pop-ups with a one-month store appropriately named FLASH. Disney has done it to feature movies like *Tron*, and Godiva opened a pop-up boutique for Valentine's Day on Fifth Avenue in New York. Even designer Kate Spade set up an igloo for three weeks in New York's Bryant Park in the middle of winter and handed out hot chocolate to warm the customers. The pop-up accomplishes three main goals for the brand or retailer. First, it creates buzz around a specific brand, product, or designer; second, it creates a sense of urgency because it has a finite life; and third, it generates revenue. It is likely that we will continue to see new and unique forms of temporary tenancies as brand retail continues to attempt to grab the customer's attention away from their PDAs.

**Pop-ups, like other temporary tenancies, are not new. Al and Lou Stein were opening seasonal Christmas toy stores in vacant storefronts fifty years ago**

*Underused Asset Utilization*

The term *underused asset utilization* is a novel and rather curious one that has surfaced of late. It describes the new sharing economy that focuses on leveraging assets that otherwise may be underutilized. The web has inspired a whole new generation of businesses that facilitate the sharing of available apartments, meals, tools, cars, clothes, and couches. There is currently another greatly underutilized asset in our midst—vacant retail space (by the millions of square feet). This empty space in our malls and centers could be reimagined and put to productive use. These ideas, if conceived and executed correctly, could become a solution to a whole series of interconnected problems and challenges facing national brands, retailers, and shopping center owners today.

For the shopping center to truly reinvent itself for a changing retail world the terms *dynamic* and *kinetic* must replace *passive* and *static*. They will need to create unique events, changing venues, and brand engagement that is personal and highly relevant to an increasingly demanding and changing audience. This will ultimately drive the concept of pop-up stores and temporary tenancies to new and more highly evolved levels. Leveraging social networks, blogs, and other virtual gathering spaces to drive traffic to special, spontaneous events, performances, and product previews can motivate like-minded brand advocates to act together, and it will serve to energize a mall or shopping center. These initiatives, combined with emerging technologies discussed in previous chapters, will provide retailers with new methods of customer engagement and personalized offerings.

Creating entertaining and highly engaging yet temporary venues for brand interface can become the antidote to decreasing mall traffic and visit lengths, while simultaneously complementing existing permanent tenants. These interactive venues can introduce new products to an audience for testing and feedback (think traveling trade shows usually reserved for industry insiders). In addition, they become havens for like-minded people to gather and interact. This creates an obvious paradigm shift for the shopping center industry as management's role moves from leasing to orchestrating high-impact events and experiences (something few are trained for). But it is becoming clear to me that the nature of the shopping center can evolve to become more of a blending of product, entertainment, and soft branding in a dynamic and celebratory fashion. This will fulfill the needs of a highly diverse audience seeking new and genuine means of socialization and human interaction while still having a brand experience, whether or not the mall happens to be the final point of purchase.

*RaveRetail®*

In March 2011, I spoke at Global Shop in Las Vegas, the big annual retail fixture tradeshow, and my address was titled, *TechnoTrend Convergence: Retail's New World Order*. I posed the (rhetorical) question, "With the point of sale conveniently tucked away in the backpack, back pocket, or purse, what is the retailer, brand bearer, or mall to do to engage this new highly mobile consumer?" The answer (surprise) is RaveRetail®.

RaveRetail® responds to rapidly changing trends in consumer behavior influenced by social networking and the seismic growth of e-tail and MEtail[SM], which are having a highly disruptive effect on store-based retailing. It will create, organize, facilitate, coordinate, and market high-impact branded events located in and around malls, shopping centers, and other public gathering places (e.g., Zumiez Couch Tour). RaveRetail® will be the matchmaker and intermediary between the retail space holders (malls

**The web has inspired a whole new generation of businesses that facilitate the sharing of available apartments, meals, tools, cars, clothes, and couches.**

297

and shopping centers) and potential space users (retailers, brands, major manufacturers, and entertainment entities). It fills a market void by matching leading brands with strategic retail venues for short-term, high-impact, temporary tenancies with transformational, highly engaging brand events. It will strategically manage, repopulate, and ultimately increase the value of huge amounts of retail square footage that is currently vacant or underutilized in the country's shopping malls and centers.

RaveRetail® will orchestrate events for brand entities of every size, category, and audience. They may last hours, days, or weeks. The pop-up nature of these events has the capacity to bring like-minded fans and brand advocates together en masse to drive traffic and populate single- or multiple-tenant spaces in a matter of minutes from its virtual and actual unveiling and netblasts. They may be single- or multi-brand events that can be choreographed within or across categories to create an experience focused on a specific consumer psychographic or product category.

RaveRetail® events will be turnkey in nature, involving single or multiple locations in a given city or region of the country or worldwide events. The soup-to-nuts approach will include location analysis and procurement, brand venue design, complete venue fit-out, entertainment booking, security, and tactical coordination with all parties to ensure desired brand impact and event buzz. The design, planning, and marketing will use the most complete psychographic data available to score available retail locations throughout the country and strategically align any brand with its highest-value consumer to ensure maximum event impact and reach. Brands may provide their marketing databases to prioritize announcements to consumers based on previous RaveRetail® events or preferred customer status. RaveRetail® will become the leading clearinghouse and agent for orchestrating exciting brand events and revaluating millions of square feet of undervalued retail real estate nationwide. In 2010, I applied for trademark protection and in November 2012 the RaveRetail® service mark became federally registered with the U.S. Patent and Trademark Office (Reg. No. 4,242,786); the concept also has U.S. patent protection.

A visit to deadmalls. com provides a sad and sobering reflection on our retail culture's all-too-recent past.

## DISCARD TO REPURPOSE

It is undeniable that the importance of recycling has become ingrained in our public and private institutions, in manufacturing and consumer products, and in our general attitudes. Many may argue that it is too little too late for a planet that is in peril, but we are beginning to think more about the life cycle of products and systems, and consequently, are becoming more responsible and proactive about what we make and how we make it. This thinking is behind the cradle-to-cradle design initiatives that seek to create essentially waste-free holistic methods of design and manufacturing. Lately, I've been preoccupied with a rather large recycling challenge that is in our midst.

### Mall Fall Down

While RaveRetail® may indeed be the tonic to help reasonably healthy and viable malls get their mojo back, there are too many of these meccas of past consumption that are less likely to become recharged, and there are many sitting, waiting to be repurposed or bulldozed. A visit to deadmalls.com provides a sad and sobering reflection on our retail culture's all-too-recent past. It reminds me of gazing at the mangled remains of a once-beautiful sports car that was driven recklessly. You know there are likely stories of people connected to it that probably aren't pretty.

Adaptive reuse or the recycling of dying or dead malls is not a new idea. In May 1999, *Metropolis* magazine did a feature article entitled "The Mall Doctor" largely devoted to sprucing up moribund malls. To a far lesser extent, the article did explore the more fundamental question of their future viability. Both I and architect Jon Jerde, whose firm specialized in designing some of the world's premier malls and commercial development, looked beyond refurbishing to the inevitable. I commented in this article that the future of many of these environments may be repurposed as "living-working-buying environments" and Jerde referred to them as "gigantic placeholders awaiting their real life."

*Gimme Shelter*

A decade ago there were 36.3 million people ages sixty-five and older, making up 12 percent of the population. By 2030 this will increase to 71.5 million, or 20 percent of the U.S. population. Over the next two decades, as seventy-eight million Boomers undertake downsizing or right-sizing their lives, they will need a host of new services and service providers not currently in existence. They will also be searching for a new sense of community and connectedness to others.

As these empty nesters contemplate moving to condos, townhouses, and apartments, many are also taking care of their aging parents. Elder care now accounts for more lost work hours than child care. College tuitions, depleted IRAs, job losses, and inadequate retirement planning have all conspired to paint a very different picture of retirement than many of us were planning during the casual consumption years of yore. For affluent members of society, the retirement housing options are many and varied. New housing alternatives are gaining favor, including continuing-care retirement communities (CCRCs), which offer a broad range of living and care options depending on health-care needs and levels of independence. Most CCRCs require an entrance fee and a monthly fee. Entrance fees can run from twenty thousand to four hundred thousand dollars, depending on living units and community amenities. In most cases these entrance fees provide little or no equity in the community. Monthly payments can range from two hundred to five thousand dollars, also depending on levels of care and amenities.

For many Boomers who remain vital and engaged but have fewer assets, the options may not be as plentiful. Inexpensive and energy-efficient housing that is close to vital services and quality-of-life assets will be in short supply in many communities. However, numerous new forms of community-focused elder care services are emerging. These include co-housing communities, member-owned health-care cooperatives, neighborhood-based block nurse programs, and naturally occurring retirement communities (NORCs). Meanwhile, our embattled health care system is yielding to a new emphasis on wellness and prevention. This is likely to lead to new incentive (carrot-and-stick) programs for preventative care and wellness with support from insurance companies and care providers.

The rapidly growing global population combined with the emerging global middle class and changing weather patterns caused by global warming have all conspired to put an end to inexpensive food. Growing concerns over food quality and the emphasis on energy independence are driving an increasing interest in local growth and consumption of food, often called the locavore movement. This is also fueling a new trend toward home-grown fruits and vegetables, as well as public foraging for food and edible vegetation. In fact, some communities are beginning to plant more edible plants on public lands in urban areas, recognizing that an ever-increasing segment of the solidly middle class

> I commented in this article that the future of many of these environments may be repurposed as "living-working-buying environments" and Jerde referred to them as "gigantic placeholders awaiting their real life."

are doing anything they can to feed their families and make ends meet. In addition, the physical and psychological benefits derived from gardening are bringing people of all ages and economic status back into the dirt, from America's first family on down.

## New Community Form

I believe these converging trends suggest the innovative idea of the adaptive reuse of many of our darkened malls into a kind of new community form. This new hybrid lifestyle community model could be a cross between an elder hostel and an Israeli kibbutz with a dash of wellness center thrown in for good measure. The entity could fulfill the needs of America's aging Baby Boomers for a living/working and fully integrated social environment that completely reinvents the types of sterile convalescent facilities known to previous generations. The fact remains that many of today's regional malls are appropriately sized and strategically located with reusable structural cores that would enable repurposing into this new entity. The resulting communities would celebrate our diverse and highly individualized aging population while meeting a series of interconnected, dynamic social needs. These communities would focus on a generation of senior citizens who view aging differently than previous generations and who will remain active and productive for many years. It will provide for the ongoing needs of many of our 78 million aging Baby Boomers with a complete and holistic blend of services and offerings.

A range of housing options from apartments (rental and ownership) to assisted-living and full-care environments could also be offered. These developments could accommodate anywhere from 1,000 to 2,000 full-time residents or more. While the community would not be completely self-sufficient, there would be enough of a contained population to support key essential services providing able-bodied citizens meaningful employment. Services could include a clinic, convenience store, spa, fitness center, food service, library, community center, seasonal farmer's market, food processing and packaging, crafts center, media center, laundry, intergenerational daycare, and more. Links to local university systems would be provided throughout the various communities, which will promote continued education, including web-based lectures and seminars.

One of the responses to our society's excesses has given rise to a renewed interest in spirituality. These values would be fostered through study, discussion, yoga, and meditation. Additionally, with the conversion of parking lots back to green spaces; the communities will benefit from mini parks, walking and bike paths, and other outdoor communal spaces that will enhance this vital and sustainable community form. Gardening could become an essential component of the internal economy as a source of fresh fruits and vegetables for food services, resident consumption, as well as a profit center aimed at the broader adjacent community. There could also be a host of job opportunities that cover a broad range of services offered within the community. This live/work model would take on a new dimension with an eye toward becoming a self-sustaining community.

Our kids, the 87 million Echo Boomers, or Millennials, will be busy having their own families, creating a significant need for day care and support while mom and dad are at work. The new community form will borrow from an intergenerational model that has worked for centuries. Grandma and grandpa can assist with day care in the community center, which could provide teaching, learning, and bonding for both the old and the young alike. It could also become another stream of income for the community. And no vital community can exist and flourish without the arts. There could

> I believe these converging trends suggest the innovative idea of the adaptive reuse of many of our darkened malls into a kind of new community form.

be community outreach to museums and performing art groups throughout the area. Naturally, a public presentation space would be planned for use by all segments of the new community form. Residents with art, music and other creative gifts will be encouraged to share them with young and old alike.

For many people, the pride of one's high school or college years continues throughout life. Often the source of that pride stems from the bonding of like-minded people going through an important transitional period in life. The same holds true for military service veterans. I believe this type of cooperative, community living will create a similar bond and sense of belonging and shared purpose that will contribute to longer, healthier, and more fulfilling lives. And as such it is beneficial to soft brand this new form of community in ways that foster a sense of pride in the community and shared experience of its citizens. Living in these environments will be anything but a passive existence because participants will be contributing to keep the community dynamic and viable. This diverse group of aging citizens will be dealing with extended life expectancy combined with a host of new challenges that didn't even exist a generation or so ago. The combined need to provide the necessary shelter and services for aging individuals who are still highly able and productive is sure to generate some very creative thinking around these urban and suburban "place holders."

While this concept has not been taken far enough to prove its financial viability, I firmly believe there is enough anecdotal evidence to suggest that the concept is worth pursuing. The creation of this concept will be dependent on locations, size, cost of acquisition, and redevelopment. Those costs will be affected by the degree to which the bones of previous anchor department stores and specialty retail infill can be reused. There are also a host of other issues related to the sites and local communities. That said,

I believe the need for such sustainable communities is intertwined with the economic and social need to find a solution to repurposing these huge assets that are blighting many communities and having an impact on tax bases. To bring this model to fruition (particularly in its prototype form) will take cooperative efforts between private business, financial institutions, and local governments. These are the very groups that stand to benefit tremendously from the repurposing and rejuvenation of some of the largest and best-positioned building forms conceived and developed in our lifetime. It is well worth the exploration to determine whether these physical assets may become the source material to meet the host of impending needs that are only now beginning to be identified.

## THE TRIPLE BOTTOM LINE

The new metrics of business sustainability that is often referred to as the three Ps are: profit, people, and planet. This notion was originally coined in 1994 by John Elkington, founder of SustainAbility, a British consultancy firm that has gained considerable traction since the turn-of-the-century movement toward corporate social responsibility, climate change, and fair trade. The idea is that companies need to prepare three separate and distinct bottom lines. The first is the traditional measure of profits. The second measure is the degree to which a company is socially responsible in its operations both inwardly and outwardly. The third bottom line measure is how environmentally responsible the company has been. Behind this concept is the fundamental notion that you only get what you measure, hence unless strict and balanced attention is brought to each of the three Ps, a company will not be accounting for the full cost of doing business.

The new paradigm arose after the 1990s, when cost cutting was priority number one, and the costs of transferring business and

> These are the very groups that stand to benefit tremendously from the repurposing and rejuvenation of some of the largest and best-positioned building forms conceived and developed in our lifetime.

production to places like Brazil, India, and China were becoming ever more apparent. Purchasing products from countries that were habitual polluters with environmental stress brought on by shipping great distances, and exploitation of cheap labor has contributed to the breakdown of the "cheap at any price" corporate mantra. The growing awareness of this institutional malpractice has begun to put pressure on the companies who continue to utilize unregulated labor markets and where manufacturers turn a blind eye to lax social and environmental standards. This has also given rise to the fair trade movement, which supports brands whose products have been produced and traded in a socially and environmentally "fair" manner. Millennial consumers in particular expect companies to behave responsibly and enhanced brand equity will depend on it. In addition, we know companies that adopt triple bottom line philosophies benefit from increased employee morale and overall customer goodwill.

## Just Don't Do It

In the late 1990s Nike found out the hard way about just how important the triple bottom line is to its customers. When a series of articles appeared in the *New York Times* that exposed the sweatshop conditions in Nike factories in Vietnam, Indonesia, and Thailand, Nike sales began to take a hit, to the tune of a billion dollars between sales years 1998 and 1999. Product boycotts and protests that came about because of the exploitation of 400,000 Asian workers were believed to be the direct cause of the major financial loss, according to *Forbes* magazine. Nike responded by spending over two billion dollars to repair its image and reputation. Over a decade later, Nike has made tremendous strides in repairing its materials and supply chain and its practices of social responsibility. In an era of increased transparency and scrutiny both retailers and suppliers need to focus less on the cost of operating responsibly and more on the cost of *not* doing so.

**Millennial consumers in particular expect companies to behave responsibly and enhanced brand equity will depend on it.**

# TYING UP
# LOOSE ENDS

A

As this book demonstrates, I remain very optimistic about retail's omnichannel future, which I believe will include a large variety of store-based retail. And even if the store is not where the ultimate point of sale takes place, it will play a huge role in how the customer experiences and engages with the brand. This ongoing evolution and transition may become a rough road for many retailers, but the speed of change and constant uncertainty for "what's next" need not be a major disruptor if the brand has chosen the correct long-term path, and its operatives recognize and embrace the qualities of Generation Flux. Fifty years ago, the Stein twins learned to not only adapt to a changing world, but they had the guts, insight, and perseverance to become change agents and reinvent an entire retail category. With the collapse of antiquated corporate structures that both protected and inhibited many from maximizing their career potential, I'm hopeful that many newly minted entrepreneurs will emerge ready to pursue the opportunities that our ever-"flattening" world is providing.

This book has allowed me to reflect on my life, the lives that came before mine, and the ones that both my girls will be challenged and hopefully rewarded by. I regret that neither Ariel nor Brianna Stein ever knew their grandfather "Papa Al," although they both met and shared some special moments with his identical twin, Uncle Lou, who was a pretty great facsimile. I've always tried to share a bit of my dad with the girls and enjoyed talking about his outrageous sense of style. After Dad passed away in 1984 we kept some of his shall we say "singular" apparel items. This included two giant garbage bags full of his "socks of many colors," which eventually were repurposed to create the Al Stein Memorial Sock Cart. Looking like a three-dimensional Pantone color guide, it occupied a prominent position in the conference room of my first downtown office. For years I have also attended speaking engagements with a sports jacket he purchased in Palm Beach, Florida. It frankly resembles an article stolen off of the album cover of *Sgt. Pepper's Lonely Hearts Club Band*. I would have the jacket hidden under a black cape beside the speaker's podium. At the end of my presentation I would "reveal" and don the coat proudly always to the audience's bursts of hysterical laughter. "He actually *wore* that?" they would always ask. "Yep, he did," I would respond.

But the most meaningful of the wearable items were his ties, all 300 of them. Now mind you, many were made from the same silk material that adorned the linings of his suits, and because they were mostly from the late 1960s, 1970s and early 1980s, they had huge mass to complement their bold hues.

During the winter of 1994, as Cheryl and I were anticipating Bri's March arrival, Ari (then almost 5) and I hatched a plan for welcoming her new sister. We emptied the bag of ties onto the floor and proceeded to arrange them by dominant color, which in some cases became pretty difficult. I purchased a very large wire-like lattice structure used in retail display and we worked together, patiently weaving the ties in concentric rows to make a very large and very colorful wall sculpture out of Papa Al's ties. Today, nearly two decades later the tie sculpture remains prominently hung in our home for all to see and enjoy, just as Dad would have wanted. We lost Dad in 1984, and Uncle Lou in 2011. Dad passed away on January 16, just ten days short of his 69th birthday. His dear brother passed away on January 10, just sixteen days short of his 96th birthday. The numbers are all the same, just in a different order. Just as Dr. Chopra told me, there are no accidents.

**Adaptive Reuse**—The process of reusing an old site or building for a purpose other than its original intent or design

**Assisted Discovery**—The process of enabling the customer to "decode" the store and move from observer to engaged participant, achieved through an intuitive layout, logical adjacencies, and unmistakable way-finding, as well as the structured use of graphic and digital systems to enhance choice-making.

**Big Data**—High volume, high velocity, information that requires new forms of processing to enable insight, discovery, and decision making.

**Brand**—A unique and identifiable symbol, association, name, or trademark which serves to differentiate competing products or services. Both a physical and emotional trigger to create a relationship between consumers and the product/service.

**Brand Positioning**—The "market space" a brand is perceived to occupy; the part of the brand identity that is to be actively communicated in a way that meaningfully sets it apart from the competition.

**Brand Touchpoint**—Image, representation, and/or point of brand engagement, which may occur prior to, during, or after the product sale. Sometimes this is referred to as brand extensions.

**Brand Touchpoint Integration**—The seamlessness required to insure high perceived brand value across the myriad of points of brand interaction; also referred to as synchronicity.

**Bricks and Clicks**—Term associated with the early acceptance of a multichannel retailing model that integrates both offline (bricks) and online (clicks). The philosophy would ultimately be embraced (to a greater or lesser degree) by most store-based retailers.

**Common Area Maintenance** (CAM)—Fees above and beyond base rent that a mall charges the tenant or lessee based on a pro-rata share of common area maintenance expenses.

**Cradle-to-Cradle**—Design initiatives that seek to create essentially waste-free holistic methods of design and manufacturing.

**Cross Channel Retailing**—Stepping beyond multichannel retailing in an effort to bring cohesion across various retail platforms or touchpoints.

**Customer Demographics**—The study and grouping of people by gender, age, race, disabilities, home ownership, etc., in order to define purchasing trends.

**Demographic Demarcation**—The names associated with generational demographic identification commonly used by marketers including: The GI Generation, Matures or Silent Generation, Baby Boomers, Generation X, Generation Y or Millennials, Generation Z, and Generation Alpha.

**Design Process**—Objective problem-solving process undertaken by design professionals taking into consideration five key factors including: immersion, context, openness, style, and communication.

**Differentiated Offerings**—A product or service with a high price/value proposition, resulting in a strong degree of intrinsic satisfaction.

**Drive Isle**—A primary path of circulation through a retail store.

**Endless Aisle**—Leveraging the ability of the smartphone-carrying customer to utilize digital technologies such as QR (Quick Response) codes, NFC (Near Field Communications) and other digital enhancements to access a myriad of products not seen or displayed in the store.

**Four P's of Retailing**—Product, packaging, pricing, and promotion; expected to be radically impacted and reshaped by the "brick-and-mobile" world.

**Generation Flux**—Term that first appeared in the February 2012 issue of Fast Company as the feature article written by the magazine's editor Robert Safian; describes a psychographic or mindset that tolerates and even embraces the unknown. The article recognizes that the mindset is not exclusive to any demographic group.

**Gens3**—Anecdotal grouping of Generation X, Generation Y, and Generation Z into a single group, based on their innate understanding and acceptance of all things digital, thus recognizing a "digital divide" between these groups and the previous three living generations before them.

**Geodemographic Segmentation**—Psychographic tool based on census-data analysis which categorizes the U.S. population into various lifestyle, life-stage, and social groups.

**Geotracking and Geolocating**—Means whereby retailers will be able to use the new digital enhancement technologies (NFC, RFID, etc.) to engage with customers in highly personalized ways in both casual and highly targeted manners.

**Gross Revenue**—The total revenue (calculated over a particular time frame) before the cost of goods or operational costs are factored.

**Gross Revenue Per Square Foot**—Gross revenue divided by the square footage of a particular retail store. Traditional regional malls average from $350 to $375 per square foot, while Apple stores commonly exceed $5,500 per square foot.

**Halo Effect**—The perceived positive features and characteristics of a particular item positively impact the broader brand.

**Home Sourcing**—Big businesses deploying telecommuting and outsourcing as a means of stripping away the excesses that corporate America built before the global economy began to impose a new cost-cutting diet.

**INTERDES**—Acronym to define the essential components of an exceptional brand, including: identity (knowing who you are); nuance (subtle points of differentiation); transcendence (going beyond boundaries); emotion (connecting on a primal level); relevance (what people want); design (the key differentiator); endurance (being in it for the long haul); and soul (the whole is greater than the sum of its parts).

**Internet Pure Play**—The high-profile web-only storefronts (like Amazon) that received a great deal of attention in the late '90s, largely funded by the dot.com boom. They included names like Buyitnow.com, FreeShop.com, boxLot.com, and Mall.com.

**LEPSync**—The blueprint used to guide the customer through the assisted discovery "funnel"; includes four key aspects of wayfinding and making a choice: lifestyle and brand imagery, empowerment content, product information, and shelf-facing labels.

**Lessor**—References the landlord, shopping center, or mall.

**Lessee**—References the tenant or retailer.

**Market Fairness Act**—U.S. Congress bill S.743 (legislation pending) authorization to require the collection of sales and use tax; essentially taxing online goods in a manner similar to the way offline sales are taxed. This is widely believed to be the means of leveling the playing field between online and store-based retailers.

**MEtail**[sm] —Acronym for mobile electronic retailing which recognizes the impact smartphones are having on all aspects of retailing.

**Multichannel Retailing**—Retailers that utilize multiple platforms to engage their customers; first demonstrated in the early twentieth century by catalog retailers Montgomery Ward (1925) and Sears & Roebuck (1926) through the opening of their first stores.

**Near Field Communications** (NFC)—Micro-digital tag that emits a small current, which creates a magnetic field that is recognized by the customer's smartphone and turned back into electrical impulses and ultimately data, instantaneously; both passive and active (one way/two way) forms are in use. The "cashless society" that futurists have talked about is likely to become a reality by employing active NFC technology. Google Wallet and MasterCard PayPass are two examples of NFC technologies that allow for instant, cashless transactions.

**Neurological Connectivity**—Refers to the way our brains work when all our senses are engaged (sensory sync)—sight, sound, smell, taste, touch, and the sixth sense, that of the mind—thus producing a strong psychological and physical response.

**New Community Form**—Term for the planned, adaptive reuse of darkened malls into a new hybrid lifestyle community model; a cross between an elder hostel and an Israeli kibbutz with a dash of wellness center thrown in for good measure. The entity is intended to fulfill the needs of America's aging Baby Boomers for a living/working and fully integrated social environment that completely reinvents the types of sterile convalescent facilities known to previous generations.

**Omnichannel Retailing**—The ultimate synergy between and across retailing platforms or touchpoints in recognition of the fact that the customer identifies first with the brand, and that the nature and point of platform engagement is dynamic, unpredictable, and constantly changing.

**Pop-up Retail**—Temporary/short term tenancies intended to accomplish three principle goals for the brand or retailer: it creates buzz around a specific brand, product, or designer; it creates a sense of urgency because it has a finite life; and it generates revenue.

**Preemptive Distribution**—Getting the product or service to market ahead of the competition.

**Product turns**—Number of times a given shelved item (SKU) is sold and replaced.

**Profit margin**—The spread between the cost of an item and its selling price, before other operational costs are factored.

**Psychographics**—The study of personality, values, attitudes, interests, and lifestyles.

**Radio Frequency Identification** (RFID)—Embedded micro computer chips used for tracking everything from cargo and cattle to house cats; commonly used in retail for data transfer and back-of-house operations, including pallet identification and a host of inventory-control issues. Has future potential for communicating with a customer's smartphone.

**RaveRetail®**—Solution to repopulating underperforming retail centers; a matchmaker and intermediary between the retail space holders (malls and shopping centers) and potential space users (retailers, brands, major manufacturers, and entertainment entities). It will create, organize, facilitate, coordinate, and market high-impact branded events located in and around malls, shopping centers, and other public gathering places. RaveRetail® responds to rapidly changing trends in consumer behavior influenced by social networking and the seismic growth of e-tail and MEtail[sm], which are having a highly disruptive effect on store-based retailing.

**Retail Theatre**—Term attributed to architect and veteran store designer Kenneth Walker describing the interplay between customer, space, and product when exceptional product-staging heightens customer engagement and product value.

**Showrooming**—Practice of real-time online price-checking, utilizing smartphones while shopping in a retail store.

**SKU** (Stock Keeping Units)—The term for each unique item in a retailer's inventory.

**Small Office/Home Office** (SOHO)—The phenomenon associated with the surge in business start-ups, as a result of corporate downsizing in the mid- to late-'90s. This was aided by the Internet-created "digital democracy" that was allowing individuals to do things that were once the exclusive providence of corporate America.

**Solution/Lifestyle-Based Retailing**—A contextual approach to merchandising that recognizes the "lifestyle" and personal milieu involved in the purchase; this approach also recognizes the added value associated with "retailer as expert." This contrasts to a more traditional component or product-based approach, which often results in commoditization.

**Staged Experience**—The highest level of differentiated offerings which may create a "transformational experience" for the consumer. Disneyland and Starbucks are successful examples.

**Store–Within–Store Concepts**—Contained branded environments within multi-brand spaces, often found in department stores or big-box environments; driven by the feature brand's desire to control brand message and value.

**Swat Audit**—Used in relation to an overall assessment of a retail store from the standpoint of layout and circulation, fixtures and merchandising, brand positioning and appearance, and overall customer experience. Became a pivotal ingredient to the in-STORE[sm] initiative of the early '90s.

**The Third Place**—Term attributed to American urban sociologist and writer Ray Oldenburg in his books Celebrating *The Third Place* and *The Great Good Place*. Oldenburg describes home as the first place, and work the second place. The third place is the heart of a community and includes casual gathering places such as pubs, cafés, coffeehouses, and even post offices; these are deemed important to a civil society and civic engagement. It could be argued that Starbucks has institutionalized the third place.

**Trend Convergence**—When multiple trends converge, their influence may become greater than the sum of their parts. The intersection of a number of micro trends can combine to produce a macro trend of far greater significance, and cultural impact.

**Triggers and Treasures**—Costco-speak for the 75/25 mix of staples or "triggers" that dominate the inventory, contrasted against the here-today-and-gone-tomorrow "treasures" that drive traffic.

**Underused Asset Utilization**—Often used to describe the new sharing economy that focuses on leveraging assets that otherwise may be underutilized; inspiring a whole new generation of businesses that facilitate the sharing of available apartments, meals, tools, cars, clothes, and couches.

**Undifferentiated Commodities**—The bottom of the price/value proposition where product is essentially the same and price is the principle differentiator.

**VALS** (Value, Attitudes, and Lifestyles)—The first "attitudinal" metric developed to look at lifestyle types that transcend issues of gender, age, race, and location; developed in 1978 by futurist Arnold Mitchell and his colleagues at Stanford Research Institute. It is arguably the first psychographic marketing tool.

**Value Chain Control**—Controlling the entire value chain from conception to consumption; also referred to as vertical integration. The ability for a retailer or manufacturer to control every aspect of the value chain to insure brand continuity.

## WORKS CITED

Abernethy, Samantha. "Downtown Target Opens In Carson Pirie Scott Building." *Chicagoist.* Gothamist LLC., 25 July 2012. Web. 30 July 2013.

Agrawal, Rakesh. "Who's Afraid of Amazon Locker?" *Venture Beat.* Venture Beat, 12 Nov. 2012. Web. 19 Mar. 2013.

"Bakers Footwear Reports Fourth Quarter Net Sales." *Business Wire.* Business Wire, 4 Feb. 2010. Web. 03 May 2010.

Balch, Barbara. *Buildings for Best Products.* New York: Museum of Modern Art, 1979. Print.

Barreneche, Raul. "Restoration Hardware's Boston Flagship Store." *Architectural Digest.* Conde Nast, June 2013. Web. 30 July 2013.

Black, Sam, Ellen P. Gabler, and Mark Reilly. "Best Buy to Launch Health Store." *Minneapolis/St. Paul Business Journal.* American City Business Journals, 3 Oct. 2004. Web. 27 May 2013.

Boylan-Pett, Liam. "As Barnes & Noble Closes Stores, Independent Bookstores May Be the Ones to Pick Up the Slack." *PolicyMic.* Mic Network Inc., 6 Feb. 2013. Web. 26 July 2013.

Chaey, Christina. "What You'll Pay for Fancy Target Products." *Fast Company* May 2012: 26. Print.

Chopra, Deepak. *The Seven Spiritual Laws of Success: A Practical Guide to the Fulfillment of Your Dreams.* San Rafael: Amber-Allen Pub., 1994. Print.

*Consumers of Tomorrow: Insights and Observations About Generation Z.* Grail Research, 2011. PDF file.

"Country Club Plaza." *Wikipedia.* Wikimedia Foundation, Inc., 12 Mar. 2010. Web. 05 Apr. 2010.

Cuprisin, Tim. "Glendale Drive-in Served as Inspiration for Hangout in 'Happy Days'." *Journal Sentinel.* Journal Sentinel, Inc., 19 Aug. 2008. Web. 31 Jan. 2013.

D'Innocenzio, Anne. "Target Goes Local, Nationally, with Boutique Shops." *Bloomberg Businessweek.* Bloomberg L.P., 12 Jan. 2012. Web. 22 July 2013.

Davis, Stacy V. "Penzeys Spices Owner Says He's Reached a Deal to Buy Northridge." *The Business Journal.* American City Business Journals, 8 May 2013. Web. 9 July 2013.

DiNardo, Anne, ed. "JC Penny Turnaround: Part 1." *VMSD- Visual Merchandising and Store Design.* Sept. 2012: 8. Print.

"Edison Brothers Stores, Inc." *International Directory of Company Histories.* Vol. 56. N.p., 2003. Web. 04 Apr. 2010.

Edwards, Greg. "Former President Sells His Story of Edison Brothers' Fall." *St. Louis Business Journal.* American City Business Journals, 27 Aug. 2009. Web. 3 May 2010.

Ewoldt, John. "Shopping More at Smaller Stores." *Star Tribune* [Minneapolis] 28 Oct. 2012: D1+. Print.

Firestone, Mary. *Dayton's Department Store.* Charleston: Arcadia Pub., 2007. Print.

Flaherty, Jackie, comp. "Edgewood Middle School Picks Up STEAM." *Natural Awakenings: Twin Cities Edition* May 2012: 6. Print.

Foster, Christine. "A Life of Spice." *Forbes.* Forbes.com LLC, 19 May 1997. Web. 9 July 2013.

Friedman, Mildred S., ed. *Nelson/Eames/Girard/Propst: The Design Process at Herman Miller.* Vol. 98-99. Minneapolis: Walker Art Center, 1975. Print.

"F.W. Woolworth Company." *Wikipedia.* Wikimedia Foundation, 08 Mar. 2010. Web. 21 Mar. 2010.

Gabler, Ellen. "Best Buy Pulls Back from Health and Wellness Test Stores." *Minneapolis/ St. Paul Business Journal.* American City Business Journals, 19 June 2006. Web. 18 June 2013.

Godagama, Shantha. *The Handbook of Ayurveda: India's Medical Wisdom Explained.* London: Kyle Cathie, 1997. Print.

Grant, Danielle, Babangida Bafarawa, Claudia Prieto, Yoselin Gonzalez, and Manikandan Sivasankar. "Songa Asks: Can Fashion Be Sustainable?" *Triple Pundit.* TriplePundit, 24 Apr. 2013. Web. 7 Aug. 2013.

Halverson, Dean, and Wayne Glowac. *Healthcare Tsunami: The Wave of Consumerism That Will Change U.S. Business.* Madison: Wave Marketing, LLC, 2008. Print.

Hindle, Tim. "Triple Bottom Line." *The Economist.* The Economist Newspaper Limited, 17 Nov. 2009. Web. 7 Aug. 2013.

Isaacson, Walter. "The Real Leadership Lessons of Steve Jobs." *Harvard Business Journal* Apr. 2012: 92-102. Print.

Janowitz, Neil. "Rolling in the Depot." *Fast Company* May 2012: 38. Print.

Kellog, Craig. "Matters of Design- Up To Speed." *Interior Design Magazine* Feb. 2012: 124-26. Print.

Lee, Thomas. "Aura of Apple Takes Big Bite out of Best Buy Sales." *Star Tribune* [Minneapolis] 21 Sept. 2012: D1-D2. Print.

Lee, Thomas. "Behind the Turmoil, Best Buy Shows Upside." *Star Tribune* [Minneapolis] 20 May 2012: D1+. Print.

Lee, Thomas. "Best Buy Bets Big on Store-within-store Concepts." *Star Tribune.* StarTribune,14 July 2013. Web. 22 July 2013.

Lee, Thomas. "Target Tackles Future of Retail Like a Start-Up." *Star Tribune* [Minneapolis] 10 July 2013: A1+. Print.

Lindsay, Greg. "Swedish Modern Comes to Town." *Fast Company* Mar. 2013: 50-52. Print.

Lindsay, Greg. "Working Beyond the Cube." *Fast Company* Mar. 2013: 34-38. Print.

"List of Defunct Retailers of the United States." *Wikipedia.* Wikimedia Foundation, Jan. 2008. Web. 05 Apr. 2010.

Mareydt, CL. "Generation Nicknames." *Gather.com.* Gather Inc., 09 Jan. 2012. Web. 06 Feb. 2013.

McPartlin, Susan M., comp. *Retailing 2020: Winning in a Polarized World.* PricewaterhouseCoopers LLP, 2012. PDF file.

"Melville Corporation." *Wikipedia.* Wikimedia Foundation, Inc., 03 Dec. 2009. Web. 05 Apr. 2010.

Mitchell, Stacy. "After 20 Years, Congress May Finally Pass Internet Sales Tax. Is It Too Late?" *Institute For Local Self-Reliance.* Institute For Local Self-Reliance, 13 May 2013. Web. 26 July 2013.

Mitchell, Stacy. "Top 10 Reasons to Support Locally Owned Businesses." *Institute For*

*Local Self-Reliance*. Institute For Local Self-Reliance, 10 Dec. 2012. Web. 26 July 2013.

Morozov, Evgeny. "Keep Calm and Carry On... Buying." *The New York Times*. The New York Times Company, 09 Mar. 2013. Web. 22 Mar. 2013.

Novak, Jill. "The Six Living Generations in America." *Marketing Teacher.com*. Marketing Teacher Ltd., n.d. Web. 6 Feb. 2013.

O'Donnell, Jayne. "National Retail Federation CEO Tracy Mullin Retires." *USA Today*. USA TODAY, 7 May 2010. Web. 7 May 2010.

Persaud, Christine. "The Rise of the Independent Retailer?" *Market News: Connection Business and Technology*. Bomar Publishing Inc., 04 Feb. 2013. Web. 26 July 2013.

Pine, B. Joseph, II, and James H. Gilmore. *The Experience Economy: Work Is Theater & Every Business a Stage*. Boston: Harvard Business School Press, 1999. Print.

Pineiro, R.J. *01-01-00: The Novel of The Millennium*. New York: Tom Doherty Associates, 1999. Print.

Pitner, Kolean and Bruce N. Wright. *Peter Seitz: Designing a Life*. Minneapolis: Minneapolis College of Art & Design, 2007. Print.

Raines, Claire. "Claire Raines on 10 Predictions for Generation Z." *AMACOM Books Blog*. American Management Association, 14 Mar. 2013. Web. 8 May 2013.

Rosenblum, Paula. "The Independent Retailer Lives On." *Forbes*. Forbes.com LLC, 1 July 2013. Web. 18 July 2013.

Rossman, Jo. "Seducing Shoppers Through Technology." *Retail Environments* Sept. 2012: 14-16. Print.

Rudnick, Michael. "Best Buy Taps Into Wellness Market with EQ-Life Store." *HFN The Weekly Newspaper for Home Furnishing Network* [Minneapolis] 31 Jan. 2005: n. pag. The Free Library. Web. 27 May 2013.

Safian, Robert. "Generation Flux." *Fast Company* Feb. 2012: 60-71. Print.

Safian, Robert. "Retail Therapy." *Fast Company* May 2012: 55-60. Print.

Schlender, Brent. "The Lost Steve Jobs Tapes." *Fast Company* May 2012: 75-82. Print.

Shopping Center World Staff. "Cheers to 100 Years... 20th Century Timeline." *National Real Estate Investor*. Penton, 01 Dec. 1999. Web. 20 Mar. 2010.

Shoulberg, Warren. "Why Home Furnishings Can Save Sears & Kmart... And Why It Will Never Happen." *The Robin Report* Sept. 2012: 22-23. Print.

Simon, Paul, and Art Garfunkel. "Fakin' It." *Bookends.* Columbia, 1967. Vinyl recording.

"Southdale Shopping Center." *St. Louis Park Historical Society.* N.p., n.d. Web. 25 July 2013.

Stein, Lou. Telephone interview. 10 Mar. 2010.

Strickler, Jeff. "Meditation Goes Mainsream." *Star Tribune* [Minneapolis] 30 May 2013: E1+. Print.

*Transforming the Customer Experience with RFID.* Motorola Solutions, Inc., 2013. Print.

Verdon, Joan. "Online Retailers Extend Reach with Delivery Lockers." *Star Tribune* [Minneapolis] 17 Apr. 2013: N.p. Print.

"Victor Gruen." *Wikipedia.* Wikimedia Foundation, 18 July 2013. Web.

Vignelli, Massimo, and Michael Bierut. *Design: Vignelli.* New York: Rizzoli International Publications, 1981. Print.

"Walmart Corporate." *Walmart Corporate.* Wal-Mart Stores, Inc., 2012. Web. 07 Aug. 2013.

Weitzner, Mitch (Producer), & Quintanilla, Carl (Correspondent). (26 Apr. 2012). *The Costco Craze: Inside the Warehouse Giant* [Documentary film]. United States: CNBC.

"Welcome to NearFieldCommunication.org." *Near Field Communication: What Is Near Field Communication?* NearFieldCommunication.org, n.d. Web. 19 May 2013.

Wells, Melanie. "In Search of the Buy Button." *Forbes* 1 Sept. 2003: 62-70. Print.

Whitaker, Jan. *Service and Style: How the American Department Store Fashioned the Middle Class.* New York: St. Martin's Press, 2006. Print.

adaptive reuse, 136–138, 299–305
advertising. See Branding; Lifestyle approach; Marketing
Albrecht, Jeremiah, 258–259
Amazon.com, 190–191, 196, 285
ancestry, search for roots, 288–289
Apple Company, 117–119, 120, 125, 163–165, 199
assisted discovery, 213, 224–229, 252–253
authenticity, 287–292

Baby Boomers, 24, 206–207, 300–305
back-end fulfillment, 195–196
Bedbury, Scott, 102–103
Best Buy, 179, 245–246, 269–270
BEST Products, Inc., 144–148
big-box retailers
    decline, 284
    growth, 151, 247
    store-in-store approach, 269–270
    unique BEST approach, 144–148
    use of history, 289–290
    See also Target
bottom-up retailing, 279–280
brand commoditization, 89–90, 115, 120–121
branding
    development, 39
    differentiators, 41
    emotion, 112–115, 249–250
    endurance and soul, 121–126
    graphics hook, 226
    heritage, 290–292
    holistic, 135, 163–165, 213–214
    identity, 103–105
    Life Enhancements project, 241–245
    national brand syndrome, 276–277
    in niche areas, 272–276
    nuance, 105–108
    reinvigorating, 262–263
    relevance, 115–121
    sensory sync, 160, 198

single brand at location, 255–259
    touchpoint connections, 211
    transcendence, 108–111, 126, 161–162
    value chain control, 199–200
    See also Lifestyle approach
Brunswick Corporation, 89–90, 97–98, 254–259
bump-backs, 171–172
business sustainability, 26–27, 305–307

Calhoun Square project, 142–143
cars, 20–23, 35, 53, 91, 130–131, 166–168, 288
casual shopping, 220–221
Cherry, Les, 78–79
component-based vs. lifestyle, 214
CompUSA, 115–116, 120
consistency, importance of, 102
Cordaro, Jim, 182, 244
Costco, 106–108
Country Club Plaza, 51
Cowell Industries, 247–254
Crate & Barrel, 123–124
creative process, 33–34, 76, 87–88
customer experience
    adaptive reuse projects, 136–138
    assisted discovery, 213, 224–229, 252–253
    choice and, 107, 246–248, 250–251
    e-tailing challenge, 161
    emotions and, 160, 198
    heritage story incorporation, 291–292
    importance of in-store, 213–214
    increasing experientiality, 296–299
    managing, 106–107, 115–116
    relevance, 117–119
    service culture, 174–177
customers
    attention span, 292, 293
    company ethics and, 305–307
    empowering, 95, 226–229, 242–244, 252
    increasing sales from existing, 96–98
    interface with, 18, 79–85

# Index

as participants, 164
personalizing shopping for, 215, 218, 220
preference for local, 283–284, 286–287
relationship building, 26–27, 79, 117, 167, 275
target, 81–82, 85–87, 93–94

D/R stores, 137–138
de Alcala, Steve, 259
de-architecturization, 145–147
demographic demarcations, 205–209
department stores, 10, 17–18, 53–54
design, 34, 35–37, 79, 121–126, 148
Design Consortium Inc. (DCI), 138–140
design process
    communication, 95–98, 226–229, 242–244
    consensus on objectives, 78
    context, 79–87
    immersion, 76–79
    openness, 87–90
    package, 242
    style, 90–94
discounting. See Off-price retailing
display cases/windows, 4, 84
distribution, 285
downsizing, 268–270, 280–281
downtowns, 9–10, 16–20, 24, 52

E-fficient and personalization, 218
e-tailing
    Amazon.com, 190–191
    customer experience and, 161
    mentality, 193
    mobile devices and, 212–213
    sales, 204
    sales taxes, 190, 213, 285
    store-based retailing response, 191–192, 193, 195–196
    See also MEtail<sup>SM</sup>
Edison Brothers Stores, 39, 50, 77–79
elder care, 300–305

emotion (in branding), 112–115, 249–250
endurance (in branding), 121–126
entrepreneurs, characteristics of, 8
environmental graphics, 68–69
ergonomics, 45–46
ethical responsibilities, 305–307
Everist, Margaret, 241, 243
experience economy, 158–159, 161, 197–198
extended packaging, 217

fad to lifestyle approach, 232
Farber, Damon, 138, 140
foot traffic, importance of, 5
Ford, Angela, 258–259
functionality, 45–46, 122–123

Geek Squad, 178–179
Gegax, Tom, 174–177, 240–241, 259
Geisler, Tim, 138–139
general stores in rural America, 25
Generation Dlux, 194–195
Generations X–Z, 207–209
geodemographic segmentation, 86
geotracking and geolocation shopping, 220–221
Gerber, Mort, 142–144
Ghirardelli Square renovation, 136–138
GI Generation, 205–206
Gilmore, James H., 158–159, 161, 197–198
giveaways, 26
Goodman, Arthur, 83–85
graphics, use of, 226–229, 295
Gruen, Victor, 52

Hayne, Richard, 105
health care retailers, 271–272
heritage stories, 290–292
Home Depot, 247, 250, 252
Hutton, Brent, 181–182, 253, 256–257

identity (in branding), 103–105

IKEA, 270–271

In Sync and MEtailing, 218

indie retailers, 283–287

*in*STORE℠, 152–153

INTERDES (branding essentials), 103

InterDesign, 67–69, 138

Internet, 188–189, 196–197, 205, 209–210
    See also E-tailing

Jewelry and Toy Center, 4–5, 8, 37–38, 159–160

jobbers, 37–38

Jobs, Steve, 117–119, 125, 263

Junkyard, 135–136

layaway plans, 159–160

LEPSync, 226–229

Levitt, Mary Ann, 142–144

Life Enhancements project, 241–245

lifestyle approach
    authenticity as part of, 287–292
    branding, 290
    component-based retailing vs., 214
    from fad to, 232
    graphics, 226
    in paint industry, 249–250

lighting, 49, 84

Limited Brand companies, 133–135

"living-working-buying environments," 299–305

localism, 277, 279–288, 301–302

Lowry, Cotty, 140

Mall of America (MOA), 135–136, 171–174

malls
    bump-backs, 171–172
    decline, 266–267, 276
    growth of, 53–54
    lease requirements, 79, 148, 152
    RaveRetail®, 297–299
    repurposing, 299–305
    shopping centers turned into, 132
    Southdale as prototype, 52–53

margins, 37–38, 284–285, 305

market-of-one promise, 215

marketing
    analytic tools, 81–82, 85–87
    events, 294–295
    1950s style, 20, 21–23, 35, 63–64
    pop-up stores, 295
    See also Branding

Matures, 206

merchandise
    add-ons and profit margins, 284–285
    amount of choice, 246–248, 250–251
    bottom-up inspiration, 288
    cross-selling, 252
    depth and mix, 41, 86, 107
    lifestyle/personal style component, 214
    placement/staging, 42, 105, 119, 159
    pricing and purchase, 283, 284–285
    retailing specialized, 271–276
    single brand at location, 255–259
    story, 112
    temporary dynamic initiatives, 296–299
    turnover rate, 38, 293–294
    variety, 41

MEtail℠, 161, 198, 212–213

middlemen, 37–38, 200–201

midsize regional retailers, 151–152

Millennial Generation, 207–208

Millennium brand, 111

multichannel retailing, 210–211

name, importance of, 41–42

NFC (near field communications) tags, 219–220

Nike, 306–307

NIKETOWN, 163

Northland Center, 51–52

nuance (in branding), 105–108

off-price retailing, 18–19, 104–105, 268

See also Target
office landscape, 46
omnichannel retailing, 211, 221–223, 285, 292

paint and decorating industry, 247–254
Penzeys Spices, 273–276
percentage rents, 51
personal brands, 43
Pharmaca, 272–273
Pill & Puff, 8, 41–44, 48–50, 64, 103–104, 130, 131–132
Pine, B. Joseph, II, 158, 161, 197–198
plan-a-grams, 42
Plexiglas, 63–65
pop-up stores, 295
preemptive distribution, 198–199
price
    brand commoditization, 89, 115, 120–121
    experience economy and, 158
    MEtailing and, 213
    purchase and, 283, 284–285
    quality and race-to-the-bottom, 79
    transparency of e-tailing, 204
PRISM (geodemographic segmentation), 86
private brands, 199–200, 227, 235–237
products. See Merchandise
profits, 37–38, 284–285, 305
psychographic market segmentation, 85–87

QR (quick response) bar codes and sales, 214, 215, 217

RaveRetail®, 297–299
Rechelbacher, Horst, 113–115
recycling, 136 138, 299 305
Red Wing Shoes, 291
relationship building, 26–27, 167
relevance (in branding), 115–121
rents, 51
Restoration Hardware, 289–290

retail theater, 109, 144–145, 172–174
retailing
    early, 9–11
    four Ps, 223–224
    future of, 223–225
RFID (radio frequency identification), 217–218
roadside advertising, 63–64
Rubin, Bruce, 182, 244
Runkel, Craig, 171

sales
    benefits of product to customer, 23, 49
    e-tailing, 204
    increasing from existing customers, 96–98
    instant cashless, 219–220
    new technology and, 217–221, 228
    price and, 283, 284–285
    selling walls function, 94
    store design to drive, 79–80
sales taxes, 190, 213, 285
Schildkraut, Cal, 43
Schultz, Howard, 187–189
Sears & Roebuck, 9, 210, 260–263
Segal, Gordon and Carole, 123–124
Seitz, Peter, 67, 68–69
Select Comfort, 180–183
selling walls, 94
Semon, Ben and family, 25, 30
sensory sync, 160, 198
service economy, 158, 165–168, 171, 174–179
services. See Merchandise
shelf-facing labels, 228–229
showrooming, 212, 221
signature shops, 281–282
Silent Generation, 206
Sinegal, Jim , 106–108
small retailers, 10, 37–38, 247, 248, 255–259, 269–270, 281–282
social media utilization, 294, 296–297, 298
social responsibility, 305–307

social synergy, 219
Sony, 115, 116–117, 123
soul (in branding), 121–126
Southdale Center, 52–53
space/product/customer triad, 79–85
speaking in one voice, 180–183
specialty retailers
    in big-box stores, 269–270, 281
    downtown, 18
    growth, 39
    health care, 271–273
    malls and, 53–54, 133, 267
St. Anthony on Main project, 149–150, 237–238
staging experiences, 163–165, 214
Starbucks, 187–189, 282
Stein, Sanford, 31–33, 40, 44–45, 47–49, 58–59, 60, 61–72, 148, 151, 153–154, 168–171, 238–239
Stein family, 4–5, 11–14, 14–16, 25–27, 30, 37–39, 41–44, 49–50, 58, 59, 126, 141, 147, 148, 151, 153, 161–162, 240–241, 277–279, 293, 295, 310–311
Stephens, Robert, 177–179
store-in-store, 269–270, 281–282
Stransky, John, 97, 255–257, 259
suburban shopping centers, 24, 50–51, 132–133
    See also Malls

Target, 52, 117, 236
    branding, 104–105
    first, 19
    health clinics, 271
    national/proprietary brands mix, 199–200, 227
    pop-up stores, 295
    product inspiration, 288
    signature shops, 281–282
    urban stores, 268–269, 280–281, 289
targeted shopping, 221
team building, 175

technological parity, 285–286
tell-show-involve training method, 176
the third place, 187–189
Thom McAn, 39
Tires Plus, 174–177
top-down retailing, 279
touch-point connectivity, 135
Toys R Us, 196
transcendence (in branding), 108–111, 126, 161–162
transcendental meditation (TM), 70–72
trends, 187–189, 232, 245–246, 267
triggers and treasures, 107–108
underused asset utilization, 296–297

VALS (values, attitudes, and lifestyles), 85
value building, 167
value chain control, 199–200
vertical integration, 293–294

Walker, Kenneth, 108–111, 119, 159, 180–181, 180–182
Walmart, 104, 268
wellness movement, 232–237, 238–241, 245–246, 272–273
Wexner, Leslie, 133–135, 136
Whole Foods, 235–236
Woolworth's 5 and 10 cent store, 18, 19

Zara's, 293–294
Zumiez Couch Tour, 294